G000271672

ZEN ENTREPRENEURSHIP

Walking the Path of the Career Warrior

REVISED EDITION

RIZWAN VIRK

BAYVIEW

BOOKS

Published by Bayview Books, an imprint of Bayview Labs

First Edition, Copyright © 2003 Rizwan Virk

Second Edition, Copyright © 2013 Rizwan Virk

Cover Art, Copyright © 2003 Ellen McDonough

All rights reserved.

ISBN: **0983056919**
ISBN-13: **978-0983056911**

For my Dad, who brought us from the East into the West.

Table of Contents

PART III: THE WARRIOR'S PATH 206

APPENDICES 282

ACKNOWLEDGMENTS

Many people contributed to this book over the years and I am grateful to all of them, though I cannot list them each individually.

First, I want to give a special thanks to all of my teachers over the years, each of whom has contributed to the philosophy that's reflected in this book. On the spiritual side, this includes Bill Kennedy, Andrea Siever, Vywamus, James Forgy, and especially, Rama for opening my eyes to meditation and career success. More recently, I'd like to thank Robert Moss for his inspired teaching on shamanic dreaming and the folks at the Barbara Brennan School of Healing for their insights. I'd also like to thank all of the students of my online course, the Path of the Career Warrior, who helped shed more light on the philosophy of the Career Warrior, and provided the encouragement to finish this book.

On the business side there were many mentors who helped and I'd like to extend a thanks to them all, including Dean Redfern, Brad Feld, Sundar Subramaniam, John Donovan (Jr. and Sr.), my collaborators at Brainstorm, Mitch Liu, Irfan Virk, Kirk Goodall and even Mario Girasa, plus many others in the years since. On the writing side, I'd like to thank all of those who offered encouragement, feedback, and inspiration through the process, including Wendy Keller, Joyce and Pam LaTulippe, Christopher Papille. For the second edition, I'd like to thank Caroline Kessler, Wendy Piatek, and Marguerite Wainio, and I'd also like to thank the many readers who contacted me with their own personal stories about meditation, entrepreneurship, and career success.

Finally, I want to extend a special thanks to Ellen McDonough (http://www.placesoflight.com) for all her hard work on the cover art, web site design, and most importantly, for being there through it all!

.

INTRODUCTION

If you are called to the spiritual life, perhaps the most difficult (and interesting) challenge you face is how to bridge the gap between what you do during the day in your ordinary life — your job, work, career — and what is happening in your non-ordinary life, that part of you which exists in the spiritual worlds. How you walk between these worlds will give you insights not only into how successful you are but also how successful and fulfilled you *feel* in this life.

This book is a compilation of lessons I learned about how to bring the magic and mystery of the spiritual worlds into the business world, where many of us live on a daily basis. These lessons, taken together, represent the Path of the Career Warrior. A Career Warrior is someone who can harmoniously bring the insights gained through spiritual practice into the every day world. And someone who can take the challenges and insights gained in the wonderful world of work with them into the hidden worlds. It's a two-way street.

How this book came about

In 1993, I started on an interesting journey in the business world: at the age of 23, I became President & CEO of my first high technology company, called Brainstorm Technologies. My co-founders and I grew this company rapidly and for a time we were known as one of the 'hottest' start-ups on the East Coast. As the company grew, so did my understanding about the business world and how it worked. I learned a series of lessons over the next few years that I'd like to share with you.

However, around the same time, I began another journey of personal growth, which became inextricably entwined with the growth of my business. In fact, it led me to some startling lessons about entrepreneurship as a path of personal growth; I learned a set of spiritual practices, techniques, and principles, which had to do with what my mentors called 'the hidden worlds'.

Eventually, I realized that these lessons were part and parcel of what I learned in the business world, and the only way for me to explain one is to also explain the other. Though my chosen career, high-tech entrepreneurship, is more risky (and potentially more rewarding) than most careers, I believe the lessons that I learned were universal and can be applied to any 'life path' — with the result being that anyone can walk the Path of the Career Warrior.

It took some time for these lessons to sink in, and it was not easy for me to come to the realization that success or failure in the business world is not simply about 'dollars and cents', that it could in fact be an integral part of a path of spiritual growth and personal discovery.

I discovered that starting a business is as much an act of self-expression as it is a professional one. I found that our beliefs, energetic patterns, and our thoughts manifest themselves in our careers in ways that I couldn't have imagined. I also realized that many of us feel the need to bring more spiritual consciousness into the workplace, so that each of us can contribute to the world in ways that are more self fulfilling and holistic. This inability of our current system to let our individuality shine through is, in my opinion, one of the most important failures of our current private enterprise system.

How to use this book

This is the story of what happened in the everyday world, and how it led to a gradual awakening of what was happening behind the scenes, in the hidden worlds, during my formative entrepreneurial episode. I have re-arranged some events to draw out the spiritual lessons, and have combined characters (including rolling several of my mentors into a single personality) in order to bring coherency to the story, but this book is otherwise based on my own experiences.

The chapters taken together not only represent what happened as I started and grew my first company, but they also represent the crucial elements of the Path of the Career Warrior, as I learned it. Since the first edition of this book, the thing that most readers asked for is more commentary and clarification on the various principles and practices mentioned in the story. As a result, I have added a summary section at the end of each chapter to draw out the lessons from that chapter.

If you like spiritual adventures, you can simply read this book and enjoy it as a *tale of power*. If you like business stories, you can simply read and enjoy this as a most unusual tale of entrepreneurship. On a first reading, you might want to skip the summaries altogether and just enjoy the story and let it sink in.

On the other hand, if you are further called to understand the relationship between your own experiences in your career/job/business and your own path of personal growth, then you'll want to re-visit the summaries and comments at the end of the chapters that speak to you the most. Each chapter deals with an important issue that you may come up with in walking your own Warrior's Path, the unique combination of the lessons you are here to learn (your soul's development) and the contribution you are here to make (your life's work).

In addition to advancing the story, each chapter introduces a conceptual model, often contains one or more assignments, and represents a level of awareness that you can carry with you into your own life and career. In this expanded second edition, in addition to the chapter summaries and comments, I've added an appendix with a recap of all the major lessons from the book—the Principles of the Career Warrior. Because many of us learn better visually (even more so now than during the time this story takes place), I'm often asked to give more up-to-date movie assignments. I've refrained from doing that in this book, but will make those available online for those interested.

I started on this path because I thought that *meditation* and *spiritual development* could help me to achieve my goals in the business world. I ended up realizing that the business world and all aspects of life are there to help me with my meditation and my spiritual development, leading me to my own unique 'Warrior's Path'. May these words help you to do the same,

—Riz Virk, *Palo Alto, CA, January, 2013*

Part I:
Baby Steps

1 MEDITATING FOR MONEY? A STRANGE ENCOUNTER
MAY, 1993

"I trust you've been meditating?" he asked as he gestured for me to sit down in the chair facing his desk. Behind him was a wall of glass that revealed a stunning view of the Charles River and the Boston skyline.

The late afternoon sun was reflecting off of two of Boston's tallest (and most famous) buildings: the Hancock and the Prudential. There were so many small sailboats dotting this stretch of river that it resembled a maritime parking lot. And though each boat had its white sail raised and was obviously 'sailing', each also seemed to be standing still within its own plot of water.

"I've been meditating a little bit, based upon the instructions that James gave at the meditation center," I responded as I sat down in the cushy black leather chair facing him.

Normally, at an opportunity like this my eyes would be taking in the breathtaking scenery just outside; but this time they were glued to the enigmatic man I had come to visit. He did not look at all like I expected. When I first heard the name, Ramaswami, I immediately assumed that he was from India. Instead, Ramaswami was a tall, skinny white guy with curly blond hair, wearing a double-breasted, designer suit (which I would later find out was Italian).

I was a bit taken off guard by his looks and his demeanor. I knew, from James, that he had been teaching meditation since he was 19, and I guessed that he was in his early forties now. And I knew, also through James, that he had started several technology companies and had made millions of dollars from them, which explained how he could afford such a luxurious office.

James had been studying meditation with him for a number of years, and when he mentioned his teacher, Ramaswami, I immediately wanted to meet him. I thought that anyone who taught meditation *and* knew how to make millions in the business world was someone I wanted to meet.

I was 23 years old at the time, and was on what I hoped would be a fast-track career in the high tech industry. Ever since I was 12, I have wanted to start a software company. Some of my earliest memories of junior high school are of reading about the founders of companies like Apple Computer, Microsoft, and Lotus Development Corporation, which were started in the midst of the personal computing revolution of the early 1980's. Not only had these companies gone on to create whole new industries, but their founders had also made many millions of dollars in the process, a fact which was not lost on me, given my modest middle-class upbringing.

This ambition propelled me to learn about computers at an early age. It fed my desire to study computer science at MIT, which was located at the center of Cambridge, Massachusetts, a hotbed of technology entrepreneurship. And it persuaded me to quit my well-paying computer consulting job in order to join a small startup in Cambridge called DiVA Corporation, for virtually no pay. I only spent a few months at DiVA, but my working there had unexpectedly put in motion a chain of events that brought me face to face with this interesting, if unorthodox, teacher of meditation.

He leaned back in his chair and put his arms behind his head, as if he was evaluating me. The light streaming in from the window made it difficult to see the details of his face.

"I ... I've been thinking of starting a company..." I continued. Before I could say any more, he interrupted.

"Yes, yes, you have." He started waving his index finger in front of him as he talked. "And you thought that because I too

3

have started a company, many companies, in fact, and you are, indirectly, a student of mine, because you have been learning meditation from James, and James is a student of mine ... that I might be able to help you, maybe even give you some startup capital, correct?"

It was the longest run-on sentence that I had heard in a while, but he was essentially correct. "Yes, I..." I started, but he held up the palm of his hand, as if to silence me. I could tell he was used to having his way, and his manner made me a bit nervous.

He closed his eyes and turned his chin slightly upward. It was as if he was gazing into and beyond the spot just above my head. Of course, he couldn't have been looking at me, because his eyes were closed. He slowly turned his head to the left a bit, and then just as slowly to the right, as if he was a video camera, scanning an image of me.

"What are you doing?" I asked, not quite sure how to proceed. Everything about this initial encounter was off, and I began to wonder if it was such a good idea to have visited him after all.

He held up his left hand again in a motion that could not be mistaken: *wait a minute, don't say anything, let me finish.* Then, after a few moments, he smiled and started to nod his head, as if he approved of the picture he was seeing in his mind's eye.

He opened his eyes, lowering the hand that was stopping my barrage of questions, and gave me a childlike, almost innocent smile. He reminded me of a little kid who had gotten just what he wanted, and was now very pleased with himself.

"Well," he started, extending both hands out in front of him, as if offering me the chance to make the next move.

"Well, what?" I asked, still not sure where he was going with this behavior. In my mind, I began to rehearse what I had come to tell him about: my idea for a new business.

"Hmm..." he started, and now I was thoroughly confused and a bit miffed that he wasn't going to offer me an explanation. He still seemed to be moving his face slightly to the left and slightly to the right, this time with his eyes open but clearly gazing behind me and not looking at any one thing in particular.

"What were you doing?" I ventured, trying to buy some time before I jumped into explaining my startup idea.

4

"Aha, of course. Let me explain." He got up and walked around his desk. Then he leaned back on the desk, and crossed his arms. *How odd*, I thought, when I noticed that he had been sitting at his own desk, in his own office, *with his suit jacket on.*

His manner now changed to that of a friendly teacher, having a quiet fireside chat with a pupil. "I was studying your energetic patterns, and trying to determine probability of success of your new business," he said, matter-of-factly. He moved his hands in the air in front of him as he talked, pointing to things that only he could see. His gestures and general demeanor reminded me a little of Jeff Goldblum in *The Fly*.

I hesitated for a moment, trying to understand what he had just said. I understood probabilities, but *energetic patterns* was a term that I wasn't familiar with. This meeting was getting stranger by the minute. I looked at the door to make sure I had a clear escape path in case things didn't go well. "Isn't it typical for a venture capitalist to ask about the potential market, the competition, and my experience, in order to determine the probability of success of a business?" I asked politely, trying to sound knowledgeable.

"Yes, that's what a typical venture capitalist does," he nodded and laughed. "But, I am not a typical venture capitalist. How many VCs do you know that also teach meditation classes?"

I had to admit I knew none. But then again, I didn't know any venture capitalists at all. I was only a year out of college and hadn't yet started my first software company. My mind turned to the chain of events that led me to meet him in his office.

I had been in Europe in the fall of 1992 working for a consulting company, shortly after my graduation, when I suddenly decided that it was time to join a small startup in preparation for starting my own software company someday. I quit my job in Europe and came back to the Boston area to work for DiVA, a multi-media software company that was spun off from the MIT Media Lab. I had only been there a few weeks when I noticed that the office next door had a sign that read 'Boston Meditation Society', and a poster that advertised 'Free Meditation Classes'.

The first time I noticed the sign, I didn't pay much attention to it. Then one evening, around 7 p.m., I was talking with some of my co-workers when a gentleman wearing a gray suit that looked a little too small for him wandered in. Technology startups, particularly in Cambridge, aren't known for dressing up, and we were all dressed very casually in jeans and t-shirts. He introduced himself as James, from the Meditation 'studio' next door. I had no idea what a meditation 'studio' was but studied his appearance to see if I could learn anything.

He had dark hair, a hawk-like nose, and always seemed to be leaning forward on his toes, as if he was wearing sneakers and was about to spring forward. I looked at his feet to see if in fact he had gym shoes on; he did not, his black wing-tips were 100% business-like.

"That's a strange way to dress for meditation," started one of my co-workers, Lisa, who seemed to know a little bit about the subject. I knew very little about meditation, but listened with interest.

"Huh?" he looked confused for a second. Then his eyes did a complete 360-degree circle at a pace slightly quicker than the pace of his head, which was also circling in the same direction, while he lifted himself up on his toes. At the end of the strange circling motion, he stopped, fell back on his heels, and looked directly at her.

"Oh," he smiled and laughed. "You mean the suit! No, I'm a computer consultant, as many of the members of my meditation group are. We only do meditation classes at night. I'm still dressed up from work. I just wanted to invite you guys over for a free 'how to meditate' class sometime. It's at 7 p.m. every night."

Then he went on to explain how their meditation wasn't like normal meditation, how they used it to help them get ahead in their computer careers. It was difficult for me to pay attention to what he was saying, because of the weirdness of his facial expressions and movements. He kept leaning forward and turning his head in arcs both clockwise and counterclockwise in between (and sometimes during) his sentences. He was obviously very passionate about the benefits of meditation.

After he left, Lisa laughed at how odd it would be to try to learn meditation, which was supposed to be about relaxation and peace of mind, from someone who was so *wired*. And *weird*. Then she went on and on about how she felt this guy didn't understand meditation at all. "Meditation isn't about making money," she explained, "it's about giving up your worldly possessions and being spiritual! And if you're really committed, you go up into the mountains to meditate, not wear a suit and brag about how meditation helps you with your career!"

She had obviously written him off. In her mind, making money and meditating did not mix at all. They were two completely separate things. I, on the other hand, was secretly intrigued by the idea that there was a group of computer consultants who had formed a meditation group. James had insisted that meditation could help me grow personally, reduce stress, and help in my career. Of the three, I quickly latched on to the two practical ones: reducing stress and helping in my career, and I decided I would check out his class sometime. I didn't mention it to my co-workers because they didn't seem to think too highly of the ideas that James was presenting.

On a Tuesday evening during the following week, I wandered in to the studio and there was James. As I was the only student to show up that evening, he taught me a basic meditation technique and spent a lot of time asking about my background. If I was interested in learning more, he said, I should show up again the next week. I started meditating for a few minutes each day and followed his instructions, but wasn't sure if I was doing it correctly, so I kept coming to his classes.

I soon noticed that he kept mentioning his teacher, particularly in the context of esoteric teachings. James would always begin with "My teacher always says...", then go on to talk about something that I had either never heard of, or if I had heard of it, wasn't sure I believed: things like auras, energy lines, astral travel, past lives, and on and on. He alluded to so many of these things that I lost track of them quickly.

One day, several months after I had started meditating (and had moved on from DiVA to work at Lotus, which was one of the largest software companies in the world at that time), I told him that I was considering starting a software company with my roommate, and asked how, if at all, he thought meditation could help me.

That got him really excited. He started telling me about his teacher, who was an accomplished entrepreneur in the computer industry, and how he had formulated a path that that combined career success with spiritual success. Finally, after about fifteen minutes, he told me he'd introduce me to his teacher to see if he would help me start my company.

I didn't know (or really care) much about spiritual development, but I figured that if this teacher could teach me 'advanced' meditation techniques that could help me start my company — I'd be there in a heartbeat! And, if he was that accomplished an entrepreneur, maybe he could teach me about business, or better yet, could give me some start-up money so that I could get my company off the ground!

With that in mind, I found myself in Ramaswami's office trying to ask him for business advice but getting some strange reply about how my 'energetic patterns' would influence my success in the business world, before I'd even had a chance to explain my business idea to him.

This meeting, which came at the very beginning of my journey into the business world, was also the start of a hidden journey that kept pace with what was happening with my entrepreneurial activities. I call it a hidden journey because Ramaswami would explain that his path of teaching was as much about the 'hidden worlds' (another term that I didn't fully understand) as it was about the world around us.

His teachings introduced me to a whole new side of meditation, human relationships, career paths, spirituality, and what can only be termed, for lack of a better word, the 'occult'.

This journey would go through the rocky rise of my first company, Brainstorm Technologies, which during its time became one of the fastest growing and well-known startups on the East Coast. I didn't realize it at the time, but my success and failures in the business world would be intertwined closely with my mastery of a set of 'spiritual principles' concerned with these 'hidden worlds'.

I started meditating, a path of personal growth, because I thought it could help accelerate my career. By the time I was done, I would begin to view my career as a way of accelerating my personal growth. I realized I had it backwards.

But all of that comes later. As I stood in his office, overlooking the Charles River with the Boston skyline in the distance, I was simply wondering how and if Ramaswami could help me to get my business up and running.

"I guess I don't know any VCs that teach meditation classes," I answered sheepishly.

He nodded and then asked me to go ahead and describe my business idea. "Since you are so convinced that it's important for me to hear about your idea, the potential market, *et cetera, et cetera*, then I will listen."

I didn't even recognize that he was only humoring me and didn't really care if I had a coherent business idea or plan at this point — he was just trying to get to know me better.

I was now working for Lotus and was excited about their collaborative computing platform, Lotus Notes. I had come across Notes before, when I was still a college student, and thought it might make for the start of an interesting business someday. I rapidly described my idea to him, which was to build a link between Lotus Notes and various products that were sold by Microsoft. I explained in detail how companies spent so much money on both Microsoft and Lotus products, but had difficulty making them work together. "These companies," I finished, trying to sound business-like, "aren't leveraging their investments."

He was nodding his head slowly but remained silent.

"Well, what do you think of the idea...?" I asked, thinking that I made a good sales pitch. "My business partner and I are planning to do some market research starting next week," I added, hoping to impress.

He rubbed his chin slightly. "You know, it doesn't really matter what I think of the idea ... the only thing that really matters is your energetic patterns at this moment in time, superimposed onto the energetic patterns and timing of the marketplace."

It was not the answer I was looking for.

"Look, people think that starting a business is simply a career decision and that factors in the market determine the success or failure of a business. But do you know why most businesses fail?"

I had to admit I did not.

"Because of the energetic patterns of the founders, of course! Their patterns cause them to fail. Bad management is the #1 reason why business fail in this country. They don't know themselves well enough, and this causes them to do stupid things."

He waited for it to sink in, then went on: "That's so important that I want to repeat it! The #1 reason why business fail is: *entrepreneurs do stupid things.* Now, most entrepreneurs aren't stupid people — yet they do stupid things. Isn't that interesting?"

"I ... guess so," I responded.

"Why is it that most businesses implode? Because starting a business isn't really about starting a business. What makes you do these things are your karmic patterns, your energetic patterns in the hidden worlds, and your hidden beliefs about this world. That's why I was studying your energetic patterns to determine how successful I think you will be."

I had no idea what he was talking about, but ventured a guess that 'energetic patterns' were a way of talking about different management styles, and/or different personality types. "And, what did you learn ... will I be successful?" I asked.

"Are you sure you really want to know?"

"Are you saying," I responded, regaining my confidence, "that you can tell the future?" I was a little flabbergasted that he would make such a ridiculous statement.

Suddenly he hunched down, puckered up his lips and face, and walked in front of me as if he were a very old man with a cane. He waved the imaginary cane in the air and spoke slowly with a raspy, deliberate voice delivered from the back of his throat: "Al-ways ... in ... motion ... is ... the future ...!" Then he waved his imaginary cane at me, smiling.

"Huh?" I responded involuntarily and then I had a flash of recognition. "Yoda," I replied, recognizing his impression of the character from Star Wars.

"Yes, yes..." he replied in his normal voice. "It is not possible to know the future exactly ... because it is always in motion ... but it is possible to see how things are likely to play out, given today's situation." He walked back to his chair and sat down before continuing.

"I learned that you will have some success in your business venture ... but it will take longer than you think, and will lead you down a path that you're not expecting to be on ..." He chuckled as if he knew something I didn't know.

I didn't understand what he meant. "You mean that I will end up creating different products than I'm envisioning now?" I was naturally thinking about the inevitable evolution of a business concept. I had read many books about how the first idea is not necessarily the one that makes you successful.

He broke out in laughter unexpectedly. The he stopped, folded his arms, putting the elbow of one arm in the hand of the other, with his fingers tapping his chin. "Such a serious young man," he said, in mock-seriousness. I could see that he was enjoying his feigned look of concern.

"No, kid, I'm not talking about what products you'll make — that's the content of the business. I'm talking about the form and structure of your business and your life." He stopped to see if I had grasped his meaning. I had not.

"I'm talking about your energetic patterns. You will have some success, to a degree, and may even make some money, but what you will learn on this journey is the most important thing! I'm talking about personal, even spiritual twists and turns. Let me ask you a question: why do people start businesses?"

I answered without hesitation. "To make a lot of money and retire early so they don't have to work anymore!"

He started laughing. "What you don't realize is that there is no such thing as *not working* for someone like yourself ... Your Energetic Pattern won't let you stop working! Okay, let's say that is the obvious reason for starting a company. It is a universal law, I repeat, a uni-ver-sal law, that every obvious thing, has a hidden counterpart. So what is the hidden reason to start a business?"

I had no idea what he was talking about and told him so.

"The hidden reason, my young friend, for starting a business, is that it is simply a step along a path. This journey is not unlike the journey spiritual seekers embark upon when they begin to meditate, and they do something like committing to go to a monastery. They think they are doing it because they want to gain something; in their case, the thing they want to gain is Enlightenment, the Big E, or in your case, it's Money, the big M." He smiled as he emphasized the word.

I still had no idea what he was talking about.

"For most spiritual seekers, they see Enlightenment as some goal that, once attained, will give them freedom. In your case," he was now pacing back and forth in front of the window, "you see money as a goal that, *once attained*, will give you freedom!"

I thought I was beginning to understand. "But money will give me freedom," I replied quickly and went on to describe how without money, I wasn't free to travel when I wanted, wasn't free to spend my time in my own way, had to get up in the morning and go to work, and so on.

He slammed his hands on his desk so hard that I almost jumped out of my chair. "Hogwash!" he yelled. I eyed the door, planning my escape route from this madman, but he calmed down just as suddenly and resumed his very cerebral, almost soothing tone.

"The real reason that you are about to embark on this path has a lot to do with your future, much more than you know. I saw things in your aura which confirm this. Starting a business is like a stretch of a road, you could call that road your career, or you could call it your life. Each of us who embarks on it learns lessons that are much more important than whether you make a ton of money or not. Sometimes, how much money you make isn't directly under your control – it's all about the market you're in."

"Saw things in my aura? How did you do that?" I asked, now a bit intrigued. I had heard of auras, recently from James, but hadn't met anyone who claimed to be able to see them. And I had never heard of them mentioned in a business context.

"Yes, in your aura. Let me ask you another question: what was your favorite activity in high school?"

I thought back to my high school days. I had been quite active in a number of extracurricular activities, but my favorite had always been speech competitions. My success in those competitions had helped me to get into MIT so that I could study what I thought was my real passion, computer science.

"Yes, yes, that's it. When you have some time, think about that—your past is inevitably linked to your future, in ways that you can't even imagine..." He was turning his head from left to right in a strange way that I didn't understand again.

"Your business idea. We will talk of it again, when you are more ready," he said.

"But I am ready!" I exhorted.

"I have students all over the country who are teaching introductory meditation classes. It was no accident that you met James — James will act as your mentor as you learn some basic techniques. Remember this, it's the second universal law: there are no accidents. Do you like movies?"

I nodded my head. "It's the only way to get through to you Generation-X'ers," he blurted out. "You're all so visual, it's the only way to get you to tap into a state of mind. I will give you a movie assignment. The fact that you recognized my Yoda impression means that like most computer geeks, you're probably a fan of science fiction and fantasy, am I right?"

Though I didn't like being called a computer geek, it was true. I did like science fiction and fantasy movies. I didn't realize it at the time, but time and again he would use things that already intrigued me to teach me about this particular path of spiritual development, which he called the Path of the Career Warrior.

"Your assignment is to rent and watch *Excalibur*. Have you seen it?"

I hadn't. But I was more than a tad disappointed. I hadn't expected a movie assignment. I had come to talk about business, and all he had done was utter strange remarks about auras and told me to go see an old movie about King Arthur. Not that I disliked medieval adventure movies, but I had a thousand and one questions for him about business, and unfortunately, it was clear the meeting was over. He dismissed me abruptly.

CHAPTER SUMMARY
A STRANGE ENCOUNTER

Is it possible that career success and spiritual progress are not mutually exclusive but inter-related?

Like my co-worker in this chapter, we all have a deeply ingrained picture of a serious spiritual seeker: someone who renounces his worldly possessions and goes off into the desert or to a monastery to meditate or pray.

This chapter introduces a new idea: that you can be successful in the world and be deeply committed to your own spiritual growth. What we need are mentors and role models who have travelled this path before. Ramaswami was one for me, and that's why I wrote this book for you.

Similarly, this chapter introduces the heretical idea that it's okay to ask "what's in it for me?" when exploring spiritual practices like meditation, Yoga, martial arts, or even prayer. It's okay to start a spiritual practice because you think it might help you in some way as long as it sets you firmly on a spiritual path. If you travel the path correctly, the process itself will change you. What we need is a "way in" to the hidden worlds — once you're in, you can't help becoming a totally different person.

Starting a business is a journey, not a destination. So is meditation.

Many of us think that the reason entrepreneurs start a business is to become rich, to make enough money to have the freedom to do whatever we want to do. The reality is that only a few entrepreneurs get rich; most don't. It's the journey of a startup that is always rewarding in and of itself, chock full of lessons about ourselves that we didn't even know we needed to learn.

Similarly, some people view meditation as a way to reach "Enlightenment" or freedom from the world – freedom from what Buddhists call the endless cycle of life and death. But meditation is also a journey, and the process is as important as the destination. If you do it right, or even if you do it wrong, you'll learn lessons about yourself that you definitely didn't expect!

Everything that is obvious and visible to us has a hidden side.

Every single mystical and religious tradition in the world tells us that what we see around us is not "all there is." In eastern traditions, everything travels through the causal and astral realms before becoming physical reality. In some Native American traditions, everything that is going to happen in the physical world happens in the dream world first, before it shows up in physical reality. Shamans journey into these other realms and they are referred to as non-ordinary reality. Meditation is a practical way to clear our minds so that we can open up and sense what's happening in these other, normally "hidden" worlds.

Success in our career may have as much to do with our Energetic Patterns as it does with external factors.

This chapter also introduces the idea of the Energetic Pattern. If there are hidden worlds all around us, then our Energetic Pattern defines our character and personality in these worlds – the sum of all of our hopes, fears, experiences, tendencies, aptitudes, and even our destiny in this life. More to the point, our Energetic Pattern impacts how we make decisions about our careers and our lives, and manifests itself in the world around us as External Patterns of success, failure, and repetition in our lives as a result of our decisions.

As Ramaswami warns me as a would-be entrepreneur: "Why is it that most businesses fail? Because of the Energetic Patterns of the founders, of course! They don't know themselves well enough, and this causes them to do stupid things … what makes you do these things are your karmic patterns, your energetic patterns in the hidden world, and your hidden beliefs about this world. That's why I was studying your energetic patterns."

While our Patterns affect the future, the future is always in motion!

Our Energetic Pattern isn't so much about destiny or free will, as much as it is about how we interact with the world around us, and how that world affects us. Yoda's famous statement about the future always being in motion may be

15

obvious on one level, but it has powerful implications for all of us. What this means is that what we do, how we think, how we interact with other people, is constantly causing our future to shift. Although our energetic patterns have influence on this, we can change those patterns and thus change the future!

2 A LITTLE DÉJÀ VU
JUNE, 1993

James called me at 3:30 p.m. and asked how I was doing. I was actually quite bored with my work at Lotus; even though I hadn't gotten in to work until 10:30 a.m., my mind had already wandered. His call was an interesting distraction.

"Swami asked to meet you this evening after work," started James. "Are you available?"

It had been several weeks since my meeting with Ramaswami, and I was quite surprised to hear he wanted to meet with me again. During the first week following the meeting, I thought about it incessantly: what had he meant by my energetic patterns? What did he think about my business idea? Did he think I'd make a good entrepreneur?

The abruptness with which he ended our meeting convinced me that the meeting went poorly, and that he wasn't going to help me get my business started. Given his strange philosophy on what it took to be a successful businessperson, I wasn't completely convinced that I wanted his help yet. But, my own need for approval led me to obsess with whether I 'sold' him on my business concept or not. He was the first really experienced entrepreneur I had presented the business idea to.

"Ah, sure," I answered, after hesitating for a moment, "I can make it. Did he say what it was about?"

"Yes, he's taken a very strong personal interest in you. I

don't know what you said but it definitely left him with the impression that you are someone he wants to work with!"

I was a bit surprised. "But, I didn't say anything to him! Half the time he had his eyes closed during our meeting, and when I tried to ask him questions, he cut me off and abruptly ended our conversation. I was sure that we didn't mix well."

"Oh," James laughed. "Don't worry — that's what he always does — he was using his third eye to look into your past lives and your future selves..."

"Huh? Past lives and future selves?" *Here we go again*, I thought. "Say, James, do you really believe in that stuff?"

He suddenly became non-committal. "Well, why don't you ask Ramaswami about that..."

We were to meet at the Christian Science Center in Boston, which is one of the more interesting places in the entire city. Built over a hundred years ago, the land that it occupies is now worth a fortune.

It consists of several magnificent (and imposing) church buildings and a large open courtyard. On one side of the courtyard there is a line of lampposts that look like trees. On the other side, pillars of stone line the side of one of the long buildings, which serves as the administration offices for the center.

The size, scale, and architecture of the place give it a feeling that is somewhere between a gothic medieval church and an ancient Egyptian temple.

In the middle of the courtyard is a long rectangular pool of water that has some unusual characteristics. The pool is actually raised above the ground, and the structure containing the water looks like a large air mattress, made out of reddish-colored marble. The water spills off of the sides of this stone mattress and disappears into invisible drainage devices located slightly below ground level.

The top of the pool is a smooth surface that gives the appearance that it is not moving, but the water is actually constantly in motion, draining off the sides. The sound of the water, combined with this smooth surface, makes it a very soothing place to go for a walk. That's exactly what

Ramaswami had in mind when he asked to meet me there.

"Look around," he instructed me as we started to walk along the length of the pool. He was dressed, as usual, in a designer, double-breasted suit. It was sunny that afternoon, and the grayish-olive complexion of his suit seemed appropriate. As usual in those days, I was dressed in tennis shoes, khakis, and a T-shirt. The two of us must have looked like an odd pair: a tall skinny white guy dressed immaculately, and a much shorter, brown guy dressed like the computer programmer that I was.

"What catches your eye?" he asked and gestured all around us.

I wasn't sure how to answer. "Well, the water does."

"Yes, what about the water?" he pressed.

"Well, hmm..." I thought about it for a second, trying to think of the kind of answer he would want to hear.

He saw me and interjected. "No, no, don't think about it too much. Use your intuition — what's the first thing that comes to mind?"

I took a deep breath and said the first thing that came to mind, surprising myself. "It's very strange to be in the middle of a city, on a concrete courtyard, and to have this pool be here ... it's almost futuristic..." I took another deep breath: "and ancient at the same time."

"Yes, that's good," he smiled. I wondered if he would have said that no matter what my answer was. "Have you seen it before anywhere?"

I wrinkled my forehead and looked down as I tried to remember. Then I looked around. I had a vague sense of déjà vu — as if I had been in a similar place a long, long time ago. But I could not remember a specific time and explained my feeling to him.

He listened to my explanation and nodded his head as we walked. "The past and the future are linked together, sometimes we can remember the future in the same way that we remember the past..." he paused to see if what he had said had registered.

"But that's of no consequence right now. I'm here to teach you about different kinds of meditation and the path that I believe you will want to follow."

"Wait-a-minute! Hold on!" I had yelled it so loud that the

people around us all looked over to see what the commotion was about. I was a little embarrassed, and waited for them to look away before I continued.

We were standing now just beside one of the shorter sides of the rectangular pool. In the ground was a small circle made out of red-colored bricks. It had markings along its perimeter, as if it was a compass, or a clock.

"How is it possible," I started, standing smack dead in the middle of the circle, "to remember the future? That's just new-age mumbo jumbo. If it hasn't happened yet, how can you remember it? That's impossible!" Now I thought I had caught him.

He was standing at the outer end of the circle and started walking around it clockwise. "Inkling, my friend. Inklings are what we remember. In the business world, the ability to see the future is of paramount importance. Of course, the future is not set in stone, like I said last time ... *always in motion is the future.*

"We all start businesses because we see a certain vision of the future ... of how things are going to be. But we're not all successful because the future isn't always what we expect it to be!"

He paused as if wondering whether to go on. Then, he spoke rapidly. "But that's not what I'm talking about here ... I'm talking about the direct experience of a future or past self," he sighed. "This is a bit difficult to explain in your current state of mind, and even more difficult for you to understand. We'll have to continue this discussion about the past and the future when you are ready."

Secretly, I believed he was copping out. I had heard of past lives — reincarnation was a belief that was held by a large number of people around the world, and though I didn't personally believe in it, at least it seemed plausible. But future selves? That absolutely made no sense. Part of me wanted to get into an argument about the logical inconsistencies in what he was saying.

"This is all I can say now. Do you understand causal links? It goes something like this: A causes B to happen. However, under rigorous mathematical definitions, there is no constraint that says A has to happen in time before B. A can actually happen after B, but still be the cause of B! It doesn't break the causal link." He saw me trying to grasp the concepts and laughed.

"Come on," he replied, "you're the MIT guy ... just do some research on quantum physics and report back to me when you've had a chance to ... for our purposes, let me just say that you are thinking about starting a business around Lotus Notes, right? Now, when was the first time you were intrigued by Lotus Notes?"

I thought about it. A logical answer would have been my current assignment doing work at Lotus. But I had, in fact, been exposed to it much earlier, while still in college. My college roommate and I wrote a business plan for a competition and I had identified Notes as an interesting technology platform that let people work together more effectively. I explained that I had been intrigued by it even then, and when I got the chance to get my current job at Lotus, I jumped at it.

"Now, one way to look at it," he said walking clockwise around the circle, "is that you took this assignment at Lotus partly because you had noticed an interest in Lotus Notes many years before. The cause is what happened to you in college. The result is you taking the contract at Lotus, which is in turn the cause of you starting a business based around Lotus Notes, right?"

I agreed that this seemed reasonable.

He stopped his clockwise walk, and then began to walk around the circle in the opposite direction. "Or, it can be said, that the reason you took such an interest in Lotus Notes all those years ago, is because one of your future selves, this one," he pointed at me and touched my shoulder, "was, one day, possibly going to start a company ... related to Lotus Notes.

"Now, in strict mathematical terms, you cannot distinguish one from the other. What caused what is up for debate — it depends on your perspective."

I found it all more than a little bit confusing, and I was sure that under strict mathematical terms, he was wrong. I could not, however, remember any laws or theorems or equations that I could use to counter his arguments, other than simple common sense.

He continued. "The key is that you *took notice* of it back then, just as you *took notice* when this contract at Lotus was offered to you. Do you remember the feeling when you first noticed Lotus Notes?"

I could not remember what I was feeling at the time, beyond the fact that I was intrigued by it and wanted to learn more about it.

"Well, that feeling of noticing something in your environment is like a message from the hidden worlds. Of course, a message like that could mean many things." He stopped walking around the circle and stepped back.

"Now, it could also be said that the reason this place looks familiar to you—" he pointed out the Christian Science Center complex all around us, "is that you've had some connection to it. Most people in the spiritual community would say that déjà vu means that you have had some previous experience here, perhaps even in a past life. But it is just as valid to say that perhaps you will have a future experience here and that little tug you feel in your mind, which you call déjà vu — is actually remembering the future. You see?"

I did not know what to say. I didn't agree and went on and on about how the future could not cause the past — it was a logical impossibility, but my arguments fell on deaf ears. I used the improbabilities of time travel to the past as an example. But he stood firm and insisted that I go to the MIT library and see if I could find any strict mathematical or physical constraint that said that A had to happen before B if A was the cause of B.

As I could not convince him otherwise, and he could not convince me of his point, we were silent for a few minutes.

"Have you ever been on a treasure hunt?" He asked, seemingly changing the subject.

"Huh? What do you mean?"

"As a kid, do you remember when you were on to something and you had a map to follow or a puzzle to solve?"

I did in fact remember the feeling, as I was an avid solver of puzzles. When I was young, my friends and I would bury something, and then draw a 'treasure map' that showed its location. It made us feel like adventurers on a quest. I described this feeling to him.

"Aha. Yes. Well, that's more to the point, then," he said and started walking around the pool again, hiding a smile.

"Oh? Which point is that?" I followed him, completely forgetting about the frustration I had been feeling during the past-future conversation.

"Why did you want to meet with me in the first place?" he asked from a few paces in front of me.

"Ah… well … I thought maybe you could help me start my business."

"Yes, and so far, you're probably wondering why I haven't given you any practical business advice?"

"Ah … well … yeah," I said, fumbling for the right words.

"You see, I do teach principles that can be applied to the business world, particularly to the process of starting and growing a company.

"But the most important part of my teaching is that starting a business is *not really simply about starting a business, it's about discovering and walking your own unique path in this life.*

"I teach about using the business world as a way to learn more about ourselves, and using this knowledge to ultimately be more successful in the business world. Only when we truly know ourselves, when we're aware of our own destinies can we really, truly feel successful in the business world. Otherwise, we'll end up being either unsuccessful, or even worse, unfulfilled."

"What do you mean?" I asked. The concept that someone could be successful but not fulfilled was lost on my young mind.

"Well, the Path of the Career Warrior is the path of a seeker. If you follow my instructions, I will show you how to bring that feeling of excitement, of adventure, that you had when you were a little kid on a treasure hunt into your daily life. The process of starting a business will become more like a treasure hunt than a risky undertaking."

I was now intrigued by what he was saying.

"What is it that I'll be seeking on this path?" I asked.

"Oh…many things…business success…success in your meditation. Personal growth. Finding your true self. All of these things and more. You have already taken the first step, by learning to meditate. The second step is to pay attention."

"Pay attention?" I replied, thinking that he was admonishing me for letting my mind wander. "But I am paying attention."

"Not to me! It's important that you learn to pay attention to yourself. To the *feelings* that you have inside you. Many meditation teachers will tell you to simply meditate and things will get better. In the real world, it's not so simple. In the business world it's not so simple. You have to use meditation as a mirror ... to clear your mind so that you will be able to see the clues that are all around you and more importantly, inside you."

He stepped up on the concrete platform that surrounded the pool and walked on the narrow ledge with his arms extended in different directions, looking very much like a little boy who had found something new to play with. I walked alongside him slowly contemplating what he was telling me.

"To walk this path is to be a treasure hunter. And as a treasure hunter, you are to look for clues. When you find a clue, you should write it down in a diary or a journal. Do you keep a journal?"

I had experimented with keeping a journal at various times of my life, but only inconsistently.

"Okay, that's good. Now I want you to start keeping one again, and to use this journal to find and record clues."

"Clues ... what kinds of clues?" I asked.

"Clues usually start with something in the everyday world around us. But how we notice if it's a clue is by paying attention to how we feel inside. For example, remember the feeling that you had been in this place before? That's a clue. Write it down. Remember the feeling when you first were intrigued by Lotus Notes back in college? That's a clue too. Write it down."

"What exactly should I write down?" I asked, glad that he had given me a specific task to do that I could get my hands around, but unsure exactly how to accomplish it.

"Write down the event, place, or item, that causes you to have these feelings. Each of these feelings is a clue. And then write down how you feel in response to these external things. It's simple. This is a basic exercise."

"But how do I know if I should write something down or not?" I asked.

"Oh, you'll learn over time. The key is that if you have an *unusual feeling* toward a place, person, thing, or even to an event, you should write it down. If it's a feeling that you have all the time, then it's probably not unusual or significant enough to be worthwhile. If, however, it's something unusual, you should write it down."

"But how will I know if it's significant…?" I asked him.

"At first, you may not, but that will come. Try it out. Write down things that intrigue you, or are out of the ordinary. Even if a coincidence happens that seems a little too *coincidental*, write it down. Whether it is actually significant or not is something that only hindsight will show you. And even then you might not recognize its significance."

I liked the idea of having something specific to do, but his directions seemed vague and I still wasn't sure if I grasped what he meant.

"Have you ever met someone and felt as if you'd known them for a long time?" I had to admit that I had. "Okay, that's something to write down. That's the type of feeling that is a clue from the hidden worlds."

"What am I supposed to do after I start writing these things and feelings down?"

"You're going to look for patterns. For example, the feeling that you have in this place is unusual. Where have you felt it before? When you start to notice and write these feelings down, you will be able to go back into your notebooks and see when you had this type of feeling before."

"Will this help in becoming an entrepreneur?" I asked.

"Oh … absolutely. Without a doubt. But you are not *just* becoming an entrepreneur. You will be noticing the messages from the hidden worlds that will give you clues about what important issues you need to deal with during your entrepreneurial journey."

"But why do I need clues? Can't I simply learn about how to start software companies from talking to people who've done it before?" It seemed like a much more reasonable approach than 'writing down my feelings.'

"Yes, and no. You are not looking to start *their business*, you are looking to start *your own business*. The lessons that you need may be different than the lessons that those folks need. Starting a business is not simply a mechanical thing; it's part of your path of personal growth. The clues that we're seeking are markers along this path."

I wasn't sure if I believed that there was any connection between the Christian Science Center and either my past or my future. But I did agree to start writing down what he called 'clues' as best as I could remember them.

"Remember two universal principles that I always insist my students understand: One, that everything that happens in the everyday world has a counterpart in the hidden worlds. Every unusual event probably has a significance in the hidden worlds. A significance that is unique to you. And Two, when something repeats, it may be even more important, because these events are linked together in ways that modern science has no way of comprehending.

"These links aren't figments of our imagination, they actually exist in the hidden worlds. This is equally true with clues from the past or clues from the future."

I resumed my argument that it is not possible for something in the future to cause something in the past.

He sighed. "Think of time as a river. It flows in only one direction. But let me ask you, if you are a drop of water in the river, can something that happens downstream affect you even though you haven't gotten there yet?"

"I guess if there was a dam or if something fell in the river that affected its flow, that would affect me," I answered. "However, if I knew that the river was going to be blocked up ahead, I'd find a way around it."

Again, he insisted that though the future wasn't fixed, it was certainly possible to be impacted by it. "Even though the blockage of the river is still in our future (because we haven't reached it yet), it can cause us to do something in the present, namely finding a way around it."

I found that applying his analogy to time seemed like nonsense. I made a note to look up the mathematical principles that would prove him wrong.

He nodded and then changed the subject again: "I always give movie assignments that start with obvious, non-subtle elements so that my concepts can start to sink in at a subconscious level while suspending your disbelief! That's why I start with science fiction and fantasy, because they are *obviously* fiction. Right?" He smiled and waited to see if I had gotten his intonation of the word *obviously*.

"I watched *Excalibur*," I told him. "I enjoyed the movie, but what does it have to do with starting a business?"

"Fantasy is a good way to start to get a sense of what the hidden worlds are like. Without a mastery of the hidden worlds, you might be successful in your business, but it will be extremely unfulfilling to you, because of your particular energetic patterns. I cannot underestimate the danger of success without purpose for you. You will learn this lesson the hard way, but it would save you a lot of trouble if you just listened to me now."

I thought I *was* listening and told him so.

"Is there anything you saw in *Excalibur* that relates to our discussion of future and past?"

I thought back to the movie. King Arthur. The sword in the stone. The lady of the lake. Sir Lancelot. Then it occurred to me "Yes! Merlin. Merlin travels backward in time — he goes from the future to the past, right?"

"Yes, that's right," he said, as we resumed our walk around the pool. "Now, if it wasn't possible for something in the future to cause something in the past, how could Merlin travel backwards in time?" he asked.

I frowned and realized that he must be provoking me. "*Excalibur*," I started, "is fantasy. It's not real. It's not like the physical world all around us," I assured him, wondering that I would have to explain this to someone almost twice my age.

"Are you sure?" he asked. "The reason I assign movies is that it makes you aware of things that seem impossible to you; but because they are presented as fiction, you are able to understand the concepts and have a point of reference first, before you are able to accept them as true."

I was about to go off on a diatribe about the fact that simply seeing something in a movie wasn't enough to make me accept it as reality when he started laughing.

"Come, come, let's leave issues of the future and the past to theoreticians for now." He picked up his pace considerably, and I strained to keep up.

"But what about Merlin, how does that relate to success in the business world?"

"It doesn't — at least not yet — I just wanted you to have a point of reference about the flow of time for when you understand the hidden worlds better."

He saw my disappointment. I had been hoping for something more practical. "The movie assignments are so that you can adopt the proper perspective ... a filmmaker imbues a movie, and certain characters with a particular state of mind. You can tap into those states of mind by watching the movie and focusing in on a certain character or aspect of it."

He made me re-affirm that I would start to seek out clues in the environment and write them down, whenever and wherever they happened. I agreed to do so, even though I wasn't quite sure what constituted a 'clue' and what didn't.

"And, since you like sci-fi movies so much, your next movie assignment is to watch *Prince of Darkness*, by John Carpenter, and tell me if it has anything to do with what we talked about here today." I had seen the movie once before and remembered it as a badly-made B horror movie and told him that.

"Nevertheless, that is the perfect movie for you to watch ... and see if you can find something interesting or meaningful about it related to *messages*."

We agreed that soon he "would teach me a different meditation technique, one that was attuned to my work." This sounded interesting and I got quite excited about it and wanted a preview now.

"Nope. You have to wait. For now, you have to start collecting clues about your future." Our second meeting was over.

CHAPTER SUMMARY
A LITTLE DÉJÀ VU

To become a Career Warrior, turn your career into a treasure hunt. To find the treasure, follow the clues!

To turn your career (and your life) into a treasure hunt, you have to look for clues. Clues are usually internal feelings, hunches, intuition, feelings of déjà vu. I like to refer to these as glitches in the "matrix." Clues are the easiest way to tune into the hidden worlds, and they are beckoning to us all the time, if we can learn to quiet our mind and tune into them. Usually a clue is triggered by something external that your subconscious mind tells you is important.

There are no coincidences. The future is always calling you.

The ability to recognize clues means recognizing not just internal feelings but synchronicity at work in the world around us. The past and the future are linked in ways that we don't always understand.

We live in a world where we think time flows only in one direction — the past and the present create the future. While this is true, as we delve into the quantum level of physics, reality becomes much more complicated than this. The placement of subatomic particles in space (at a particular point in time) is not as absolute as we might think; rather it is based on probabilities. As a result, causation is not as clear as we might suppose at the subatomic levels Some physicists have theorized that there are multiple parallel universes operating at the same time. If so, then *clues* are tools for tapping into these other realities. The funny feelings which we get may in fact have something to do with the hidden worlds as much as the world around us.

The business world and the world of science, art, and literature are full of examples of unique people feeling like they were "called" to start a business, write a book, or make a particular movie. Finding your future isn't a matter of logic; it's a matter of intuition. What is your future calling you to do? Use your intuition, follow the clues and you will find out!

EXERCISE: Keep a journal of important clues.

In the movie, *Indiana Jones and the Last Crusade*, Indy's father, played by Sean Connery, had a "Grail Diary" which included the clues he'd been gathering all his life pointing to the location of the Holy Grail.   Your own journal of clues will lead you to your own Holy Grail — the deeper part of you that knows what you need in this life and what you are here to accomplish!

1. To start, get a notebook (or if you already have a diary or journal, use that).

2. As you go through the day, start to notice strange feelings that you have about things which have no logical basis. Clues are usually internal feelings triggered by something in the environment around us.   These might be hunches, feelings of déjà vu, funny feelings, etc.

3. At certain points of the day (lunch, sunset, before bed), reflect on the day and what you have noticed.   Write down strange feelings you have experienced during the day, and what triggered those strange feelings. These are your *clues*.

4. How do you know what to write down and what not to? The two most important factors are:

- *If something feels unusual, it's more likely to be a clue.* As Ramaswami said, "The key is that if you have an unusual feeling about a place, person, thing, or even an event, you should write down."

- *If something repeats, it's more likely to be a clue.* The universe is like an echo chamber. The stronger it wants to send you a message, the more it will send you "clues" that reverberate around you. This is why it's important to pay more attention to sequences or series of clues, rather than just one clue in isolation!

3 ENGINE TROUBLE
JULY, 1993

Over the next few weeks, I started to write down enigmatic feelings that I got from people, places, and events around me. During that time, I took a day-trip up the Maine coast with a friend and had a strange, inexplicable feeling at a restaurant in a town called Ogunquit, Maine. I wrote it down along with a host of other items that didn't seem particularly relevant to my entrepreneurial journey, as I had promised Ramaswami I would.

That was when I began to notice a few 'clues' that started to point me more and more toward the direction of launching the business.

The first of these had to do with a friend of mine at Lotus named Mario. A few weeks after my experience at the Christian Science Center, I noticed an 'unusual' tug at my attention when Mario abruptly left the company because of a disagreement with our boss.

Mario and I had often talked about starting a company together in this market-space. As we went out to a farewell lunch, I had the strange sense that his departure was somehow related to my attempts to start a company. I wrote it down in my notebook with the word 'CLUE' in big letters at the top.

I decided that his departure was fortuitous and that maybe he could help my roommate, Mitch, and I start this business as a 'third partner'. I called Ramaswami and told him about these 'clues' that I had written down. He said, "That's very interesting ... you're getting into the right habit. Keep this up with other things you notice, not just clues related to your company."

"But," I protested. "The main reason I'm doing this is to help me become an entrepreneur, right?"

"That's one reason," he responded.

"Do you think that Mario leaving could be a sign that the time is right for me to launch the company?" I asked him.

"The feeling that you had was certainly a clue related to your wanting to start this business ... but that doesn't mean that you're ready to launch the business this minute."

"Why doesn't it?" I asked.

"Because, most entrepreneurs need a whole host of clues before they're ready to go, not just one or two."

"But I've been thinking about this idea for months!"

"Yes, but you haven't been tracking clues for months yet, have you?"

I had to admit that I hadn't.

"More importantly, starting a business is not just about having a great idea that you're convinced is a great idea and then jumping in! In fact, most entrepreneurs try to get a business off the ground for months, maybe even years before the circumstances are right to launch," he explained to me patiently.

"Why are you so against me starting a company now?" I said, not happy that he wasn't encouraging me to jump into the business.

"You've misinterpreted me," he explained. "I'm not against you starting the company now. But you're using Mario's leaving as a potential 'excuse' to start the company. The fact is that you're looking for other people to help you start the company, which isn't a bad thing, but you already have one partner, Mitch. The fact that you want another partner shows me that perhaps you're not there yet."

"Not where?"

"The point of no return. Until the point of no return, you place conditions on starting the business: only if this happens or if that happens will I start the company. Many folks think that entrepreneurs just jump in and start their company once they have a good idea! But it's not that simple. Certain conditions have to be met too."

"Is it a bad thing to have conditions?" I asked.

"No not at all. It's essential to have conditions. Particularly conditions about testing the market and making sure you have a good product idea. But it's even more important to have conditions related to how ready you feel, internally to start this considerably difficult journey. If you start and the timing isn't right, you might as well not have started at all. It just means that you aren't there yet. It doesn't mean you won't get there."

I didn't agree that I wasn't there, but decided to keep up this line of questioning. "But how will I know when I'm there?" I asked.

"Many entrepreneurs jump through many hoops before leaving their jobs to start a company. They try to convince others that it's a good idea to start the company and to give them money to start the company with them, but very often, no one believes them and no one is willing to sign on until they have some momentum behind them.

"Then, as a last resort, when the clues about how great of an opportunity this is become so overwhelming, then the entrepreneur has *no choice* but to jump in and start the company. That's often the point of no return."

"No choice?" I asked.

"*No choice* and *right timing* are two of the keys to deciding when to start a business," he replied.

"Huh?"

"Entrepreneurs reach a boiling point internally and decide they have to start this company, because the timing of the market is so great that they'll miss out on the opportunity. It starts to nag them day and night. More importantly, their internal timing is right; they are ready and able to make a change in their lives."

"Don't you think I'm there yet?" I asked.

"Only you can answer that," he said cryptically.

I ended the conversation convinced that I could convince Mario to join Mitch and I in our entrepreneurial journey as a third partner. He had more experience with Lotus Notes than either of us, seemed very entrepreneurial, and had five years more experience in the 'real world' than we did.

I discussed this idea with Mitch over lunch one day. Mitch,

who wanted to do more market research before we started, was enthusiastic about having another partner to 'share the risk' and to help us with this market research.

A few weeks after Mario had left Lotus, I tried to track him down. *This could be the 'sign' that helps us launch our business,* I thought, as I practiced my sales pitch to Mario to convince him that he could make millions of dollars by joining us.

I called his number. Unfortunately, no one answered. When I asked around, the only reply that I got was that Mario went to take a 'long vacation on the beach'. Mario had disappeared, and both Mitch and I got too busy over the next few weeks to even think of starting the company by ourselves.

Perhaps, I thought, I had been too eager to 'latch' onto this clue. Perhaps it wasn't like Ramaswami said at all. Perhaps that little 'tugging' feeling that indicated a clue was just crap, I told myself and resolved to ignore the clues and decide by myself when the timing was right.

A few weeks afterward, it happened again. I had the unmistakable feeling that I was being pulled to start the company. By now, I could clearly identify the feeling that Ramaswami had referred to as a 'clue' and I wrote it down.

PCWeek, one of the best known magazines in the computer industry, wrote a front page article about how Lotus had been promising some way to integrate other applications (like Microsoft applications) with Notes. Lotus was over a year late with something, and this article didn't see a solution coming anytime soon.

"It's perfect!" I told Mitch one evening. "This is exactly what I've been talking about. All we need to do is build the product and I'm certain I can get us an article in a magazine like this," I told him.

We began to discuss in more detail how we might get the product done. I wanted to be the CEO of the company, and Mitch wanted to be in charge of marketing, but neither one of us really wanted to write the code to build the product ourselves. Mitch had a co-worker, Joel, who was a very good programmer and we decided that perhaps he could be the 'third partner', the one who actually wrote the code to make the product work while we concentrated on the business side.

We described the project to Joel and he was very enthusiastic about writing the code part time, but he certainly wasn't ready to leave his job to jump on the bandwagon. Neither were we, but I took this to be a major 'clue' that the timing was right.

I called Ramaswami and met him for coffee in Harvard Square at Café Algiers, an Algerian coffeehouse. The interior of the building was decorated with Arabic designs and it was populated with a mixture of students and tourists.

We found a table in the smoking section upstairs. We noticed that they had *hookahs* for smoking in one corner and though neither of us smoked, we sat down next to one. Ramaswami, dressed in his usual double-breasted suit, seemed completely out of place, though he seemed to be enjoying the idea of *hanging out in Harvard Square with the students*. "I haven't done this in a while," he said, looking around at the youngsters all around us.

I was eager to describe my latest 'clues' to him. These consisted of the PCWeek article and the emergence of Joel as the 'third partner'. Ramaswami listened as I described how the timing was definitely right now that these two things had happened and simply nodded his head.

"Well, what do you think?"

"Hmm ... the timing does look better, and the PCWeek article definitely is a tip-off that customers may want something like this. But tell me one thing ... Joel is going to do the work of building the product, right?"

"Yes, part-time."

"But you and Mitch are the primary partners, and Joel will not be an equal partner, correct?"

"Yes," I answered.

"Then why is Joel doing all the work?"

"He's not doing all the work," I replied. "I'm going to be the CEO and concentrate on strategy."

He laughed. "Well, maybe I could understand that if you weren't capable of doing the technical work. But my impression is that both of you are capable of building the product, so why are neither of you working on building the product?"

"Because we want to concentrate on the business side," I replied.

"What exactly does that mean to you: *the business side ... strategy?* What will you actually be doing on a day-to-day basis?" he asked.

"Well, designing the product, doing market research, managing the developers, getting an article in the newspaper..."

He nodded as he listened. "It's not a bad idea to have one of you doing the business side and one of you doing nothing but the technical side. But once you verify that the market is there, my sense is that you and Mitch have the skills to launch the business, but you're hesitant to do it for some other reason."

"No, no ... we're not hesitant ... but wouldn't it be better if we had someone like Joel concentrate just on the technical side?" I asked.

"It is good to have someone concentrate just on the technical side, yes," he repeated. "But why would he accept a lesser partnership if he's going to be doing the bulk of the work, unless you guys are going to pay him for it...?"

I thought about it. We had no money to pay Joel for the work, but we were sure that his piece of the pie, though much smaller than ours, would pay off for him down the road.

I felt that Ramaswami was unnecessarily convinced that 'something was holding us back'. I assured him that we were ready, as long as the pieces were in place.

He sipped the rest of his hot chocolate and said, "We shall see." Then abruptly changed the subject. "How has your meditation been going?"

I had to admit that I hadn't been meditating much lately, feeling too rushed in the morning and being too scatterbrained after work to feel comfortable sitting down.

"I'd like to teach you a different meditation technique, one that is much more attuned to meditating at work. I'll be in California for the next few weeks, but perhaps we can meet when I get back? Meanwhile, try to start meditating again."

I agreed to start meditating again. As we got up to leave, he asked if I had done the movie assignment.

"Yes, I watched *Prince of Darkness*," I answered. For some reason, I actually enjoyed watching it this time, despite some of the bad acting.

"And?" he started, as if waiting for me to continue.

"And what?" I asked.

"Well, was there anything in the movie related to our conversation last time?"

I drew a blank as I thought back to the movie. I had been enjoying it so much that I forgot to look for the meaningful bit. He could see that I was searching and offered me a clue: "Was there anything in there about, say, the future?"

I was about to object that it was just a science fiction movie when I remembered something. "Yes, they were all getting messages ... messages from the future, right? In their dreams?"

"Yes, that's correct! Exactly." He nodded smugly, as if I had gotten the lesson.

"But what does that have to do with anything?" I asked.

"Oh, you'll find out," he said as he waved goodbye to me and walked off.

I shook my head and turned my attention back to the business. I left the coffee shop feeling that the timing was right and we were finally going to have the pieces in place to launch the company.

The next day, Mitch and I were both asked to do a part-time contract for a start-up company, helping them write some code for an interactive children's game. The pay was great, and I figured we could use some extra money, especially if we were going to launch our business soon.

I worked at Lotus during the day and on this other contract at night. It was a fun contract, and we were making good money, even though it had nothing to do with our intended product idea. Meanwhile, Mitch agreed to start on the market research, and Joel agreed to start looking into the technical side of building our own product in his spare time.

We identified 15 potential customers. It took us some time to get through to the customers, and even then we only reached five of the fifteen. They all reacted positively to our idea. One person in particular, who worked for a very large company was extremely enthusiastic.

"If you had that product *today*, I'd buy it *today*! I have three potential projects I could use it for *today*!"

After this conversation, I felt an unmistakable pull; the timing seemed right. His emphasis on the word 'today' seemed enough to increase our sense of urgency. I wrote down this latest indication that we were on to something as yet another 'clue' that we were on the right track.

Two weeks later, things unexpectedly slowed down. I was extremely tired from working on this other contract at night, in addition to my full-time work at Lotus, and was starting to run out of steam. Joel hadn't made very much progress on the technical side, and Mitch was having trouble reaching any of the other 10 potential customers.

That week, Joel asked to have dinner with both of us to talk about his arrangement.

"I think it's a good idea, and I think you will be successful, but I have a problem…" he started. "I'm getting married in a month, and my fiancée doesn't think that I should be spending all of this time on this project at night without getting paid. Plus I want to spend more time with her."

"But Joel," I replied. "Think about what this could mean if we're successful. You just said that it's a good idea."

At the end of the meeting, we agreed to pay him a certain hourly rate for his work, in addition to his equity stake, to be paid only after the product was shipping and successful. I hoped this would be the end of that discussion, for now. Of course, between now and the time the product was done, I'd have to figure out how to get the money to pay him.

Several days later, Joel asked us to go to dinner again; this time he had another issue. His fiancée, he told us, thought that this was too risky of a project to be working on under this 'deferred payment' arrangement, and he politely bowed out of the project.

It was now near the end of July, and though we had high hopes to get the company off the ground that summer, our lead programmer had just quit. We were both committed to delivering a lot of code for this other contract, and all of this work was tiring me out considerably. I also hadn't kept my promise to Ramaswami to start meditating again as I had become extremely frazzled by all of this.

We decided that perhaps the timing wasn't quite right for us to launch yet. I felt a great weight lift off my shoulders when this happened, and found it very easy to start meditating again for some reason.

CHAPTER SUMMARY
ENGINE TROUBLE

When starting a business, you should consider both external and internal factors that are you unique to you!
Most books about startups focus on the external considerations: how to set up the business, write the business plan, analyze the market, approach investors, manage employees, allocate equity, etc. These are all important, of course, but equally important are the inner factors of entrepreneurship.

Starting a business is not just about starting a business — it's part of your path in life. Starting a business is as much a creative act as drawing a painting or writing a book. No two artists would make the same painting, no two writers would write exactly the same book, and no two entrepreneurs would start a business in exactly the same way.

Start-up is a misnomer. It's really a stop-and-go process.
The myth of startups goes like this: Entrepreneur comes up with big idea. Entrepreneur starts company. Company releases product. Product is a big success. Everyone retires fat, dumb, and happy.

In reality, starting a company is usually a complicated start and stop process, not a smooth one. There are multiple steps along the way — you come up with an idea, you try to validate it, you try to convince other people to join your company, you try to find as many customers and employees as you can before jumping in. More often than not, people tell you that you're crazy and that your idea won't make a "viable business." The most important thing is that you don't get discouraged by every start and stop, but use this motion to help you to get the right factors in place to launch your business when the timing is right.

The dual principles of No Choice and Right Timing are the two most important factors to consider.
Starting a business may be the biggest financial and emotional and lifestyle decision you'll make, so it's worth getting it right.

I used to encourage people to jump in and start a business if they were enthusiastic about an idea. Now I tell them to wait until the point of "No Choice." This is a point internally where the entrepreneur has been pursuing the opportunity in his spare time, doing his homework, and is convinced that now is the right time to jump in. The entrepreneur will usually reach a boiling point internally and can no longer pursue this idea part-time, and he (or she) starts to think about it day and night. The pressure builds and the entrepreneur is worried about "missing out."

Of course external timing (hitting the market at the right time) is critical in any technology related business. But, just as important is your internal timing. You have to be ready and able to make a change in your life and be prepared for the low pay and long hours. Looking for *clues* can help point you in the right direction for both internal and external timing.

Clues are not excuses, they are indicators of direction.

In a good mystery, where does one clue point? Usually it points to ... another clue! Each clue gets you one step closer to the goal. As you write down clues and find important ones, especially ones that are pointing you towards changes in your career, you'll be tempted to use the clues as the decision maker. However, you should think of clues as just that: indicators of direction. You still have to confirm the direction and follow through to see if it's leading you closer to the treasure or not.

The more clues you have pointing in a particular direction, the more likely that is the right direction for you to go!

Partnerships are tricky but indispensible.

Understanding the motivations of each person that you ask to partner with you in the early days of the business is critical. In this chapter alone, we see Mario, who I thought was going to help us launch the business, and Joel, who was going to help us with the programming. In our story, both of the main partners, Mitch and I, were at similar stages of life, so it was easy for us to think about jumping in and "dividing up the work", as you'll see.

Too often, though shares don't get divided appropriately in a new company — the best way to deal with this is to make sure you understand everyone's motivation and timing: are they getting married, did they just buy a new house, do they want to go do something else in a few years? This can lead to much more effective partnerships.

4 A NEW KIND OF MEDITATION
AUGUST, 1993

I was back with Ramaswami at the Christian Science Center a few weeks later, and it was clear that there was something specific he wanted to teach me. I was still working two jobs and was hoping this would be an interesting break in my recently very stressful life.

"The reason you're studying with me," he said as we started pacing along the length of the pool, "is because you think that I can teach you something that will help with your career. That's okay. In our culture, everything needs to begin with self-interest. But your career is more than just a career, it is the key to happiness in your life. What percentage of your waking hours would you say you spend at work?"

His question brought me back to the present, and I did a quick calculation.

"Well, eight hours a day, five days a week, begins to add up..."

"Yes, that's right. In fact, the two things we spend the most amount of time doing in our lives are *sleep* and *work*. Freud once said that life consisted primarily of work and love — but in reality, it consists mostly of work and sleep, with a little bit of love thrown in from time to time.

"The path of meditation that I teach is not just about meditation. I call it the Path of the Career Warrior — it's a coherent path that brings together many different aspects of the hidden worlds into a practical path. And both sleep and work are part and parcel of this path!"

He stopped and paused as if ready to make a point. "As far as *love* goes, you're on your own for now!" he chuckled and then started walking again.

"Today, we'll talk about work. Once you've mastered these basic techniques, we'll spend a lot more time on what happens when you sleep ... but your mastery of the world of sleep is, believe it or not, tied directly to your mastery of the world around you."

"What do you mean? Are you referring to dreams?" I asked.

"Yes, dreams are very important. But dreams are tied directly to what happens in the waking world. If your time in the working world is disjointed and frazzled, then your dreams will be frazzled. I'm going to teach you today about a different kind of meditation technique — one that will help you take an important step on this path."

"There are, as you might have guessed, many different kinds of meditation: chanting, sitting, visualizing, walking, with eyes open, with eyes closed, breath meditation, object meditation, insight meditation, and on and on..."

"I've heard of some of those," I replied, "isn't chanting what the Hare Krishnas do?"

"Yes, that's right. They chant and dance ... losing themselves in the moment, in the song, and even in their group energy." He closed his eyes as if recalling the feeling. "After chanting for some time, it is possible to lose yourself completely in the chant. You are in a place without self, without ego — you don't have to think about being in the moment ... you *become* the moment!"

"Wait a minute," I interrupted. "Are you telling me that you chant just like the Hare Krishnas?" It came as a shock to me. Standing next to me was a successful businessman, dressed in proper business attire, who had started and run several companies; I could not see him out in Harvard Square with a shaved head, dancing around in circles, clad in white cloth.

"Do you find that hard to believe?" he asked.

"Extremely."

"Well, as you've probably guessed I haven't done that in a long time. You see, I tried most of these techniques in my teens and my early twenties. It wasn't until the age of 29 when I started to focus on the business world. I've spent the last 12 years working in the high-tech industry and teaching meditation, and assembling a spiritual path that integrates these two worlds into one."

"So you haven't done that recently?" I asked, still curious and a bit repulsed. To my scientific way of thinking, the world of the Hare Krishnas was one that the rest of us pointed to and laughed. It was inconceivable that someone from that world could be so successful in the arena that I wanted to play, the business world. He might as well have told me that he had been abducted by aliens, and this helped him succeed in the business world!

He laughed. "Oh, I still chant ... sometimes it's the only way to quiet your thoughts. You should try it sometime..." He was smiling and goading me, as he could clearly see my distaste for the practice.

"What type of meditation or path do you teach?" I asked. I had been looking at various books on meditation and had seen references to a number of different religions, paths, and philosophies, and wanted to understand where he fit in.

"Not an ordinary one," he replied quickly, as if he had been asked this many times before. "The teachings are probably closest to some forms of Buddhism, but I have tried out techniques from many different philosophies. Some are variations of eastern techniques, and some are based on Native American shamanic practices.

"The point, though, is not which religion we are studying. The real point is understanding *your* path in *your* work and in *your* life — what I call your unique Warrior's Path.

"Most gurus and meditation cronies will tell you one of two things: either 1) there are many paths up the mountain and it makes no difference which one you take, you still get to the top of the mountain. Or 2) they will tell you that theirs is the best meditation technique and every other way is inferior.

"I know they'll tell you this because when I was a young man, I searched long and hard and that's all I could find. My teaching is a bit different. We actually will try multiple meditation techniques, taken from different traditions. Let me ask you a question: if there was a mountain, and one side of the mountain was covered with snow, and the other side was rainforest, which would you climb?"

Not only did I not expect the question, I had never climbed a mountain through either snow or rainforest and told him so.

He looked up for a moment and then directly at me: "Never mind, here's another analogy. Think of two different sports — say running and tennis. Though they are both good exercise, and they will both help you to stay fit, your experience will be different depending on which one you choose. And, most importantly, the muscles that you develop will be different. Though all meditation techniques are similar, they develop different muscles..."

I was still a bit confused. "But what muscles do meditation techniques help you to strengthen...?"

"The eventual goal of all spiritual techniques is always the same: awareness. Awareness of a greater part of yourself. But you will find that certain techniques *gel* with who you are right now better than others. For example, chanting is probably not something you can even see yourself doing right now. It's not a technique that's aligned with who you are at this moment."

"How will awareness of a greater part of myself help me in my career?" I asked, still looking for some practical advice on how to go about starting my business, which had stalled. So far, we had talked only of vague concepts like energetic patterns, past lives, future selves, and tracking of clues, but I wasn't sure if this brought me any closer to my goal.

"Significantly. First, we will build your ability to concentrate. That is almost always the first *mental muscle* that is strengthened during meditation. This will also help you to visualize a goal and to stick with it through times of trouble. This is a mental muscle too.

"Most importantly, though, awareness will help you to perform self-reflection, to be aware of your own patterns and tendencies, and to see how they might be obstacles to either your career success or to your spiritual success. This is what I meant by your Energetic Pattern."

"I've heard that visualization is a key part of any goal

setting," I replied, excited that he had linked meditation back to something respectable that I could believe in. I didn't notice that he was shaking his head, as if I had missed the most important part of what he was saying.

By now, we had walked out of the Christian Science Center area and were heading up Massachusetts Avenue towards the river and the bridge to Cambridge, known as the Harvard Bridge.

"In the hidden worlds, the same principle applies that is true here in the everyday world: *practice makes perfect.* Although the eventual goal of meditation is awareness, the immediate goal is concentration, or, in the words of a famous Yogi, Mehar Baba, *one-pointedness of mind to the exclusion of all other considerations.*

"If that's the initial goal, then it is not enough to concentrate for 10-15 minutes in the morning and 10-15 minutes at night and expect that to be enough. I want you to meditate for eight hours each day to really hone your skills of concentration!"

"Eight hours!" I yelled out, incredulously. I had found it difficult to sit still for fifteen minutes at a time. "How can I do that ... I'd have to quit my career and become a professional meditator!"

He laughed as if I had made a great joke. Just when I thought he had stopped, he started again, slapping his thighs. "Yes, that's it. I want you to become a *professional meditator!*"

Then he became serious again and pointed to some students who had just come out of the Berklee School of Music, which was located right on Mass Ave. "Musicians have very good concentration. Do you know why? Because they are forced to spend hours at a time focused in on one thing: playing their music. During that time, they become engrossed and do not worry about other things — back to *one-pointedness and the exclusion of all other considerations*.

"If you were to go off to the Tibetan mountains and find a master, he would give you tasks to do all day long. These might include chopping some wood, carrying some water, cleaning the latrine, or some other such day-to-day routine, in addition to the meditation exercises you would do. The obvious reason for doing these things is to get them done, but like everything in life, there is a hidden purpose here. Do you remember the movie *Karate Kid*?"

Of course I had seen it, as most people my age who had grown up in the eighties had. "In that movie, Daniel had a taskmaster, Mr. Miyagi, who was to teach him karate. What did he make Daniel do? He asked him to wax the car, paint the fence, and then sand the floor! Remember?"

I remembered the scene well. He continued. "The obvious reason for doing these things was to wax the car, paint the fence, and then sand the floor. The hidden reason was to teach Daniel about karate, remember?" I nodded again.

"The taskmaster used these tasks as a way to teach the pupil something at a deeper level. Well, the essence of the path that I am teaching you is to use your life and most importantly, your work, as a taskmaster to teach yourself things that you wouldn't otherwise have grasped."

"You must learn to concentrate while at work on the task you are doing to the exclusion of all else. This way you will not even notice the passing of time and will be developing your concentration of mind."

This struck me as interesting. "Well, that sounds reasonable," I started. "Sometimes, when I'm programming, I get so involved in my work that many hours pass by and I don't even notice."

"Exactly! But it's not just the programming — suppose you have some phone calls to make or a memo to write. You start writing the memo, then the phone rings and what do you do?" He acted out the events in a comical manner. "You stop writing the memo, you pick up the phone and talk to someone for a number of minutes." His exaggerated movements looked silly and made me smile.

"When you finish the phone call, you go back to your computer, but your email icon is blinking. You then check email and find that you have two emails — a joke from a friend and a note from your boss — you read the joke and laugh. Then you read the note from your boss and cry." He held up his hands to his face and imitated a crying baby, enjoying both the scenario and his ability to show off his (very forced) acting skills.

"Now, someone walks by and you talk to them. Then it's time for lunch. When you get back from lunch, you make a phone call, handle a few more interruptions, and maybe you get back to your memo, but then you remember your boss's email and go to see him. Do you get the drift?"

"Are you saying that I'm not getting any work done?"

"Not exactly. You're getting some work done, but you are using your work inappropriately. You are fooling around with work, and not being nearly as efficient as you can be..." I nodded in agreement. Efficiency was something I understood.

"But, that's not the point!" he finished.

"Huh?" I thought that was exactly the point.

"The point is that you are not developing any skills of concentration, focus, or push-back, which are critical skills in both the hidden worlds and in the business world."

"What should I do differently?" I asked.

"It's simple. In the same way that you sit down to meditate for a fixed number of minutes, and then try to exclude other thoughts, you need to focus at work on tasks for a certain time, trying to exclude other thoughts and considerations.

"Otherwise you won't just feel frazzled, you'll appear frazzled too. In today's business world if you want to be an entrepreneur you are going to have thousands of things to take care of — unless you can allocate time to focus, you will just move from reacting to one crises to another."

He continued his immediate lesson: "So, start by saying that I will do a draft of this memo. Don't answer the phone — let it go to voicemail. If someone walks by, ask them to come by later. If your email beeps, bring your mind back to the element of focus. If your mind wanders to the cute girl in the cubicle across the hall, bring your mind back and focus. This is the essence of meditation!"

"But Ramaswami, I thought that part of meditating was to stop thinking?"

"That's one way of describing a state of Samadhi, which is one of the goals of meditation. Some forms of meditation do lead to a complete cessation of thought, but that's not going to happen until you've been meditating for years and years ... so initially we want to train ourselves to concentrate on a single thought.

"This is extremely important, because thoughts are things. When you learn to isolate each thought-form, you will learn one of the Keys of Manifestation. For now, think of every task you have to do at work as having a hidden purpose: to develop your ability to concentrate, *capesh*?"

"But what if I have to take a phone call or my boss interrupts me, or I can't concentrate?" I asked, worried that I wouldn't know how to follow through on his tasks. "How will I know I'm doing the right thing?"

"You engineering types are always over-analyzing!" He sighed. "Here is the test — at the end of a day of work, how do you usually feel?" he asked.

"Sometimes I feel tired, sometimes frazzled, sometimes really good," I replied.

"Okay, the test is this: you should leave work feeling more refreshed than when you arrived. If you did this, then you were using your work as meditation. If you leave frazzled, then you did not do a good job. Understood?"

I resolved to try this new 'meditation technique' at work and practiced it whenever I could over the next few weeks.

Initially, my attempts at mastering this new meditation technique ended in failure, as I was unable to concentrate for any extended period of time.

I found it extremely difficult to not read my email as soon as I heard the 'beep' indicating that it had arrived. When the phone rang, there was an uncontrollable urge for me to pick it up, no matter what I was working on at the moment.

It did, however, make me very conscious that my entire day consisted of a series of decisions of where to focus my attention, and this decision was being made unconsciously based upon when the phone rang, when an email came, etc.

Each of these *decisions of attention* by themselves were not very meaningful, but taken together they had a profound impact on how much work I got done and more importantly, how frazzled I felt at the end of the day.

In fact, I found that I often didn't get very much work done over a period of several hours, and I had to stay late in order to 'catch up' (well, later than usual anyways, since I didn't start work very early to begin with).

Gradually, every time I made a decision to stay focused and to let the signal from the outside world pass by until I was ready to pay attention to it, I won a little victory. And with each little victory it became easier for me to choose the right decision when given a choice.

This process wasn't unlike what I did when I sat down to meditate. I was letting thoughts and distractions come and go, and gently refocusing on whatever the subject of the meditation was. It was as if there was, as Ramaswami described, a mental muscle that I had started to exercise regularly.

Years later I would visit top managers at many large corporations and notice that they minimized interruptions and had an incredible ability to clear away distractions and focus on the task at hand. I was starting to use the mental muscles from my meditation for my work, and starting to use my work as a way to improve my ability to meditate.

CHAPTER SUMMARY
A NEW KIND OF MEDITATION

The Career Warrior skillfully utilizes the two largest parts of our lives — work and sleep — for spiritual growth.
Numerically, our lives consist mostly of sleep and work, with bits of time left over for everything else. The Tibetan Buddhist concept of "skillful means" refers to putting aspects of the ordinary world to use in your spiritual development. If we are serious about meditation as a path to explore our inner selves, then we can't ignore these two very large chunks of our lives. In this chapter, we explore the idea of using your work as part of a meditation practice. In subsequent chapters, we will explore putting dreams and sleep to work.

There are many different forms of meditation. Most start with concentration but the eventual goal of meditation is awareness.
If you have never meditated, it's a good idea to experience it in some form, before learning to use your work as meditation. The Career Warrior does a sitting meditation of some form each day.

Examples of meditations include meditating on the breath, meditations on *chakras* (energy centers in the body), meditation on specific parts of the body and physical sensations, meditation on an external object (like a rock), meditation on images or *mandalas* (complex patterns put together by Tibetan monks), and even meditation on music.

There are also more active meditations, such as walking meditations, chanting of mantras, and so on. Each of these provides a different quality of experience — none better or worse than others — and each develops different "mental muscles."

The important thing is that you start exercising the mental *muscles of attention*, which will lead to greater clarity and coherence in your mental state. A disjointed and frazzled mental state during the day at work leads to disjointed and frazzled dreams at night, which leads to a vicious cycle. Eventually, a calmer and more attentive mental state will lead to greater awareness.   Awareness of what?   That's what you're supposed to find out.

> **EXERCISE: Start with a simple sitting meditation for 10 minutes a day, focusing on either the breath or energy centers.**
>
> If you've never meditated before, there are many resources available in books and on the Internet about meditation. In my opinion, most overemphasize form over substance. Here's a simple first form of meditation on the body. I think it's easier for Westerners to use a concrete thing like a spot on the body for meditation (even though most Eastern traditions start with meditating on the breath):
>
> 1. Sit on a chair or on a cushion on the floor, put your hands on your thighs or knees. Close your eyes. Find a spot on the body to concentrate on – let's say you start with your navel (yes, that means your bellybutton). Focus in on it and feel any sensations that are there. If you do this for a few minutes, you will soon find that your mind has wandered.
> 2. It may have wandered to thinking about what's for dinner, what you did yesterday, your friend Jenny that you haven't talked to in a while, the latest action movie, or more likely some transient worry. The real trick is to notice that your mind has wandered, and bring it back to the point of attention, in this case your bellybutton.
> 3. After a while, your mind will wander again. The trick is not so much forcing your mind to think of nothing else; instead, you are simply, gently bringing it back.
> 4. Do this for 10 minutes each day, and that's it! You're now doing the sitting meditation. It sounds extremely simple and it is, but this simple act of bringing attention to what you are thinking about, and consciously directing the attention rather than just letting it wander, has a powerful effect.

Use your work as a form of meditation.

Mindfulness is a term that means to simply focus on what you are doing, and not to get distracted by other mental thoughts, emotions, or external stimuli. In addition to a sitting meditation each day, try mindfulness at work as a way to expand your period of meditation beyond a simple sitting meditation.

To do this, choose one thing to work on at a time, for a given period of time. In this chapter, the example of email interruptions was given. This story took place in the 1990's, when email was relatively new. Today, with smartphones and tablets, instant messaging, text messaging, social networks, push notifications and more, choosing one thing to concentrate on is even *more* difficult, and in some ways *more* important.

Our lives and our work are too often "interrupt-driven". This is a geek term that refers to a CPU (Central Processing Unit, as in a computer) that's trying to do its thing, but is constantly "interrupted" by something like a mouse movement or printer request or a network connection. Are you interrupt-driven at work? Try to change that and focus your CPU on one thing at a time.

To meditate eight hours a day, let your work be a series of moments of concentration, and practice saying "no" to interruptions and distractions. This is not as easy as it seems. Set your IM status to "unavailable", close your email and browser windows, set your cell phone to silent, while you concentrate on whatever task is at hand. The key is to consciously direct your attention during the day rather than letting it be strewn about by circumstance.

If you are a programmer or doing a job that requires some amount of manual labor this may not be that difficult. If you are in a job that requires interacting with people this can be more difficult. If you're running a startup, it's even *more* difficult since there are dozens of fires to fight simultaneously.

Nevertheless, you can make an effort to both increase your productivity and improve your mental and energetic state, which eventually will lead to more awareness.

How do you know when you're doing it right? You shouldn't end the workday feeling frazzled. Of course, no one is able to do this fully on the first day, or even after the hundredth day; in today's world something unexpected *always* happens. That's okay. It's the effort to do this that is the real goal.

EXERCISE: Turn your work tasks into Warrior's Tasks.

A Warrior's task is one that has both an obvious, outside purpose, and a hidden purpose. It's easy to take any task you have to do at work and give it a hidden purpose — to maintain or to enhance a certain state of mind. Think of Mr. Miyagi's tasks for Daniel in the original Karate Kid.

For example: suppose you have to enter numbers into a spreadsheet. See if you can do it while concentrating on the task at hand — use it as an exercise whose real purpose is to sharpen your mental state. I remember one of my students doing this with mindless data entry, and her boss remarked how much she'd improved and even gave her a raise because she did her tasks so well!

Every day, pick a task at work that you "have to do" and find no pleasure in. Now turn that task into an exercise of attention and be mindful while doing it. Try not to let your mind wander. You've now turned it into a Warrior's Task!

---

5 INTRODUCTION TO ENERGY
AUGUST, 1993

One day in late August, I was exhausted and decided to go home from work early. I tried to figure out why I was so exhausted, but I could find no good reason. I hadn't been out late the night before, I had not been doing anything extremely tiring over the last few days. I had even been using my work as meditation, just like Ramaswami had instructed me. It usually helped me focus quite a bit and gave me a way to bring the benefits of my sitting meditation (which I did in the morning), with me into my workday.

I left Lotus and decided to take a walk along the Charles River; I was on the Cambridge side and as usual, the view of Back Bay always induced a sense of wonder. This was not a new phenomenon for me; every three or four weeks I would find myself completely out of energy and so I would take the day off. It was only noon, but I knew that I couldn't work any longer. When this happened, I would usually make up for it some evening or weekend.

I thought of the email that Ramaswami had sent me earlier today. It seemed to hit on the issue that I was dealing with. It said something like this:

> *The study of Energy is the central issue for the student of the Path of the Career Warrior. If you understand energy, you begin to understand the hidden worlds. If you can master the hidden worlds, you can master the visible worlds. And vice versa.*

As usual, it had confused me. I wonder if he sent it out to all of his students or only me. It was a hot August day and I couldn't walk in the sun for long before stopping under the shade of a tree. I came up to the Longfellow Bridge, which is one of the more interesting bridges that cross the Charles. Every fifty feet or so, there are two little towers, one on each side of the bridge. These little towers, when seen from either side of the river, look like salt and pepper shakers, causing this bridge to be referred to by locals as 'the Salt and Pepper' bridge.

I thought about this moniker as I sat in the shade hoping for a breeze. I had walked the bridge many times, particularly when I was a student at MIT, and I remembered once trying to find a way into the little salt and pepper towers. They were built of brick and had long slits for windows, as if they were part of a medieval castle. Peeking into the windows revealed nothing but darkness inside. I wondered if the towers had any purpose other than decoration.

Suddenly a breeze came across the Charles and I felt its coolness through the sweat that had built up on my forehead. *Boy, am I glad that software companies don't make us dress up on a daily basis. Wearing a suit in this humid weather is useless. Maybe it's the humidity and the heat that's making me so tired*, I guessed. But then I realized that my periodic tiredness happened in the winter, too.

Suddenly I had an impulsive thought: *It might be a good idea to find out what Ramaswami might have to say about my lack of energy.* I walked over to the original meditation studio where I first was exposed to meditation and career success while working for DiVA.

Back in the late 1800's and early 1900's, Cambridge had become quite an industrial town with a number of brick-lined factories dotting the landscape. Most of these buildings had long since been torn down, but the ones that remained had by now all been converted into class-A office buildings, even though they often kept their original name. The American Twine building, where I had worked and where the meditation studio had been, was no exception. I walked in past the security guard, who had seen me there many times before and worked my way toward the studio. But the room was completely empty, as if it was not being used any more.

That's odd, I thought to myself. It was only six months ago that I stepped in to learn to meditate. I decided to go next door to the startup DiVA that I used to work for — but they too had moved out (in a strange palindromic turn of events, they had been acquired by a company whose name consisted of the exact same letters spelled backwards: Avid, which was poised to go public that year).

This depressed me a little bit, and I decided to head home and take a nap. As I left the building, I noticed a familiar face in a gray suit walking into the building. It was James, who first taught me the meditation techniques and introduced me to Ramaswami.

"Hi," I called out. He stopped and surveyed me for a few seconds. "Boy, you do need to learn a little bit about energy. You seem very worn out."

"Huh?" I answered. I *was* very tired, but didn't realize it showed.

"Ramaswami asked me to come here to fetch you — he said that I needed to come to your Energetic Rescue, but I didn't understand what he meant. Now I know!"

"Come here to fetch me? Be rescued? How did he know I was here?"

"He didn't," started James as he led me outside. "Actually, maybe he did, but he didn't tell me. It was my *occult task* to find you and to bring you to the mall."

"What's an occult task?" I asked as we both walked out of the American Twine building.

"An occult task is when you have to show your understanding of the principles of the hidden worlds by accomplishing something in the everyday world."

I didn't comment as I thought about what that would mean from a practical point of view.

"It can be something really simple, such as finding the highest energy spot in a location, or something more complicated, such as finding you on a hot summer day when I had no idea where you were."

He could see that I still didn't seem to grasp the concept. "It could also mean being guided to just the right job or finding just the right person to fill a particular job."

"How did you find me?" I asked, changing the subject.

"First I called you at Lotus, but you had already left. Then I went to the river near Lotus, but you weren't there. Finally, I went to the mall, figuring you might be eating lunch there at the food court, but I didn't find you there either. Ramaswami has asked me to bring you to the mall so that he can teach you a lesson about energy."

"So how did you find me then?" I repeated.

"Well, I found the highest energy spot in the food court area, sat down and started to access my third eye, looking for you. It's the seat of all clairvoyance, you know."

I found it a bit difficult to swallow that he had used clairvoyance to find me, and I sensed a little bit of mischief in his voice, as if he was challenging me to believe it. "Well, it makes sense that I might come here ... it's only logical," I explained, reasoning it out in my mind. "After all, I used to work near here and the meditation studio used to be here."

"Ah...yes, logical to the end. Well, I didn't see the picture I was waiting for, so there was no clairvoyance. Not really...then I had the urge to come here and meditate, thinking it may lead to me some insight to help me accomplish my occult task." He smiled as we walked down the side street back toward the mall. "Do you know why we had the meditation studio here in the first place?" he asked.

"No, but I'm beginning to think that it was no accident, right?"

He repeated Ramaswami's favorite expression: "There are no accidents." Then he pointed to the brick building we were passing "Here, in this building alone there are several startups. Very few of these companies will make it past adolescence, but the ones that do will make their founders very wealthy." He then pointed to the big building that we were approaching. I knew it well — it was Lotus, the mother of all successful software start-ups in Cambridge, where I was working at the time.

"The energy in this place exudes the start-up mentality, and so Ramaswami wanted us to meditate here. This is a power spot, you know."

"A power spot? What do you mean...?" I asked.

He ignored my question for a minute and took a cell phone out of his briefcase. This was in 1993, when the cellular phones were still quite large. He dialed a number quickly and I heard his side of a very short conversation: "Hello, Ramaswami? I've found him. Okay. Okay. We'll meet you at the mall ... in the food court. Okay. Okay. Okay."

He jumped back into our conversation without missing a beat. "The energy of the location itself tends to be very conducive to the types of things that go on here. If it wasn't conducive it would be very difficult for all of these companies to thrive here."

"Okay, now, hold on!" This was a bit much, I thought, as we entered the mall. Disagreeing with him seemed to help pick up my energy a little bit.

"The reason Cambridge has been such a haven for start-ups," I explained, "is because MIT is here, and MIT tends to attract technical types. Look at Silicon Valley, with Stanford. A good technical university is the underpinnings of a healthy technological startup eco-system! It has nothing to do with energy and power spots!"

"Oh, really?" he asked, half smiling in his own bizarre way. He stopped and started at me, then he raised his eyebrows and turned to me with a scratchy voice and funny expression, "So certain are you?"

I recognized his impressions instantly. He was doing an impression of Yoda, from the Star Wars movies. I was in no mood to laugh, though, and I felt I had him in a corner.

"Yes, I am certain!" I replied.

"And why was it, my good MIT alumnus," he started, "that MIT was built here in the first place?"

"Why? I don't know why."

"You have a lot to learn about Energy. It is true that the energy in this place has accelerated over the past 10 years with the PC revolution," he was dead serious now, not imitating any movie character. "But all of it is part of the same pattern, as it speeds up, it attracts more and more of the same type of energy. After a while, it seems only logical that certain types of people and enterprises are attracted there, but logic has nothing to do with it." He turned and continued walking.

We came to the food court and stopped to look out at the many tables.

"Okay, I have an occult task for you," he started. "You are to find the highest energy location here."

I looked around. It was after lunch, and the crowd was starting to thin out.

I wasn't sure what he meant, but I immediately was drawn to the area against the windows that was as far away from the cooking and the heat as possible. I looked at the tables against the wall and liked the sunlight that was coming in, and the fact that it was next to the trees, so it wasn't too warm. I immediately led him to the tables against the glass wall.

"Yes, that's good," he said after we sat down. "Why did you choose this one?" I explained my reasoning about its location.

"Yes, that's almost right. You forgot one thing — there are very few people here. Do you know about auras? If we sit in a crowded place, we are sure to have our auras bump up against the auras of the people around us. But this table has no one sitting around us, so it's aurically cleaner than many of the others. Finally, the trees have auras of their own and their auras can have a refreshing quality to them. They can energize you — so the best table would actually have been outside, under the trees — but this is a good second!"

I thought about what he said. "Auras, trees? Hmm ... can you actually see these auras?" I asked, wanting to probe further and see if there was any way to verify what he constantly was referring to.

"Not yet. But Ramaswami can, and sometimes when I'm meditating with him around, I have seen auras. It's only a matter of practice."

"So," I continued my cross-examination, "you don't actually know that there are auras ... you're just taking his word for it?"

He smiled. "Ah, you MIT guys are all alike. I was working with another student who went to MIT and he grilled me endlessly too." He stopped to think about how he would phrase his answer.

"You don't have to see the hidden worlds in order to

experience them. I have verified that I actually feel better, freer over here than I would, say, over there, in between those tables that both have teenagers sitting at them. I have come to recognize this feeling as somehow feeling less constricted — so I have verified it in my own way — just as you have to verify it in your own way."

Just then, Ramaswami walked up, as always, dressed in a pastel double-breasted designer suit. He looked anything but spiritual, I thought.

"Hello there my fine feathered friends," he said cheerily. James face turned serious, yet expectant at the same time. I had noticed this familiar look of devotion in spiritual practitioners when their guru, or teacher was around. I wasn't sure if I liked it, and vowed that I would not become devotional, that I would view Ramaswami like any other teacher — someone to impart knowledge. James stood up to offer him his chair, but the teacher stopped him with his hand and grabbed a chair from the next table and pulled it up.

The smile on Ramaswami's face indicated that there was some joke going on that I didn't know about. I looked at James, but he too didn't seem to know what the joke was about either. "My fine feathered friends ... how fitting!" Ramaswami said, and started chuckling to himself.

"What do you mean," I asked, but he was too amused with himself for having said that to explain. "How fitting for both of you. You'll understand what I mean some day!"

"Uh ... Swami, I have found him, like you asked. Unfortunately, I have a meeting I have to get ready for later this afternoon." When the teacher didn't answer, James seemed to get visibly worried. "I ... I can cancel the meeting if you need me here ..."

"No, no, not at all," said Ramaswami. "This could be a very important meeting for you, am I right?"

James nodded.

"Go ahead, I have a few things to teach Riz-Wan here," Ramaswami said, emphasizing the two syllables of my name as if they were two separate words. James wandered off to his meeting.

"So, I see that you are a bit tired today, no?" he started.

"Yes," I replied. "How did you know that I was so tired — do you have one of your students working at Lotus?"

He laughed as if I had just made a joke. "No, no ... you'll understand eventually, it was written in your energy field. I was simply *seeing*," he replied, and had a particular emphasis on the word 'seeing'.

"Just as it's quite obvious from looking at you in the physical world that you are tired," he pointed to me and how I was slouching now in the chair, "It's also quite obvious from looking at you in the hidden worlds as well."

He paused to see if I would argue with him. Actually, I found this to be a bit odd but was too tired to argue with him in my usual fashion. "This ties directly to the next lesson that I was going to teach you.

"The study of Energy is *the central issue* for the student of esoteric lore — of the hidden worlds. This is doubly true for the Career Warrior. If you understand energy, you begin to understand the hidden worlds. If you can master the hidden worlds, you can master the visible worlds. And vice versa."

I had a vague sense that he had already told me this.

"I'm here to give you your first lessons on Energy ... I don't usually do this in person, but I have a feeling that you're going to become quite an interesting pupil, so I wanted to talk to you face to face."

Then I remembered the email. "Aha, that's why you sent me that email earlier today!" I replied. He curled his forehead and made a face, "No, I did not send you an email today, not that I can remember."

"But I remember reading it just as I got up to leave Lotus for the day!"

"Are you certain?" he asked, leaning back in his chair, chin turned upward, arms behind his head, in a familiar position.

"Absolutely!" I remembered it clearly. The beep-beep of email had gone off just as I was about to leave to go on my walk. I went up to the computer and read it. I decided the only way to prove it to him was to repeat what the email said:

"The study of Energy is the central issue for the student of the Path of the Career Warrior. If you understand energy, you begin to understand the hidden worlds. If you can master the hidden worlds, you can master the visible worlds. Or vice versa."

"Yes, yes, that is all part of what I'm trying to teach you. It's what I just said now. But I did not send you an email with that message on there! I try not send lessons electronically. It is always done either in person, in a group, or through a mentor like James!"

I was now energized unexpectedly and swore that I had seen the email. He laughed and said that this wasn't an unusual event. I was 'a quick young man' who always seemed to be jumping ahead. It was one of my patterns, he told me, and so it didn't surprise him at all that I would have received a portion of his teaching before he gave it to me!

I was highly dubious about his explanation and was sure that he had sent me the email. In order to get past the argument, we agreed that I would go back to Lotus when we were done, look at the email, and then forward it back to him.

"Now, there are a number of things you need to learn about Energy before you are ready to become an entrepreneur and strike out on your own!"

Now that he was talking about business, I sat up and started listening intently. "The reason you are so tired is simple: your energetic configuration – which I like to call your Energetic Pattern. This includes how much energy you have in the morning and how you go about leaking energy during the day."

"What do you mean my energetic configuration?" I asked.

"It's a little hard to explain without actually showing you in your aura, but you can't yet see auras so I will try to explain: You were born with a pattern that leaves you with less energy than others your age."

I found this to be a strange statement and one that I didn't agree with. "Now, I'm not saying that you start with less energy, I'm simply saying that your pattern leaves you with less energy," he said, but I didn't hear his last sentence at all.

I protested. "But that can't be! Everyone comments on how I'm always fired up, how I'm always the one coming up with ideas, organizing things, getting people going, etc."

"Yes, yes, calm down, kid. Take a deep breath. Listen to

me." He held his hand up and didn't say anything for a few minutes. It seemed to slow me down. I suddenly remembered how tired I had been only a few moments ago.

"It's not that you start with less energy ... in fact, by Gen-X standards, you're a real go-getter, with a ton of energy! But it's that you somehow *end up* with less energy than others your age." He paused, and quoted from some unnamed source: *"The candle that burns twice as bright burns half as long..."*

He paused again waiting for something. I had heard that phrase before ... but where? Then it hit me. "Blade Runner!" I said, referring to science fiction film from the 1980's.

"Bingo!" he said, ringing an imaginary bell. "Okay, so ... what happens is this: your energy burns itself off and then you are left with none. Then you have to go take a nap or take the day off to 'recharge' your batteries. You are very intense for a period of time, and then you go to the other extreme and cannot do anything, am I right?"

I had to admit that he was right.

"It's one of your energetic patterns. You'll learn, by studying with me, that the only things you really need to understand in life are patterns. If something happens once, it's not a pattern. If something happens twice, it *might be* a pattern. It's only when something happens three times that it starts to be a pattern. How often has this been going on?"

I tried to remember, but couldn't locate an exact date. I just knew that it had been going on since high school. Despite being almost hyperactive with extracurricular activities in high school, every few weeks I would just be too exhausted to go to school. I missed so many days in my senior year that, despite already being admitted to MIT and having one of the top grade point averages, I almost didn't graduate because of a bad attendance record. I explained this to him.

"So," he continued, "it definitely qualifies as a pattern."

"I'd like to teach you a technique that you should do at least once a day. It's away for you to 'recharge your batteries'. If you do this every day, then you won't be as likely to burn out so quickly."

"But wait — I still don't understand how you could know all this. And I don't understand what you mean by energy, exactly

... does this have something to do with auras?"

"It has everything to do with auras," he started, smiling. "And it has everything to do with everything. Before we talk about energy in the hidden worlds, let's talk about it in the world around us. What does it mean for 'someone to have a lot of energy'?"

I didn't answer. "It's not a trick question," he answered. "It simply means that that person is always up and about — not unlike you under normal circumstances. Now, if we say a person has low energy, that usually means that she moves slowly, doesn't talk fast, and likes to be sedentary, right?"

I nodded my head. "So that's the obvious meaning of energy ... let's start there. Again, every thing in the physical world has its counterpart in the hidden worlds."

He instructed me to sit up, as I had been slouching, and to put my feet flat on the floor. Then he went on to describe an exercise to fill up with energy. Per his instructions, I put my right hand on my belly and my left hand over my right, and closed my eyes. I slowly inhaled to a count of seven, visualizing orange light pouring in through my nostrils and making its way down into my belly. Then, I held the breath for a count of seven, during which I visualized the ball expanding in my belly. Finally, I exhaled to a count of seven.

I did not feel particularly different after I had done this. He had me repeat it once. Then again. By the third time, I felt much better than I had only a few minutes ago. By the fifth time he had me hold my hands out about four-six inches in front of my belly and visualize the ball expanding to that diameter as I held my breath. I repeated this seven times, then opened my eyes.

"How do you feel?" he asked.

"Much, much better!" I replied, suddenly refreshed. "That was great — I feel much more like my usual self!" I immediately wanted to figure out how I could have changed so radically.

"How does it work — is it the increased oxygen to the lungs?" I asked eagerly.

He started laughing. "Yes, and no. You are certainly back to your old self! The physical oxygen helps, sure, but the key is in the rhythm of the breathing and the visualization."

I found this hard to believe. He attempted to explain it to me. "The basic rule of thumb when dealing with energy is this: Energy follows thought. By visualizing the light coming in through your nostrils, you 'filled up' with energy again."

I didn't get it.

"And, yes, Energy follows breath. The rhythm of the breath is one of the main ways that energy comes into and out of the body and the aura. It is a key rhythm. When you stop breathing, you die."

That made more sense to me, though I was back to my "more oxygen" explanation. He decided it wasn't worth explaining any more at this point, that I would simply have to experience it often enough before I started to believe it. I assured him I would practice this technique at least once a day.

"Your movie assignment, for the next time that I see you, is *LadyHawke*. Have you seen it?" I had, but it was a decade ago and I remembered very little from it. "Watch it, and there will be an interesting lesson for you in it."

I agreed. He said that he, too, had to run for a meeting and couldn't stay. He also reminded me not to forget to use my work as meditation. I wanted to ask him more about my business idea, but he refused to talk about it, and left abruptly.

I felt well enough to return to work for the rest of the day. The first thing I did was check my email. I double-clicked on my email program, sure to find an email from him. After searching for it, I could not find it. This confused me to no end, and even though I spent the rest of the day at work, I spent it looking for the missing email message. I didn't find it.

CHAPTER SUMMARY
INTRODUCTION TO ENERGY

The study of Energy is a central issue for the Career Warrior.
If we can start to get a feeling for different types of energy, how we get it, how we lose it, and how we exchange it, we can start to perceive our own "Energetic Pattern", which both helps us and hurts us in our attempts to succeed in the world. The Energetic Pattern is not some abstruse psycho-babble, it is how we hold our energy in our field, how we hold our minds and our bodies. It can actually be seen at an energetic level by some gifted people. More importantly, our Energetic Pattern is the filter through which we see life, through which we react to the world around us, and thus, known or unknown to us, it plays a major role in how we make decisions.

Always start with the obvious, and then you can find a way to uncover the hidden flow of energy.
If you understand energy, you begin to understand the hidden worlds. If you understand the hidden worlds, you can understand the visible world much more coherently.

In this case start with the obvious definition of *energy*. Some people seem to have more energy naturally, some people naturally have less. Exercising regularly, eating well, all of these things contribute to our energy. That's pretty obvious. If you're tired, rest or sleep and you should wake up with more energy. That's also pretty obvious.

Now think about how you feel after interacting with some people? How does your energy flow ... do you feel less or more energy after or during your interaction? Does going to certain places make you feel more energetic, or more frantic? We are all like radio receivers, getting signals from places and the people who populate those places. Are there certain times of day when you come alive, and other times of day when you can't stay awake, let alone be productive? This is all about *Energy*.

To accomplish an occult task, follow your intuition, not your logic.
An *occult task* is to use what you have learned about the

visible and hidden worlds to accomplish something concrete. This is slightly different than the Warrior's Task, introduced in the last chapter (which has to do with having more than one purpose for a given, usually mundane task).

In this chapter, Ramaswami gave James an occult task to find me. I was also given an occult task: to find the highest energy spot in the mall's food court. Notice that simply trying to implement techniques is not enough to accomplish an occult task; you usually have to let go and trust your feelings. In the case of James, he meditated and tried to figure out where I was using logic, but neither of those things worked, so he gave up. Then he had a feeling to go to a particular spot to meditate there, and by going there he found me!

That's how intuition works: it's not some obvious "I am going to use my third eye now and see a perfect picture of where I should go or what I should do." Rather it comes as a feeling or hunch that you should move in a particular direction, which may not make any sense logically speaking. If you follow your intuition, you can accomplish very difficult occult tasks.

Two central tenets of Energy are: Energy is regulated by breath. Energy follows thought.

Thus, you can use breathing and visualization exercises to replenish and regulate energy in the body. The practice of Yoga very much has to do with manipulating energy in the body. In Yoga, this was traditionally done via *pranayama* (breathing exercises for regulating energy), and *asanas* (physical postures that we think of as practicing Yoga) and the *yamas* (the do's and don'ts in daily life which affect our energy).

There are many exercises that you can do to alter your energy. The one given to me in this chapter was to help me to slow down and stop the leaking of energy out of my field by pouring more energy in. The regulation of breath — by re-instating rhythm while breathing — was as important as the visualization itself.

A result of going through life is that our "energetic patterns" change over time. As they do, we introduce blockages into our energy field, which results in tightness and holding in our bodies. This results in bad breathing, which results in suboptimal flow of energy. Almost without fail, anyone can start to feel better simply by regulating the breath into a natural rhythm.

In Yoga, there are many ways to use the breath to regulate your internal state: alternate nostril breathing, abdominal breathing, paradoxical/reverse breathing, breath of fire, and on and on. If it calls to you, you should explore this area in your development of the Path of the Career Warrior (look for Chi Gung or pranayama exercises).

To try this yourself, assess your energy, and try the exercises given in the chapter.

EXERCISE: Filling Up With Energy

This is a simple breath and visualization exercise that was given in the chapter.

1. First, sit on a chair with your feet flat on the floor, and try to straighten your spine.
2. Put your right hand over your navel and your left hand over your right.
3. Close your eyes and inhale slowly to a count of 7, feeling your abdomen fill up.
4. As you inhale, visualize filling up your belly with orange (or yellow) light – notice the color that comes more naturally.
5. Hold your breath to a count of 7, and as you do so, imagine an orange ball of light expanding in your belly outwards.
6. Exhale to a count of 7.
7. Repeat 5-7 times.

Be sure to assess how you feel afterwards. Notice that rhythm doesn't always mean you will gain energy – if you have too much, you can use slow rhythmic breathing to slow down your mind and your body as well. The basic principle is, paraphrasing the words of the famous Johnny Cash: when energy is unbalanced, *Get Rhythm!*

6 AN ENCOUNTER WITH THE OCEAN
SEPTEMBER, 1993

I stood on the cliffs overlooking the Pacific Ocean. It was only my second time on the West Coast, and as soon as I had gotten my rental car, I decided that I would go straight to the ocean.

I didn't even realize the strangeness of my question when I asked the guy at the car rental place at San Francisco airport: "I'd like to go to the ocean. Can you tell me how to get there?" I didn't notice his puzzled look as I waited anxiously for his answer.

"Go west, young man," he replied, and suddenly got a look of self-satisfaction, as if he'd just made a joke.

"I want to see rocky coastline," I replied, still very seriously. "Can you tell me how to find rocky coastline?"

"Look, buddy, this is northern California, it's all rocky coastline!" he answered gruffly, suddenly getting annoyed. "If you got a few hours, you can go north of Golden Gate into Marin. It's beautiful there. Or, if you don't have that much time, go south of the city, take 380 towards Daly City, and there's some rocky coastline there."

I looked at my watch as I rushed out. It said 10 p.m.

I realized that I only had a little while before sunset. I did the calculations in my head, "It's 10 p.m. back east. It's September. The sun sets by 7:30 at the latest back in Boston. That means it probably sets by about 8 here." I had always been intrigued by sunsets and so could quickly figure out the time of sunset in just about any part of the country.

It was my first experience seeing the northern California coastline, and I was spellbound by its sheer size and beauty. I stopped at a Taco Bell in Pacifica, a town on the ocean just south of the airport, to get a bite to eat. The concept of a Taco Bell right on the beach was new to me. Surfers were everywhere. The sound of the surf rushing in, the coastline vanishing off to the north, the bright blue sky overhead — all put me into a peaceful and almost reverent state of mind.

I drove on the Pacific Coast Highway and found a little shoulder area where I could park. Then, completely ignoring the 'Dangerous - Do not climb on cliffs' sign, I stood atop what amounted to a mound of sand that separated the road from the cliffs. From there, I could look down and see the surf smashing into the rocky cliffs hundreds of feet below.

Even though I had spent the last five years in Boston, I decided right there and then that the Atlantic coastline was nothing compared to the grandeur of the Pacific. I looked out at the vast expanse of ocean, then at the dark, rocky cliffs I was standing on, and then finally at the brown hills on the landward side of the road. There was something warm and comforting about the experience that I couldn't analyze but felt deeply.

I stared at the shimmering reflection of the sun in the water, which by now was beginning to set, took a deep breath, and lost myself in the moment.

Suddenly, I was jolted out of my reverie by a voice.

"It's because I'm a friendly ocean, and you can learn much from me." It surprised me, and I almost lost my balance. I looked around to find out who had spoken to me, but there was no one around. Only the rush of the cars on the Pacific Coast Highway, and the sound of surf far below.

I sipped my Taco Bell drink, turned back to the Ocean and felt its ever-present breeze run through my hair. *Who said that?* I looked down the cliff to a little beach, but it was deserted. *I must have imagined the whole thing*, I thought, and soon fell back into my peaceful state, enjoying the scenery.

I closed my eyes, and concentrated on feeling the breeze on my face. I noticed the light of the sun through my closed lids, and listened to the surf. I have always found the sound of surf comforting. Although I was constantly in motion in those days, always doing something, listening to this sound was the one activity that could calm me down no matter where I was. Soon, I was lost in this feeling again and began to imagine the surf washing over me.

Suddenly, the voice came again, a deep voice that spoke slowly. "I am vast ... I can teach you how to conquer even the biggest obstacles. You can do it in a series of waves. If the waves keep on going, you will eventually be successful; if the waves stop, then you will not be successful!"

This time, I did not open my eyes. I realized it was only a voice in my head. *I don't believe this*, I said back to the voice-within-myself, *I'm talking to myself as if I was the Ocean...*

"No, I'm talking to you," the voice said with the next incoming splash of surf, sounding like the jolly green giant. It was silent again until the next wave came in, "And I am the Ocean!"

I'm losing my mind! I decided the best thing to do was to ignore it as much as possible.

"Relax, whenever you are in trouble, or anxious, remember the vastness of the ocean..." it started. Then: "Waves of relaxation ... I can calm you down. Think of me in times of trouble ... or if you are really stressed out, come visit me."

I don't believe it! The Pacific Ocean is talking to me! Something is definitely wrong here. I opened my eyes to make sure no one was watching me. I was embarrassed. I could feel the anxiety building up inside me — the sun was about to set; before me was one of the most beautiful scenes I had experienced in my life, but I couldn't enjoy it because I was becoming delusional.

What could have caused this breakdown?

I had been extremely stressed out for much of the summer, continually frustrated by my inability to launch the business in the way that I wanted to launch it, and exhausted from working two contracts. I remembered something Ramaswami had told me earlier: "Sometimes no one believes in an entrepreneur but himself; under those circumstances the only thing to do is to start doing it yourself. In time, if you're doing the right thing, help will arrive."

This vacation, coming at the end of the summer, was a much-needed break from all that computer programming and obsessing about the best way to launch the company. *Maybe that's what did it*, I guessed, *sitting in front of a computer terminal all through the summer*. I vowed never to do that again, and turned to go back to my car when another car pulled into the make shift parking area. Its lights were on so I could not see inside.

The figure that came out of the car looked familiar as he walked up to me. He was wearing a double-breasted suit and had curly blond hair ... and then it hit me!

"Ramaswami! What are you doing here?" I was shocked to see him. I knew from conversations with him that he came to the West Coast every few weeks. I had even heard from James that he was in the San Francisco area this week, but to see him drive up to the exact point on the Pacific Coast Highway I was standing on seemed to be too much of a coincidence!

He smiled and walked past me, taking a stand in the exact location I had been admiring the sea only moments earlier.

"Isn't it beautiful...?" he gestured toward the setting sun. The sky had turned red, orange, purple, and a little yellow, all at the same time. "Moments of beauty like this are always interesting to me. I search them out. There is a truth in beauty that cannot be thought about ... it can only be felt."

I glanced at the colors, and agreed, but was still surprised to see him here. "But ..." I started as he held up his right hand to silence me; then he motioned for me to stand next to him looking out at the ocean.

"Why is the ocean so beautiful?" he asked. "What about it makes us relax, and stare in awe?"

I was at a loss. "It's ... it's ... the size! It's so ... vast," I volunteered, embarrassed that only moments earlier the ocean had been speaking to me telling me about its vastness.

"No, not quite," he replied without moving his eyes from the sunset. "This is incredibly fortuitous that I've found you here ..." he laughed quickly, as if he had just made a joke. I didn't see it as a joke at all.

"You see, this time of day is the most interesting to me. Why? Because at twilight, the dimensions shift as day turns into night. At twilight, ordinary people with little training can see into the hidden worlds, the dimensions of night and day mix together in a way that affects us profoundly ..."

I too enjoyed the sunset, but I had no idea what he was talking about. "Day does shift into night, and it is beautiful..." I agreed, having had a fascination with sunset myself. "But, what do you mean by dimensions?" I couldn't for the life of me figure out what he was talking about.

He turned to me with an almost absent look; by now I knew that this meant he was going to describe to me something he was looking at in his mind's eye, what was referred to as his 'third eye'.

"The physical universe all around us is simply one dimension of existence. Think of it as only one notch on an axis that spreads out toward infinity. And there are multiple axes. Each notch in the axis represents a dimension of existence — we cannot perceive these other dimensions ordinarily because we are fixed in this one," he gestured all around us. "But, there are other layers of existence, all in the same space. When we meditate we begin to be able to perceive these other dimensions.

"Think of yourself like a radio. There are countless radio stations broadcasting all around us, but we are only 'tuned into' one station at a time. In our case, it is the physical world."

I wasn't buying it, and he could tell. He sighed and started over.

"Okay, as always, let's begin with the obvious, and perhaps it will reveal something to us about the not-so obvious."

"Okay," I agreed. I suddenly noticed how funny it looked to see him fully dressed in a business suit standing on the cliffs looking out over the ocean. Down below the cliffs we could see surfers in wet suits coming onto the beach from the water.

"If you had been out in the ocean on a ship for weeks, would you find the ocean so beautiful as you do now?"

I thought about it for a few seconds. "I have never been out to sea for even a few days, let alone a few weeks," I replied.

He smiled. "Yes, yes. But, if you had been out for a few weeks, you might *not* find the ocean so pretty. In fact, when sailors have been out to sea for some time, they find the scenery to be ordinary — nothing but water spreading out in all directions, and you know what? They begin to crave land! They don't get excited when they see ocean anymore, but when they see land."

"Land ho!" He made an exaggerated impression of a sailor looking out over the horizon. "And suddenly everyone is excited? Why?"

I didn't know why.

"It's a truth of human nature and the universe that consciousness finds the boundary of two things extremely interesting. When you have been on land and you suddenly see the ocean, your spirits are lifted because you have come to a transition between two very different worlds. If you had been traveling across the Great Plains and you suddenly saw the Rocky Mountains, you'd see a beautiful sight! But if you had been in the mountains for weeks, you wouldn't find the mountains to be that beautiful, would you?"

"I ... guess not." He had a good point.

"So you see, transitions are significant things. When-ever, where-ever you see a transition, you have stumbled onto something that is inherently interesting for you, and for me. Our minds crave differences, and a transition is the essence of a difference."

He turned back to the ocean as the sun sank beneath the horizon. The sky was slowly turning a brilliant red.

"Find moments of beauty like this, and you're onto something about the structure of the worlds. Now, what other transition do you notice around us?"

I think I finally saw where he was going. "The transition of day into night," I answered.

"Yes, of course. The daytime may be beautiful, the nighttime might be beautiful, but it's the transition between the two that has caught the attention of poets for many ages. Twilight has some inherent interest for us. Let me ask you a question: do you feel differently at sunset than you do the rest of the day or night?"

I wasn't sure. "Well, let me answer for you," he continued. The words seemed to flow effortlessly for him in this state.

"Twilight holds a sense of wonder that causes us to be more reflective. It's a romantic time, but also a time for self-reflection. Our consciousness is better able to slow down and reflect on things going on in our lives during twilight.

"This is not just some random thing that happens. It's a pattern that holds great significance. This is because we are able to shift our consciousness into other dimensions at twilight that we are not ordinarily able to do. We are able to perceive things that cannot be ordinarily perceived because we are too caught up in the worries of the day or the night! During the day we are working too hard, and at night we are usually attending to our families, our roommates, our dates, or what-have-you."

"You do have an interesting point about transitions." I had never thought of it that way before. "I do become more reflective around sunset ... that's why I'm here in the first place. But what do you mean by perceiving things we cannot ordinarily perceive?"

There was a glint of mischief in his eyes as he smiled and winked at me: "I think you know what I mean."

"I ... don't know what you mean." His face bid me to look toward the ocean, as his smile got larger and larger. I felt very uncomfortable and embarrassed.

When I didn't answer, he closed his eyes and turned toward the ocean. Then: "I see you've been talking to the Pacific here! She says she has much to teach you!"

I was flabbergasted. I didn't know what to say, so I quickly explained what had happened and my theories that I had been under too much stress lately.

He dismissed my explanations as 'psychological babble' and insisted that I had actually spoken to the Pacific Ocean. I wasn't so sure. "How can you speak to the Ocean? After all, it's not a living entity ... it's ... it's just water!"

He nodded and took a few steps away. I followed. "It's not just water. The Pacific Ocean is not just an ocean ... she has a spirit. It's not a traditional spirit — it's not a ghost, for example. But, the Pacific consists of thousands ... millions ... of living organisms. Someday you'll understand that the Earth itself is alive and has a spirit. Are you familiar with the term *gestalt*?"

I had to admit I was not.

"It's a borrowed German word. Here in California we use it to mean the whole of something, the totality. Gestalt therapy, for example, is a form of therapy that is supposed to be holistic ... dealing with the whole of the individual and the whole of the problem, but that's another story altogether — let's not talk about therapy here. Think of the gestalt as something that is more than the sum of its parts ..."

That much I could easily follow.

"Now, imagine a herd of animals — each of them has a consciousness of its own — but the herd moves in unison and it takes on a collective consciousness that is more than the consciousness of any individual in that group. The same is true for a school of fish.

"Now, in the hidden worlds, you can actually see this collective consciousness as another personality ... more than, but composed of, the individuals in the group. But it will be quite some time before you can perceive what's happening on those levels. Just suffice it to say that every living thing, even a group of living things, has some consciousness in the hidden worlds."

It sounded a bit far-fetched to me and I was ready to tell him so. "That seems a little unscientific, don't you think?" I responded. I explained that there are many reasons why a flock of birds can take visual cues from each other and that accounts for how they move in unison.

"There's nothing unscientific about it!" He seemed to be getting a little upset at me. "Science is about observation. I'm not speaking theory here, my young scientific friend; I'm telling you that these things can be observed. Now, just because most people can't observe them doesn't mean they're not there. Part of what I'm going to teach you is a series of behaviors, techniques, and meditations that will allow you, with years of practice, to actually perceive the hidden worlds ..."

"What does this entity look like?" I asked, not altogether convinced, but willing to humor him.

"Listen, we could be here all night talking about the hidden worlds. But it's not to be talked about. It's to be experienced. We could talk about it forever and that wouldn't make the slightest bit of difference. Now, your skepticism isn't a bad thing — in this path, it is important to verify through your own personal experience rather than taking things on blind faith. However, you should not snap to judgment until you have had the proper training. Then you will be in a better position to use your skepticism in a *healthy* way.

"Now, let's assume for a second, that what you thought happened, actually did happen. It doesn't really matter if it was the Pacific Ocean or a voice in your head. In either case, I'm telling you that it's important. Now, what did it say?"

I thought back, but couldn't remember exactly. "Something about the ocean being vast and calm, and that if I get too anxious I could come back to the ocean and it would calm me down. And something about solving problems in waves."

"Aha. Now that's a bit of wisdom that has a lot of bearing on you..." he paused and smiled, "and on your business."

"My business? What do you mean?" He had suddenly caught my attention.

"I'm simply telling you to listen to what the voice said."

"But," I countered, "it isn't exactly practical for me to fly to California every time I'm feeling anxious!"

"No, no, no! You don't have to fly out here, you only need to take a mental trip. Listen, I'm going to leave you here for a few minutes, I want you to really experience the ocean and let yourself relax. Meet me back out here at sunrise, and I'd like to talk to you more about your business idea..."

"Why can't we talk about it now?" I asked, now impatient to talk about my business.

"You Gen-Xers! Everything has to be *now* ... listen, the best way for you to comprehend some of the things that I'm talking about is for me to give you assignments, since you're a bit thick skulled and won't take my word for it." I was insulted a little but now that he wanted to talk about business, I was all ears.

"I watched *LadyHawke*," I told him. "It was a fun movie, but the music was terrible; it was obviously from the early 80's because it had Mathew Broderick, but it could have been from the late 70's, given its twinkly music!" By this time I was starting to think that he was just a fan of badly made sci-fi / fantasy movies.

"Ah, very good. It's not the music that I wanted you to pay attention to. Was there anything in the movie that relates to our discussion here today?"

I turned my mind back to the movie. There was magic, sorcery, swordplay, and animals. That was it! "Yes, the curse that was on the captain. He and his love interest, Michelle Pfeiffer, were turned into animals, a panther and a falcon, I believe."

He waited for me to continue. "The problem was that the man was a panther during the night, and the woman was a falcon during the day, so they were cursed and couldn't spend any time together."

"Except ..." he prodded me.

"Yes, except at sunset or sunrise. At the transition point. *Always together, Forever apart,*" I answered, recalling more from the movie. "But, Ramaswami, that's a medieval fantasy movie. How can you say that relates to how the world really works?"

"As I've told you many times, for now I am simply using a visual medium, movies, as an expedient way to tap into a state of mind."

"You mean watching these movies will help me start my business?"

"Not exactly. Watching movies will help you to tap into certain states of mind that I think you need to be at to comprehend what I'm telling you. I'm going to start with really obvious stuff, something that's *obviously* fiction! But, there's more to good fiction than meets the eye!"

I thought about how any of this could help me start my business. Then I thought of a movie about the business world. "I watched Wall Street several times!" I volunteered, hoping that this would impress him. He only groaned. "Listen, kid, Wall Street is a great movie, but the state of mind that it taps into, the ambition of the go-go 80's isn't exactly what you are in short supply of, right?"

I had to agree that I had no shortage of ambition. In fact, in high school I had been voted as our graduating class's most 'ambitious' student.

"Besides, what happened to Budd Fox at the end of the movie?" he asked. Budd Fox, played by Charlie Sheen, was the main character of the movie, an ambitious stockbroker who aspires to become rich like his idol, billionaire Gordon Gekko, played by Michael Douglas.

"Ah..." I hesitated. "Well, that's not really the part of the movie that I focus on," I answered.

He nodded his head. "I'll tell you. Budd Fox goes to jail! Remember the last line of the movie: I wanted to be Gordon Gekko so bad, I didn't realize that I'm not Gordon Gekko, I'm just Budd Fox. And then he went to jail! Don't let your ambition run wild! But anyway, that's not the lesson we're going to focus on right now."

"Okay," I replied, not knowing what to say and a bit disappointed that he had shot down one of my favorite movies.

"Meet me here at sunrise tomorrow and we'll talk more about your business idea. For now, I'd like you to concentrate on the wisdom of the Pacific. It'll help you in your business considerably!" He smiled and started walking back to his car.

"Wait a minute!" I followed him. "I know you were in California, but how did you find me here...?"

That made him stop and laugh. "Remember what I told you last time, there are no coincidences! But, if you must know, I came out here to meet with some venture capitalists. There is a link between Boston and Silicon Valley that I'm sure you're aware of — the technology connection. I'll tell you more about that link some other time." He turned and opened his car door.

"But how did you find me *here*?" I yelled out to him again as he entered the car. He stopped midway, stepped out of the car, looked me straight in the eyes and broke out laughing: "First of all, there is only one Pacific Coast Highway. And more importantly," he paused to make sure I was listening. "You're not the only one who talks to the Ocean!"

I wasn't ready for the lesson to end but didn't know what to say. "I'll give you your assignments tomorrow," he said and drove off, leaving me alone in the darkness standing out over the Pacific Ocean.

That night, I got a hotel room in Pacifica just north of the location of our conversation. My room at the Days Inn allowed me to look out at the beach and to see and hear the surf all night long. That night, the sound of the ocean lulled me to sleep, and with each passing wave, I became more and more relaxed. The stress of the past few months seemed to disappear, as had the anxiety of wondering whether I had lost my mind earlier. I fell asleep feeling like I was floating.

CHAPTER SUMMARY
AN ENCOUNTER WITH THE OCEAN

The physical universe all around us simply one dimension of existence.

To understand this, think of the physical world around us as only one notch on an axis that spreads out toward infinity. Like different radio frequencies, each notch is a dimension that exists in the same physical space and time. We cannot perceive these dimensions ordinarily because our receiver is fixed, or tuned into, this single physical reality. But, there are other layers of existence, all around us which we don't normally perceive.

What holds our perception into this one single dimension? It is our view of the world, our internal dialog and chatter, and by the agreement we make with society as we grow up from children into adults. As we grow older, we fix our receiver into this one frequency over the course of a lifetime. It's hard to hear anything else with all of this dialog and chatter, fear and worry, going on in our minds all the time.

To tune into other dimensions is a matter of quieting the mind and tuning into feelings and energy.

To quiet your mind, use what you've learned during sitting meditation. Once your mind is quiet, you have to learn to pay attention to your feelings at different times of day.

Seek out moments of beauty like the one described in this chapter. Whether it's a beautiful sunset, a small winding country road near rolling hills, or the corona of the full moon – beauty touches a part of us that is non-verbal. There are innumerable moments of beauty in the world — but you have to seek them out and pay attention to them. In those moments, be sure to take in how they make you *feel*. This is important because finding the pathway to the hidden worlds is not just about your mind, it involves *feelings* and *energy*.

Places have energy and people both sense and contribute to this energy, sensing and creating Places of Power.

A "Place of Power" is a location that is particularly high in energy and your mere presence there affects you. It's hard to define this more precisely in physical terms because it's more about the "feeling" in a place.

As more people congregate to a place thinking similar thoughts, these thoughts intensify and then these thoughts are literally "in the air" in those places.

There are two types of Power Places: Natural Power Places (usually a specific spot up high on a ridge or down low in a valley where there aren't too many people), and Man-Made Power Places (such as Silicon Valley or Cambridge, MA regarding technology, or other places for other vocations). Usually Man-Made Power Places have a combination of natural energy, mind-enhancing architecture (i.e. sacred geometry), and a history of many people engaged in similar activity and thought patterns.

Transitions often represent Times and Places of Power.

Sunset and sunrise are examples of transitions of day into night. We can shift into other dimensions at these times because they are natural Times of Power. More on this in future chapters!

Listen to your intuition, no matter how crazy it seems.

Intuition can come in many forms. Even in the form of an Ocean talking to you, teaching you lessons by both its waves and its inner voice.

There's a great line in a more recent movie, which serves as an excellent movie assignment: Harry Potter and the Deathly Hallows (Part 2). In this scene, Harry Potter finds himself in a vision of what looks like the afterlife, with his mentor, Professor Dumbledore, who has already died. Not sure what to think of their conversation, Harry asks: "Professor, is this *real*, or is this all just happening in my head?"

"Of course, Harry, this is all happening inside your head," answers the Professor. Then he adds: "But why should that mean it's not *real*?"

Pay attention, particularly to what goes on inside your head!

7 THOUGHT-FORMS AND BRAINSTORMS
OCTOBER, 1993

I sat in my room on my little green meditation pillow. The light from my halogen lamp was dimmed, and there was soft music emanating from my stereo in the corner. My room was sparse: the stereo, my futon, the lamp, my desk, a few books, and my little meditation area. My friends told me that its sparseness reminded them of a Japanese painting.

On the carpet in front of me sat my notebook. I had followed Ramaswami's advice and written down every single reason I could think of for not starting the company. This I had done while still in California; then when I got back to Boston, I started writing about my business idea and why it should be built. I wasn't very sophisticated in my analysis, but I had put down the following points:

-We know there is market demand, based upon market research we did in the summer
-I believe, based upon what I saw at Lotus, that we can get an article in a major magazine written about it
-We can build it ourselves in a few months
-I'm bored with my work at Lotus and really want to break out on my own

I read these points and looked out of my window at the leaves of the trees. It was now officially autumn, and the leaves in New England had begun to turn brown, orange, and yellow. The winter of 1993 would be a harsh one, as would the following two winters, but so far the weather had been mild and I looked forward to seeing the foliage, a big event in New England.

Each day, after my evening meditation, when my concentration was the strongest, I would write about the product that I wanted to build and how I would sell it, trying to get an inner momentum going.

I closed my eyes and began to visualize what the product would look like. I first tried to visualize the different components of the product, but it was difficult to do. So then I visualized an article in a computer industry magazine talking about our product, but it was still too difficult for me to do this. My powers of visualization weren't quite that strong.

Finally, I started to visualize a software box. The box was white. On the box was written VB-NotesLink in sky blue letters. In the box were disks with our software product on them. Ramaswami would tell me that I would 'know' when I found the right image to visualize by an inner feeling. Somehow, whenever I visualized the box, I felt a build-up of energy in my belly, not unlike what happened after doing the energy visualization that he had taught me a few months earlier. The more I visualized the image, the stronger the feeling became, and the more realistic it became. It became easier for me to hold the image in my mind as this momentum built up.

I thought about what Ramaswami had explained to me at sunrise almost a month ago back on the West Coast.

"One of the most important things you will learn while meditating is how to find the right image and how to hold it in your mind. This is one key part of manifestation. If you want to create a result, an achievement, even a software product, visualization can help you to build up the momentum to guide you towards your goal."

"Meditation, particularly visual meditation, builds the muscles of the mind that you will need to hold an image. Now, don't get me wrong: visualizing does not guarantee anything, but it does help focus all of your energies to attempt to bring the thing that you visualize into reality."

"Isn't that simply the Power of Positive Thinking?" I asked

"Yes, and no. It is the power of positive thinking, yes, but it is not simply that. What you will learn is that thoughts are things. How many thoughts do you have in a given day?"

I had never counted them and had to admit so.

"Even so, how many? Tens of thoughts? Hundreds of thoughts? Thousands of thoughts?"

I thought about it, but could not come up with an answer, or even a method to calculate how many there might be.

"Okay — so what percentage of those thoughts have pictures and which are just dialogue?" he asked me.

Again, I had no idea. I could not even remember most of my thoughts from the previous day, let alone count them!

"Well, you see the beauty of meditation is that it lets you focus your energy on one or two thoughts, rather than dissipating it across literally hundreds or thousands of thoughts in a given day. These thoughts are a hodge-podge of things that we pay attention to, but..." He stopped for effect to make sure I was paying attention. "The thoughts that we have on an on-going basis are the ones that will actually have an impact on us. These thought-forms lodge themselves into our auras. It is because of this that I always say: *What you focus on, you will become.*"

I told him that I had no idea what he meant when he spoke about thought-forms lodging themselves in my aura. By now, I understood what he meant by an aura: the theoretical energy field that surrounds each living thing, which certain mystics claim to be able to see. But thought-forms were a new concept.

"What is a thought-form?" I asked.

He picked up a rock in his hand. "This rock is real, you wouldn't question that, would you?" I shook my head in answer. "Well, thought-forms are things also, just not in the physical realm. Thoughts exist in higher planes of existence. A habitual thought becomes a thought-form. That thought-form has a life of its own once you've imbued it with enough energy. And there lies one of the keys to manifestation."

"The process of creating something in your life is called *manifestation.* In order to manifest something that you think about, you have to first give the thought enough attention so that it becomes a thought-form. Then, you have to crystallize that thought-form so that it comes from the higher planes to the physical planes. The only way to do that is to focus on it again and again."

I nodded my head and agreed. "It seems logical," I started, "that if you focus on one thought again and again, then your subconscious mind will grasp opportunities to bring that idea into reality. That's what positive thinking is all about, isn't it?"

He stomped his foot in the sand. "No! It's not that simple. The subconscious mind is a figment of your imagination!" he insisted and began walking on the beach. By now the sun had come up and light was everywhere.

"Thought-forms are things that exist in the hidden worlds, outside our normal consciousness. If you think something often enough, the thought-form becomes lodged in your aura, and it is actually visible in the hidden worlds. The subconscious mind is something that you cannot ordinarily perceive!"

I took in what he said, gazing out into the ocean past him. For a brief second, I suddenly noticed a fuzzy red haze all around his body. I blinked and looked again but it wasn't there. I didn't realize it at the time, but I had just seen my first aura.

He picked up a stick and we kept walking along the beach. "I am going to teach you the keys to success in your career, in your life, and the key to accomplishment. It is more than visualization, but it may take you years to really appreciate all the items that are necessary to become a master at dealing with the physical world in non-physical ways.

"Do you remember the universal laws I've been teaching you?" he asked.

For a moment I had no idea what he was asking for; I was trying to see the red haze around him that I had seen just a moment ago. "Huh? Oh yeah, that everything in the obvious world has its counterpart in the hidden world."

"And what else?" he continued. I replied: "That there are no accidents."

"Anything else?" he continued. I replied: "That there are clues all around us ... these clues usually result in some kind of internal feeling that we recognize ... these clues are supposed to lead us to something that helps with our meditation, I think." I hadn't quite understood the reasons I was looking for clues but knew it had something to do with meditation and "personal growth".

"Yes, well today's major lesson is this: thought-forms are things and you need to become aware of them; your habitual thought-forms will determine the direction of your life. Learn what they are so that you can use them to your advantage, not to your disadvantage."

He pulled out a little book from his pocket and handed it to me. I studied the cover; it said simply, *The Dhamapadda*. It was a pocket-sized book that could be carried around inconspicuously in a shirt or a suit jacket pocket.

"This book contains the selected sayings of the Buddha, making it one of the most important religious works in the world," he said, pointing to it. "Now it doesn't matter how much you know about actual Buddhism, and it doesn't matter if you believe the Buddha was divine or just some fellow wearing a loincloth who said some interesting things. Just realize that the Buddhists have spent more time understanding the hidden worlds than just about anyone — except maybe some of the shamans of native cultures — and so their teachings are inherently interesting to anyone who attempts to walk the Path of the Career Warrior.

"I'm not talking about the unnecessary crap that most Buddhists focus on day to day — that's full of ritual and not very interesting. This book cuts to the heart of the Buddha's philosophy. He could have said anything, he could have said: You are all sinners and you will burn in the hellfire. Or, he could have said: You shall convert to Islam at the tip of a sword, or you will die. Or, he could have said: The God of Abraham will bring pestilence and destruction to your people, because you aren't as cool as we are. Or, he could have said: Worship the goddess at the temple once a week or you will return as a goat. He could have said all of those things, but he didn't, and that's why I got so interested in Buddhism in the first place!"

I was taken aback. In one paragraph, he had managed to insult all of the major world religions, even the one he claimed to be a member of, Buddhism, and the one that I had been brought up under, Islam. I wasn't sure if I should be offended, annoyed, or impressed, so I didn't say anything and waited for him to continue.

"What the Buddha said, instead of all of these things, was quite interesting. Open to the first page and read it."

I opened the book, and was about to start reading the preface by Ram Dass, when he instructed me to go to the first real chapter. "We want the teachings of the Buddha, not of Ram Dass," he replied. Later I would find out that Ram Dass was a former Harvard professor who had given drugs to his students in the sixties along with Timothy Leary. Both of them were kicked out of Harvard for this. Eventually, he went to India, studying meditation with a teacher named Hari Dass, who gave him his spiritual name: Ram Dass. I flipped past his intro and started reading the first verse of the first chapter aloud:

"We are what we think.
All that we are arises with our
    thoughts.
With our thoughts we make the world."

He instructed me to stop reading. "If you can learn this, you have learned the first pillar of how to use meditation and spiritual practice to achieve success in the business world. Meditation helps you to refine the number, type, and quality of your thoughts. In the end, our thoughts, particularly our habitual thoughts, have a big impact on our success in the world."

"So how do I apply that to starting a business?" I asked.

"It's very simple, but I will show it to you as part of a larger whole," he said. He took his stick and drew a diamond shape in the sand. "To accomplish anything in the physical world — anything at all — whether it is to modify your behavior, or to create a company, or to otherwise achieve a goal, there are four points, or *keys,*" He touched each of the points of the diamond, "that you need to worry about."

He pointed to the top corner of the diamond. "The first point is what we will call *intent,* which we can focus by using visualization. In order to create a result we know we want, we can focus our *intent* by creating an image that represents this in our minds, and we can meditate on that image."

"But what image would I use for a business?" I asked.

He was almost annoyed. "How should I know," then he broke out into a small laugh. "It's YOUR business! What will your business make?"

I quickly explained the product again. It was disconcerting to me that he didn't remember it from when I told it to him back in May. *Perhaps he doesn't really listen to me*, I thought.

"So, find an appropriate image, and hold it in your mind's eye. Do this with your eyes closed right after your evening meditation, and do it during the day with your eyes open. This will create a thought-form that has the potential to become reality."

"What do you mean by potential?" I asked.

"Whether it becomes reality or not is determined by a number of other factors — factors in your energetic patterns, and in the patterns of the market, and the other people you engage in your pursuit. Some of those things are in your control, and some are not."

"Is that what the other three points in the diamond are?" I questioned, trying to guess what they might be.

"Yes, and no." He pointed to the top point in the diamond. "This first point is about *intent* — in the physical world it means visualization and meditation to create a thought form. This one," he pointed to the one on the left, "is about Patterns. It refers to inner beliefs, and external patterns in our life, which, by the way, are almost exactly the same thing since they are both reflective of your Energetic Pattern.

"You're too young to appreciate this yet, and you haven't had enough experience in the business world to truly appreciate that people's patterns often repeat in their careers with different jobs. This is the beauty and the curse of your Energetic Pattern — it is the primary factor in how we make decisions, and whether we like it or not, it ends up influencing what happens in our lives.

"This one," he pointed to the one on the right moving along, "refers to technique, which are the steps in your action plan and the real world skill sets you need to take. This is the practical, outer steps you need to take to accomplish something. For example you can buy many books on how to write a computer program or how to set up a corporation or how to make sales calls, et cetera. I call this *right technique*.

"And finally, this one at the bottom is something I call appropriateness, or *right timing*. This one has to do with where you are on your life's path, what I call your unique *Warrior's Path*. Your specific Warrior's path is the unique combination of lessons you are here to learn, and the contribution you're here to make. This part of the diamond represents how harmonious this goal is in the context of your particular *Warrior's Path*."

He could see that I was still stuck on the first point.

"The first point, visualization to build intent, leads to ambition and the manifestation of your goals in reality. The Positive Thinkers say this is all you need to do and the rest will follow. But having this pillar," he pointed to the point at the top which represented intent, "without fully understanding beliefs and patterns," he pointed to the left-most point on the diamond, "leads to self sabotage."

Again, he pointed to the first point. "Having this pillar without understanding technique," he pointed to the rightmost point on the diamond, "or having the skill sets in the world to achieve your goals, or visualizing your goal while taking the wrong steps, leads to frustration and ultimately disillusionment! You can't just visualize your goal unlike what the Positive Thinkers tell you … that's not enough!"

"Finally," he said pointing to the bottom point of the diamond. "Any of the top three, without having point number 4, *appropriateness* for our Warrior's Path… leads to unhappiness and the sense that you are drifting … not being fulfilled. How do we know if something is appropriate and we are tapping into *right timing*? We get messages. *Messages from the Hidden Worlds*."

I was still trying to figure out which image to visualize to help launch my company.

"But I see these will have to wait for another time," he said. "I'll have to teach these to you one by one as you start to make your way into the business world."

Back in Boston, I recalled all of this as I struggled to hold on to the mental image of a white box with blue writing on it. I used my power of focus, gained from meditating for a number of months, to imbue the image with energy and life. I still didn't understand what Ramaswami had meant by talking about my energetic patterns or the energetic patterns of the market. When my mind wandered, I brought it back with mental muscles I had been developing. I picked up the notebook and started writing:

What does he mean by my energetic patterns or right timing? It's true that I couldn't have developed this product back in the summer — I was too burned out. Maybe that's what he meant.

I did realize, though, that to bring this product to market and to start the company would require a level of focus that I hadn't had in anything before in my life. I still wasn't sure about thought-forms or any of those things, but I quickly figured out how to draw up that image and the more I did that, the more focus and drive I got to start the company and build the product, rather than waiting for outside conditions to be just right.

After a few weeks of doing this, I got up after my visualization and had made a decision. Or somehow a decision *had been made.* I wasn't sure which was closer to the truth.

I quickly spoke to my roommate and business partner, Mitch, and on my urging, we decided to go ahead and launch our company. We had been close friends since we were both at MIT. During our senior year, we had entered a business plan into the MIT Business Plan Competition, and had reached the semi-finals.

We had created a fictional company in that business plan competition called Brainstorm Technologies; both of us liked the name and decided to use it again.

We quickly named our new company Brainstorm Technologies, Inc. Our entrepreneurial journey had begun, and for the next two months, I held the image of the product in my mind day and night as we meticulously put it together.

A few weeks after our decision to go ahead with the company, we were sitting on two chairs in the living room programming away when Mitch suddenly stood up and started walking around the room in circles. "We need to buy another computer, so we can test our software," Mitch explained. "It's going to cost us $2,000."

Our living room had quickly become packed with computers, files, and other peripherals arrayed on a large folding table (which we bought for $35). These items had very quickly exhausted our short capital supply of $500 in our savings.

"Okay, but we don't have $2,000," I replied, sighing.

"Can you charge it on your credit card?" he asked. I had to admit that my credit limit was at $1,000 and it was already full.

"I can charge it on my parents' credit card," he offered. "If we pay it off in 30 days, they won't care."

"How are we going to pay it off in 30 days if we don't have the money?" I asked.

He sat back down, understanding my point, and was about to start programming again when his eyes lit up. "We can buy the computer, do our testing, and return it in 30 days! That way, the money will be taken off the credit card."

I immediately agreed. That was the first of many creative financing arrangements we would have to make over the ensuing months. We called this our revolving 30-day credit plan. We would buy a computer from one store and use it for 25 or 26 days. We would then go to another store and buy a computer there, and copy the files from the first computer to the second one. Finally, we would return the first computer within the 30-day period.

The next few weeks were spent in almost total immersion. We worked seven days a week (taking only Friday and Saturday evenings off) and were enjoying it. We were caught up in the excitement of starting a new company, and almost everything we did, from the technical to the business side, was new to us. It reminded me of when I was a young boy and had discovered a fascinating book that I wanted to stay up all night and read. My mother would have to make sure I stopped reading and went to sleep. Well, our mothers were several thousand miles away, and though each of us had many friends in the area, neither of us had a girlfriend, so we rarely stopped our almost total immersion.

I also made certain, at Ramaswami's suggestion, that I spent some time each day meditating, and some time 'reflecting' by writing down my thoughts. I wasn't sure how much actual reflection I was getting done during my writing periods, because I simply wrote what was occupying my mind: the building and selling of our first product, VB/Link. My notebook was filled with diagrams of how we would write the code to make it work, how we would test it, and how we would sell it, and on and on, usually in scrawny writing that was difficult to read. Sometimes I would simply write, "I have no idea how to make this part of the product work correctly" and various random thoughts about how customers might use the product.

This had some unexpected benefits. It would keep me engaged instead of discouraged when something unexpected came up. Many months later, as I started traveling the country giving demonstrations of VB/Link, I recognized that much of my 'pitch' — the reasons I gave for why our product was valuable, actually came out of the writing I did during this period. The detailed periods of writing and drawing diagrams in my notebook also helped in visualizing the product.

One night, at about 3 a.m., the visualization was so real that I noticed the product outside of our window. I closed my eyes, took a deep breath, and looked again; sure enough, there it was. Mitch had already gone to his room to go to sleep and I was finishing up testing a piece of code that used to work but now had a bug.

We had a small balcony outside of our living room, which looked out at our parking lot, followed by Route 9 (a usually very busy highway) and then a reservoir. It was very cold that night and there was a fog rising above the reservoir, which was frozen and covered with snow. I peered out into the darkness to convince myself that this was a hallucination, but sure enough there was a box in the middle of the fog that looked strikingly similar to the box I had been visualizing.

At first I laughed. But when I rubbed my eyes, it was still there! Now I wasn't laughing.

Maybe I've been working too hard. This is a sign that I've been visualizing this thing a little too much, I said to myself. I thought back to Ramaswami's insistence that thoughts were real things, and that if you think a thought long enough, it becomes real. I was sure that this, though, was a figment of my imagination. I closed my eyes and took a deep breath. Then I noticed it was still there with my eyes closed as well.

Good, it's just a thought-form, I said, too tired to argue logically with myself about what a *thought-form* really was and whether it had 'existence'. I went to my room and collapsed on my futon.

CHAPTER SUMMARY
THOUGHT-FORMS AND BRAINSTORMS

With our thoughts we make the world.

In many esoteric teachings, including Buddhism, the world is being created instant to instant and we are not just observers, but are taking part in this process. In some traditions the world is being *destroyed* and *recreated* in each instant   As the first words in *The Dhammapada* remind us:

> We are what we think
> All that we are arises with our
>   thoughts
> With our thoughts we make the world

To tune into this process of ever-present creation, we can turn from a *Career Warrior* into a *Career Sorcerer* — one who is adept at manifesting things in both physical and non-physical reality.

To do this, though, it may not be as simple as examining our thoughts. This verse is just a translation of what the Buddha said into English. By simply calling them thoughts, we are confusing them with our ordinary everyday internal dialogue, worries, and fears — which are also thoughts.   To distinguish from everyday thoughts, we often will use the term "thought-forms", habitual thoughts which get lodged into our energy fields.

Use all four Keys to the Diamond of Manifestation.

Legions of books, talks, and courses have been given about the power of visualization as a way to help you manifest wealth, power, status, career success, love, fulfillment, and even world peace!

Of course, if that's all there was to it, then everyone would have everything they've always wanted!   A quick look around the world will show you that isn't the case.   If you're like me and have tried these techniques, you've probably found that sometimes they work and sometimes they don't.   What's the difference?

In this chapter, Ramaswami describes the four points of the diamond (or Four Keys) of manifestation as a way to illustrate that the process of creation in the world around us is a little more complex than simply visualizing something and expecting it to show up in your life a few days later!

Using slightly different terminology, here is a summary of the Four Keys to the Diamond of Manifestation:

- *Right Intent* — Unlock the power of intent and create thought-forms through visualization.

  The first point of the diamond is what we commonly think of as "visualizing our goals". It is also what's become popularly known as *the Law of Attraction*. The basic idea is that if you visualize an outcome, it becomes real for you at some level. If it becomes real for you at some level, it becomes easier to attract that outcome in physical reality.

  In this chapter, Ramaswami describes the cardinal rule of attraction: "What you focus on you become." Basically by holding a thought in your mind it becomes a thought-form, which then becomes part of your energy field. If you meditate, you are able to clear away other competing thought forms and hold this one in your mind longer and more clearly.

  What you are really doing is attracting your ideal scenario to you. I have found that this point, while important, is often focused on too much in the self-help world. It is important to create the right thought-forms, but whether or not it becomes reality is a complicated discussion, which involves the other three points of the diamond. When used with the other aspects of manifestation, this can be a very powerful tool to "move mountains" and make things happen.

- *Right Patterns* — Stack the odds in your favor by riding, not opposing, your Energetic Patterns

  The most important aspect of the hidden worlds for the Career Warrior to understand is the Energetic Pattern. In the context of manifestation, this means that our own patterns will both help us and hurt us in achieving our goals in life.

For example, if you are someone who repeatedly gets excited about something new, and makes a lot of progress at first, only to then either lose interest or get "disappointed" at some point, then guess what? Your manifestation process (i.e. the process of going from visualization to reality) is likely to have a similar result. This is not a negative diagnosis, just an observation.

Alternatively, if you are someone who sticks with something blindly, no matter what's happening, even when you should abandon it, then you are likely to end up in a similar frustrated state. For you, simply repeating a visualization of the same image that's not working for a long period of time may not be the answer. You may need to adapt to changing circumstances.

Energetic Patterns are usually unconscious. Self-awareness is not easy. You have to face both your strengths and weaknesses. An ancient Chinese proverb says: "If you ignore the dragon, it will eat you. If you try to confront the dragon it will overpower you. If you ride the dragon, you will take advantage of its might and power."

- ***Right Technique*** — Do the right stuff in the world.

  Most books about starting a business focus on the outer techniques. These are of course very important. Simply visualizing your goal, but not making enough effort (and the right effort, as opposed to the wrong effort) in the outside world to turn your goal into reality is a sure-fire way to become disappointed and frustrated.

  Note that this key isn't just about making an effort in the real world to achieve your goal. It's about following the "right technique". If you want to achieve something, you can find other people that have achieved a similar goal and find out the techniques they used to get there. You can use this approach to build a software product, write a business plan, open a restaurant, become a writer, get an agent, or move into a particular career. However, the thing you have to be careful of is that every person and every path is unique. As Ramaswami says, you're trying to start "your business", not "someone else's business", which means that external advice can only get you so far. You can use a prescribed technique to set up a C Corp, but it's pretty difficult to use a prescribed technique to find the right market timing or hiring the right employee — these factors depend on you as much as what's happening "out there." There is an art to being successful that goes beyond technique. But if you don't interview anyone, or don't interview enough good candidates, you'll never get the person you're looking for. If you don't find the questions to ask that work for you, you'll be guilty of using the wrong technique.

Suppose you want to become the head of a movie studio. There are as many ways to get there as there are movie studios. I met a guy who, without much more than a high school education, had become head of a major movie studio. He started off by being driver for a creative agency, then went on to become an agent, helped start a well known talent agency, which then led to his being hired from the outside to run the studio! That isn't a technique you can simply "copy." But you can use the same principle — which was to get "close" to the talent world and find a way in. You have to find your own "way in" sometimes. And this brings us to the last and perhaps most important key.

- **Right Timing/Appropriateness** — Attack the right goals at the right time; this means both inner and outer timing.

  In the movie version of the Lord of the Rings, the elf-queen, Lady Galadriel, tells Frodo the Hobbit, of his Quest to destroy the ring: "This task was appointed to you, and if you cannot find a way, then no one can."

  In some ways, when traveling your own unique Warrior's Path, this is the most important aspect of manifesting effortlessly. We are all a sum of our experiences, thoughts, patterns, achievements in this life, and (if you believe in it) accumulated karma from previous lives — our Energetic Pattern. And if you can find the "appropriate" path for yourself at a particular time in life, you'll find that manifestation is easy. If you go down a blind alley or try to achieve other people's goals, you'll find that it isn't so easy. If you are like me, you'll have read some stories of people who created things seemingly effortlessly — from starting a business, getting into a relationship, or publishing a book. What's interesting is that they did this by ignoring the advice of the self help world or the "experts" in their field. They didn't do any visualization, they didn't go out and contact 50 agents, or go to any seminars on how to accomplish what they wanted. They never wrote a business plan and didn't have to go out and pitch a bunch of investors. But, if you try to copy them, you won't be able to because they didn't make any conscious effort. The difference is *appropriateness*. They followed their own clues that led them directly to some "appropriate" outcome for where they were in their lives. Your challenge will be follow your own clues to get to your "appropriate outcome."

Exercise: Write It Down. Remember he Four Keys of the Manifestation.

One of the main lessons in this chapter is that writing things down — whether in diagrams or in paragraphs or in abstract phrases — can really help you. To do this exercise, start with something you want to create in your life or work, and start writing about it by following the Four Keys:

- 1. Right Intent. To create an appropriate thought-form related to your goal, write down in detail what you think the product or service will look like. Include testimonials from (future customers) for your business.

Include what you would like to be doing in your business in terms of its products, its customers, its size, and what you would be doing in the business on a day to day basis.

- 2. Right Patterns. How do you know how your patterns are affecting your ability to reach this goal? There are two ways:
  - o 1) Find a pattern. Have you tried to accomplish this goal or something similar before? More than once? What happened each time? See if you can find some clues to your own Energetic Patterns here, and come up with a strategy to "ride the dragon."
  - o 2) Write down the objections that you think make your goal difficult. This is meant not to make these stronger, but to rob them of some of their power. To do this, after each – either strike it out if you think it's not reasonable or write what you can do to get around it.
- 3. Right Technique. Write down the steps that you have to take to accomplish your goal, as far as you can tell. Include things you aren't sure of how to do. The goal of writing down these steps in as much detail as you can provide is to crystallize your plan, but also to identify the holes in your current understanding. Those holes are which you can do research, find experts, to get the "right technique."
- 4. Right Timing/Appropriateness. Write down why the timing is good (or not so good for you). By timing we mean both the internal timing, and the market timing. Remember what Ramaswami said in the first chapter: To a certain extent, your success will be determined by your energetic patterns overlaid with the energetic pattern of the market. In other words, in business, as in life: *Timing is Everything*!

Part II:
Initiation

8 STANDING ON THE RUNWAY
NOVEMBER-DECEMBER, 1993

The ringing of the phone awakened me suddenly. It was cold outside and I didn't really want to leave my warm blanket, but after the fourth ring, I stumbled out of bed and made my way to the phone. As I did so, I recalled a particularly vivid dream that I had been having.

In the dream, I was in Florida, standing on the beach, enjoying the sound of the surf and the warmth of the sun's rays on my skin. As I looked down the beach, I saw a shadowy figure coming toward me. As the figure came closer, I recognized him – it was my friend Mario, from the old Lotus days! I hadn't heard from Mario since he had abruptly left Lotus a number of months ago. At that time, I had assumed that Mario might have been able to help us start the company, but he had left town for a while. Just as I recognized him, the ringing of the phone awakened me out of the dream.

"Hello…" I mumbled a little incoherently, still half asleep.

"Is this Brainstorm Technologies?" asked a woman on the other end of the phone.

I snapped to attention and feigned sharpness. "Umm…yes, this is Brainstorm. May I help you?"

I glanced over at the clock – it was 8:30 a.m. As a software developer, I wasn't used to getting up that early on *any* day. And this was a Monday; I couldn't remember the last time I had woken up before 10 a.m. on a Monday. Not that I hadn't been working hard – the previous night, both Mitch and I had been up until 3 a.m. putting finishing touches on our software product.

"Yes, I'm calling from *The New York Times*, and we have Lotus Notes and Microsoft Visual Basic, and would be interested in your product … VBLink … how much does it cost?"

I hesitated. We hadn't decided the price point yet; in fact, we hadn't thought about the marketing of the product at all.

"Well, we haven't really released the product yet, you know. How did you hear about us?" I asked.

"The article in ComputerWorld, of course." I could hear her chuckle. Maybe she realized that this was a "two guys in a garage" type of operation, without the garage.

"Oh … of course," I answered, remembering that I had spoken with a reporter at *ComputerWorld* the previous week and true to his word, he had written about us.

"Would you like to be a *beta* customer?" I asked. In the software industry, a *beta* customer is someone who uses the product before it's officially released in order to help test the software and work out any last-minute bugs.

"It depends," she answered. "How much will the product cost when it's released?"

The New York Times, this is big! I said to myself, trying to hide my nervousness at speaking with such a big-name company.

"Ah..." I started. We hadn't really figured out the pricing yet, though we had tossed around some numbers. "We're thinking of $199," I ventured.

When she didn't respond, I immediately worried that the price might be too high. "But, if you agree to become a beta customer, we'll sell it to you for a special introductory price of $99 when it's released!"

There was another moment of silence. "When will it be released?" she asked. I explained that the *beta* cycle had just started and would most likely continue for another four weeks.

"No, I don't think we'll want to be a beta customer. We don't want to use beta code against our production Notes databases," she said matter-of-factly.

Damn! I thought, a little disappointed that our first prospect wasn't going to come through. I quickly started to think of reasons why she should consider buying the product and was about to start my "sales pitch" when she responded:

"But, when it is released, we'll buy two copies at your introductory price, if that's OK. Do you need a P.O.? Can I fax it to you?" Her sudden change of direction took me by surprise. Luckily, we had bought a fax machine the previous week,

Just then, Mitch stumbled out of his room, and he saw me feverishly scribbling down information about *The New York Times*. "Who the hell is calling us at 8:30 on a Monday morning?" he asked, meandering over to the kitchen and grabbing a carton of orange juice.

"Oh, no one you'd care about..." I said casually. He mumbled something as he lifted the carton of orange juice to his mouth to drink.

"Just our first paying customer!" I replied as I set the phone down.

Suddenly, two things happened at once: Mitch was so surprised he spilled his juice on the kitchen floor. And the phone started ringing again.

It didn't stop ringing that day. Or the next day. Or the next. Over the next four weeks of our beta period, we quickly tired ourselves out from all of the activity. The phones would start ringing at about 8:30 a.m., and the days were spent trying to get new customers and supporting our existing beta sites. Evenings were spent trying to fix the remaining bugs in the product, and we were easily working until 2 or 3 a.m. each night getting the product ready for its "official release."

A few days after that first phone call, the phone rang again, this time at 8:30 p.m. We were exhausted and decided to let the answering machine get it.

"Hello, Brainstorm Technologies," came a familiar voice, mocking our answering machine message. "Hey Riz, it's Mario. I'm back in Boston and wanted to see if I could stay with you for a few days." I was startled and I vaguely recalled that Mario had appeared in a dream a few days earlier. Although I didn't recall the full dream, I remembered that he had been in Florida.

Mario, who was 28 at the time (*older and wiser* by our standards), had also gone to MIT, and though he always talked about starting a company, he had a unique working style. Mario would work for six or twelve months at a time, save up enough money, and then "take it easy" for six months or a year at a time. This take-it-easy time usually included long trips to Miami and Sicily.

Sure enough, when he arrived at our place that night, he looked recently tanned and seemed to be in a rested, philosophical mood. This was in stark contrast to the snow and cold that was all around us, and to the frenetic pace in our little apartment-turned-office. Mario was prematurely balding, yet at the same time, he had a ponytail, which added to the "fish out of water" effect.

"So you finally started the company, eh?" he said, smiling and leaning back on one of our folding chairs in our living room (we had never bothered to buy a sofa).

He looked around at our little 13-inch TV and the mess of computers, printers, networking equipment, pizza boxes, and other junk in what used to be our living room. I could see that he was amused. I told him excitedly about the company and our product idea. I asked him if he'd be interested in joining us, as he had always been interested in starting a company and had a similar technical background to mine.

He was impressed with what we'd done in a short period of time, and said he'd think about it. We decided he'd work with us over the next few days to see if the three of us worked together well.

A few days later, he told us that although he respected what we were doing, he "had to decline" the offer to join us.

"Why? I assure you the company's going to be successful!" I responded immediately, worried that I hadn't done a good job of selling him on our prospects. I was about to start rattling off reasons why we'd be successful, including the list of beta customers we'd already signed up, but he smiled and waved his hand in between us.

"Oh, I don't doubt that it'll be successful! You guys are really on to something here."

"Well, then why wouldn't you want to be a part of all this?" I asked, waving around the room at the assembled mess.

He laughed. "Well, to be honest, I've seen you guys work

over the last few days, and I'm at a point in my life where I can't handle that pace. Maybe in six months or a year I'd be able to do this level of work again."

I explained that this could be the "opportunity of a lifetime": the founders of a successful software company could make millions of dollars!

He smiled and said that he didn't doubt that and had heard it many times before. "But money isn't the only thing that's important in life," he told me. "Every so often, I get to one of those points in my life where I just *can't* work anymore. It's more of a physical or maybe even subconscious thing. It's not a conscious decision I make; I just can't do it ... and it takes me at least six months or even a year and a half before I'm ready to jump back into the rat race."

Mitch and I looked at each other blankly. Here was a perspective on life that neither of us had been exposed to.

"It's during these times that I feel the most *connected* with life. It's more of a spiritual thing ... I can't explain it. Sometimes you just have to let things come to you – rather than going after them so hard!"

I thought about what he was saying about spirituality; it was in stark contrast to the frenetic pace that Ramaswami's life took: starting companies, zipping from city to city for business meetings, and teaching meditation classes at night. Interestingly enough, I had begun to associate "working hard" and being "engrossed by work" with signs of spiritual progress.

Here was someone who took exactly the opposite view. Being a child of the eighties and having an entrepreneurial bug for as long as I could remember, I didn't understand Mario's point of view. I didn't understand the concept of "letting things come to you" rather than "going after them." Nor did I have to time to ponder it – we had an ever-increasing amount of work to do.

A few days later, as Mario prepared to leave Boston for sunny Florida once again, he explained that though he still had the ambition, he didn't feel the need to "rush things" and make his "millions" right away. If it was meant to happen, it would in "its own time."

He could see that I was disappointed and a bit perplexed. "You're only 23 now. This will make more sense to you as you get older." I listened but didn't comment. "But I'm willing to help you guys out somehow." He suddenly smiled and his eyes lit up as if he'd just had a brainstorm of his own.

"Are you going to Lotusphere?" he asked.

"Lotusphere?" I replied, not sure what he was talking about.

"Oh yeah, it's a conference that's happening in Orlando in December for people who are doing things with Lotus Notes... you guys should really get a booth there so that people could buy your product and learn about your company..."

"Set up a booth at a trade show?" I asked, having no idea what he was talking about. He could see that I really didn't know as much about starting a software company as I had let on. He explained that most software companies use trade shows as a way of getting leads for their products. He had spent a year in Paris doing European trade shows for a Boston-based start-up once before and knew all about the process and could give us advice on how to prepare.

"How much does it cost?" I asked.

"Oh, probably a couple of thousand dollars for a small booth, plus airfare, hotel, etc. You should really go..." He noticed that I was mulling over the "couple of thousand bucks" in my mind.

"In fact," he continued, more confidently. "If you want to be a player in this space, it's important that you go there!"

Until now, we hadn't realized we would have to spend any money to bring our product to the marketplace. So far, our marketing had been two fold: 1) word of mouth (we told all of our friends in the industry about it) and 2) the article in *ComputerWorld* about us, which had sparked the daily calls we were getting. Somehow, I had assumed that it would continue to be that easy and we wouldn't have to spend any more money until the "money started rolling in."

Mario spent the next few hours convincing us that we should go to Florida to the trade show, no matter what it cost. And then he was off to Florida himself, though for a very different purpose: to hang out on the beach. "Good luck," he said as he departed. "I'm sure you guys will do well!"

Ironically, though we had been planning to recruit him to stay in Boston and start the company with us, Mario had actually convinced us that we should be following in his footsteps to Florida.

The night before leaving for the trade show in Orlando, both Mitch and I were excited and more than a little stressed. We weren't able to use our "creative financing" strategy to pay for the show, but luckily had been able to borrow $5,000 from Mitch's parents to cover expenses.

I was frantically trying to track down a final bug in the software before we felt it was ready to go. Finding and squishing this bug was taking much longer than I expected, and as the night bore on, I could feel frustration slowly building inside me. I couldn't figure out why the product was crashing. Then, around 10 p.m., the phone rang.

It was Ramaswami. He asked about our progress so far and had called to wish us well on our first business trip. I explained the situation to him, telling him about this bug that I couldn't quite seem to track down. "You're tracking down a crash bug and you plan to leave tomorrow for the show??!!" he exclaimed, surprised.

"Ah, yeah…" I replied slowly, wondering if we were doing something wrong. He laughed. "Listen, it's totally natural to be making last minute fixes to a demo the night before you have to give it … it happens all the time!" I breathed a sigh of relief.

"But this isn't just an ordinary demo, it's a product release, isn't it?" he finished. Now I was getting more nervous.

"Maybe we shouldn't release it," I suggested. There was silence on the other end of the line, I could sense that he had his chin turned slightly upward and had his eyes closed, in that Ramaswami-sort of way, thinking about the question.

Suddenly he laughed. "This will be a time you most remember," he said, "Cooped up in that living room, getting your first few phone calls from customers, and releasing your first product. It is exciting, isn't it?"

I was wondering if he was trying to cheer me up by changing the subject. "Yes, it's exciting, but right now I'm more stressed out than excited. What do you think I should do?" I asked, hoping that he would give me a practical answer based upon his experience.

"The energetic configuration of your new company is quite interesting at this time," he said.

"Energetic configuration? How can a company have an energetic configuration?" I blurted out, not really wanting him to answer. I didn't really have time to argue, as we only had a few hours to get the product ready for release.

"Let me just say that every group of people has an aura, not unlike the aura that a person has, though this one isn't a physical aura. You might think of it as the *soul* of the company. And believe it or not, the success of an early-stage company often has as much to do with this *soul* as it does with anything else."

Looking at the clock, I decided not to discuss whether this was a plausible scientific theory or simply new-age babble. "Okay, so ... is our soul aligned?" I asked quickly, glad that Mitch was in the other room and hadn't heard me ask this metaphysical question about our business.

"The energetic configuration of a company," he continued, "is the sum of a number of parts, each of which has a different degree of effect on the company's collective aura: the employees, the management, the vendors, the customer's perception of the company, the market, et cetera, et cetera.

"Often, it's difficult to separate these elements out from one another as they are all related. In any case, I see your company's energetic configuration as one of a lot of energy rolled up into a little ball that is just waiting to explode. There are numerous people who are watching you and wishing you well, and even some that are not wishing you well." I could sense he was nodding his head on the other side of the phone. "Whether you know it or not, there are a lot of people out there thinking about you guys!"

He was silent for a moment. Then:

"So, here's some practical advice," he said. "I normally wouldn't say this, but when all else fails, lower your expectations."

"Huh?" Now I was confused, thinking that perhaps he didn't believe we should release the product.

"There are two ways to lower expectations: either reduce functionality down to the parts that you know work, or push back the timeframe to give yourselves more time. Either way, you're reducing an expectation that is too high for the current release of the product ... you're doing too much or you're trying to do it too fast!"

I thanked him for his advice and hung up the phone. I mulled it over in my mind – "reduce functionality, or push out the release date." I called Mitch in and explained the last-minute bug that I couldn't address.

"What do you think we should do?" he asked.

I told him Ramaswami's advice: "lower expectations." He stroked his chin which, like mine, had built up stubble over the last week, during which we had been working at a frenetic pace and taking very little time for personal hygiene. Mitch was holding a copy of our documentation, which he had just brought back from the copy center.

"Okay," he replied. We decided we would reduce functionality. I got rid of the bug that I was working on by simply putting up a message "That piece of functionality is not included in this version of VBLink."

And then that was it – we wrapped it up. Version 1.0 of our product was ready for general release. We spent the next few hours making 30 copies onto floppy disks. We had decided to sell the product at the actual conference and wanted to take a good number of copies with us.

Even though I had spent a good part of the last few months visualizing a box that had the name of the product on it, I realized that we had been so busy over the last few weeks that we had forgotten to buy boxes to put the disks in! It was too late to go to an office supply store, and our flight was leaving at 7 a.m. the next morning, before the stores would be open.

We made another last minute decision, and simply put the disk and manual into brown manila envelopes labeled, "VBLink". This became the first version of our product and we got a few hours of sleep before our flight took off for Orlando.

By the second day of the Lotusphere conference in Orlando, my voice was hoarse from talking to all of the people who came to our booth. We had been literally mobbed at our booth by engineers from companies who had been looking for ways to connect Lotus products with Microsoft products. Our strategy of bridging the gap between the giants was working.

Because there were only two of us at the booth, we often had a line of people waiting to talk to us. Many of them had heard about us from the recent press articles, and wanted to meet us. More importantly, we were able to convince a number of them to buy the product from us right there on the show floor. We quickly ran out of the 30 "manila envelope" packages of our product and still more people wanted to buy the product.

We became the talk of the show – two young MIT grads swamped by anxious buyers of their "hot new product". It reminded me of stories about the early days of the PC industry in the 80's, stories I had read about the founding of companies like Apple Computer and Microsoft.

By the morning of the final day of the conference, we had sold 60 copies of our product, and had earned enough to pay back Mitch's parents the $5,000 we had borrowed. More importantly, we had just had our first successful product release!

Though we were in Florida, we hadn't been able to enjoy the weather. We were both exhausted from the frantic pace of the conference and the past few months of work. Even though we were in 80-degree weather, I had caught a little cold, which had been aggravated by all the talking. I could barely speak by the end of the week.

We decided to skip the closing session and drove out to a beach in the Tampa area to recuperate. Our flight didn't leave until the next day, but we were no longer simply on the runway. Our company had taken off, and life would never be the same.

CHAPTER SUMMARY
STANDING ON THE RUNWAY

For most start-ups, the most important thing is to get to your customers.
This is a tough rule of thumb for engineers (like me) to fathom initially. If you speak to engineers in particular and product people in general, they will tell you that *the most important thing* for success is how good the product works/feels/looks. In reality, *the most important thing* for most start-ups to succeed is an easy pathway from a customer to a product.

At this point in the normal start-up cycle, we would have been finishing the product and struggling to find our first few customers. But when we'd come up with the business idea months ago, I had the intuition that I could get us an article in a major computer magazine. I didn't know how or why I knew this. After all, I had zero experience in PR (or start-ups for that matter). But by following that clue (the *feeling* that I could get us an article), we inadvertently turned our project into a real business the moment that customers started to find us!

Clues come in various forms.
Another important clue in this chapter was my dream about my friend Mario (whose earlier departure from Lotus to go to Florida had been an initial clue in my journey). The dream I had about him in this chapter, coming just before he returned from Florida, provided me with more reassurance that he had some role to play in the story of our startup.

Sometimes clues indicate direction, but it's up to us to figure out what specifically it's leading us to. I assumed this clue was leading towards getting Mario to join the company full time. Now that I'm *older and wiser* too, I know that may not have been a good idea, given where he was in his career. Still, his impact on the company was to convince us to go to the conference, Lotusphere, which provided the critical launching point for our company.

These two clues (my intuition that I could get an article about us, and my sense that Mario had some role to play) had very big consequences for us. That's why it's important to listen to clues and follow through on them — you never know where they will lead!

As an entrepreneur, you are constantly setting and resetting expectations.

In some ways, starting and running a business is a constant process of setting, resetting, recalibrating, and communicating expectations. A company that grows and sells for $2 million can be considered a huge success or a huge failure, depending on the expectations that are put on the business.

If an investor had bought half of your company for $5 million, then selling the company for $2 million dollars would be a big disappointment. On the other hand, if you own 100% of your business, a $2 million sale might be an excellent outcome! Valuations of businesses are in fact, just a case of numerically setting expectations. In the example of an investor buying half of your company for $5 million, he's setting the expectation that you can grow the company to be worth more than $10 million (since he spent $5 million for his half).

The same applies to product development. If a software product takes three months to build, that could be a huge win or a big disappointment, depending on the expectations. In life, sometimes we have unrealistic expectations about where we'll be and how far along we'll be at a certain time frame. Sometimes a simple redefining of expectations is enough to set us back on the right track, as it was for us when we decided not to fix that final bug in this chapter.

Don't forget to stop and enjoy the (little) victories.

There are so many things that can and will go wrong in a startup that it's important to celebrate your successes when you can.

Our "launch" conference where we sold out of our new product was definitely one of those. We took time off at the end of the conference to drive to Tampa and hang out at the beach. Though the memory of the conference itself is a little fuzzy years later, I remember the scene on the Tampa beach vividly. Someone had spotted a dolphin, and the sun was just starting to set. I could hear the seagulls and I was eating French fries. I remember tossing one of the fries on the beach and the seagulls descending on it from all directions. It was a strange feeling to have something that so many beings (birds, in this case) wanted. In a way, it was a reflection of what had happened at the conference itself.

Setting aside the wisdom of feeding French fries to seagulls (I would never do that today!), it's important to take time to enjoy the victories, big or small, as they occur in a startup.

9 MESSAGES FROM THE HIDDEN WORLDS
JANUARY, 1994

On the banks of the river Charles sat a building that was wider than those around it, calmly keeping watch on it surroundings. It looked like an Aztec pyramid, with steps on either side rising up from the ground and meeting at the top underneath the clear, wintry evening sky. The golden light reflected off the windows and made the whole structure look yellow, adding to the feeling that I was looking back on a scene from ancient Mexico.

Ramaswami's voice brought me back to Boston, and suddenly the building was back to what I knew it to be: the Hyatt Regency of Cambridge. It was located just next to MIT, and though I had seen it numerous times in college, I had never before thought of it so vividly as an Aztec pyramid. He noticed that I had been drifting, and wanted to know where I had been "mentally".

I didn't want to admit that I was seeing Aztec pyramids in modern-day Cambridge, so I answered: "Oh, just thinking about the scenery."

He smiled as he sensed that I was holding back. "Yes, but what specifically about the scenery were you thinking?"

"Oh, nothing much, just that it looks nice to see the sunset across the river..." I looked away, remembering the scene clearly in my mind.

"Yes, but I sense that you were touching into something much more interesting than an ordinary sunset," he said, turning on his indicator and passing up a truck that seemed to have found a spot of the road to perch itself on. We were in one of his cars, a black Mercedes, returning from a group meditation that he had led and organized.

"What do you mean by touching into something?" I asked, continuing my deflection.

"I mean that you are touching something with your mind. It's possible to *tap into* certain thoughts, or frames of mind ... it's hard to describe in words, but there are *places* in the hidden worlds that your mind can go.

"When you find yourself drifting ... daydreaming, you're often actually following a specific thought ... by following the thought, you're reaching out with your mind and touching the place from which the thought originated or following it to where it wants you to go."

We were now crossing over Charles River on the Mass Ave Bridge and I could see the pyramid-like hotel more clearly. For some historically unknown reason, this bridge was officially called the Harvard Bridge, even though it led directly to MIT and not Harvard at all.

"Places? Do you mean, like, physical places?" I asked.

"Maybe ... it could be a physical place in a different time. But more likely, it's a part of the hidden worlds that is *connected to* and *reminds you of* a physical place. This *place* is a collection of thought forms that were created by people who existed in the physical place, creating an energy that is similar to the energy of a specific place."

This I found strange and unacceptable, because I could not imagine what he meant by *places* in the hidden worlds. But in order to keep the discussion going, I decided to come out with what I had seen in my mind's eye. I described to him the scenery, sparked by the specific building in the Cambridge skyline. I described how the scene evoked a certain feeling, similar to the feeling I had when Ramaswami and I walked around the Christian Science Center many months earlier.

"Good," he said. "You're doing a good job at recognizing clues,"

"But how can this be a clue?" I asked him. "It's just an impression that I had about a building!"

"Easily," he replied as we arrived at my destination, Central Square. "If you recall, the reason I have you writing down clues is because they reveal something about the hidden worlds. They always begin with some feeling being sparked in between your ears," he touched the side of his head, "usually sparked by something that happens in the outside world."

I explained that though his concept of clues had never completely made sense to me, I had been faithfully writing down whenever something like this happened to me.

"That's good." He nodded his head.

"A clue ... is really a message from the hidden worlds, a message that is specifically tailored to you. Once you understand this, you've started to understand that there are underlying patterns in your life. Not only the patterns of behavior, but actual patterns that manifest all around you. When you can recognize these patterns, you've started understanding how your career and business are linked intricately to your purpose in this life."

It was a mouthful that I didn't really grasp the significance of.

He agreed that he would explain it to me the next time we met and decided that he should give me a movie assignment that would help me understand clues better. "Watch *Made in Heaven* as your movie assignment. It's a romantic comedy, sort of, with that woman from *Top Gun*."

"Kelly McGillis?" I asked.

"Yes, that's her."

"But I don't really like watching romantic comedies," I complained. "Can't you give me a science fiction movie to watch?"

He was silent for a moment and then smiled. "No. Broaden your horizons. This is the movie for you!" I reluctantly agreed and as we had arrived at our destination, our brief meeting was over.

"You like pictures, don't you?" Ramaswami asked as we walked into the classroom. It was in the evening and there were no students in sight, but there was plenty of chalk. "It's common," he went on, "for engineers to only understand things when they have a mental picture or a mental model. So let's use a chalkboard."

It was a week after I had seen the Aztec pyramid vision. We had agreed to meet at MIT to talk more on this subject of "clues" and for Ramaswami to get an update on my business. As usual, Ramaswami had driven up in a black Mercedes.

"Why is it," I asked when he pulled up, "that all of your long-time students tend to drive black Mercedes?" Initially, I had found it odd that both he and James drove similar black Mercedes.

He laughed. "I see you noticed. Well, there is a method to the madness. It's really a matter of energy."

"Energy?" So far we had talked about energy only in the context of doing breathing exercises, so I asked him if this was related to that concept.

"Yes, absolutely, it's similar. Last time, we spoke about the energy around the body, and how to do breathing exercises that can impact your energetic state. Well, there are exercises for giving you more energy, balancing your energy, getting rid of excess energy, et cetera.

"The study of *Energy* is central to the esoteric student. Both Tibetan Buddhism and various forms of Shamanism, which I have borrowed from heavily in constructing the Path of the Career Warrior, deal with this issue in different ways.

"The Career Warrior thinks about energy all the time, and not just in relation to the human body. If you go to certain places, you will notice that the energy in these places is different than the energy in other places. There is an invisible energetic signature in these places."

I frowned, recalling a very similar non-scientific discussion that James and I had some time ago. He laughed. "Oh, you're going to tell me that it's non-scientific!"

I started to get a little annoyed as I realized he had just read my mind (something else that I didn't quite believe in).

"The reason you think the hidden worlds are non-scientific is because they cannot be observed. But that's not true. They can be observed. There are traces of the hidden world all around us, but more importantly, when you learn to tap into your true self – not just your physical or emotional or mental self, but your true self – then you too can see the hidden worlds with the same amount of certainty that you see the physical world all around you."

"But, Ramaswami, how can that be? The hidden worlds

don't seem to be *real*." I was getting frustrated. "Sometimes, you talk about them as if the hidden worlds are inside our heads, consisting of things called 'thought-forms' and linking back to places like ancient Mexico. But sometimes I get the impression that they're more like bio-energetic fields like auras that we can't see but may be able to actually measure with the right equipment someday. So which are they? *Something real* or simply a *mental construction?*"

"That is not a contradiction," he replied. "It only seems like a contradiction because of your model of the world."

"My model of the world? I don't have a model that's any different than anyone else's," I responded, a little bit insulted at his superior tone.

"That's just the point," he raised his eyebrows as if he had just made a point. If he had, I hadn't gotten it.

"Let's think of it this way," he continued. "Think of dreams. Dreams seem extremely real when you are in them. You feel like you are physically in a dream when you are going through it. While in the dream, it seems like a real world all around you, but when you wake up, you think, *it was all in my head,* as if it was *only a mental construction!* "

"But dreams are mental constructions!" I replied.

"Oh really...?" He got up and walked to the board.

I sighed as I saw that he was ready for a lesson to begin. Just as he got to the edge of a desk, he banged his hand down on it for effect. "Dreams are *not* simply mental constructions. Dreams are part of the hidden worlds, and more importantly, they contain messages from the hidden worlds."

This was too much for my rational mind to accept. "But dreams are part of the unconscious," I responded, remembering what I could from my psychology class in college. "Sometimes they're the result of random neurons firing. Freud thought that they often represented wish fulfillment, or represented our anxieties and things that we don't want to admit to ourselves when we are awake ... things from our unconscious," I explained, now proud that I had an explanation that I could get my hands around. "And," I added triumphantly, "they occur when we are in REM sleep."

Ramaswami made a face, like a little girl who is trying to act haughty, and imitated me, greatly exaggerating my authoritative tone and making me sound like a stuck-up whiner: "They occur while in REM sleep ... blah blah blah!

"You're very good at regurgitation," he said resuming his normal face. "But let's see if you are just as good at learning."

"But *aren't* dreams simply a part of the unconscious...?" I asked, slinking back into my chair and wondering where he was going with this.

"Yes, and no," he replied, with what I had come to recognize as his favorite answer to my questions. "*Yes*, they are part of the unconscious, but *no*, not the unconscious like you think of it."

"How many different ways are there to think about it?" I asked.

"Oh, two ways: the way psychologists think about it, and then the right way! Psychologists use the unconscious as a way of sweeping things they don't understand under the rug. They simply call it *the unconscious,* because they don't know diddly-squat about it!"

He wrote 'unconscious' on the board and drew a circle around it. Off to one side he made another circle and wrote 'dreams' in it, drawing an arrow connecting dreams to the unconscious.

I was silent, honestly trying to digest what he was about say. "Where do dreams come from?" he mock-asked me. "Why that's easy, the unconscious!" he replied flippantly, pointing with his thumb.

"And," he started, pausing for effect, "where are our memories stored...?" He asked. "The unconscious?" he replied weakly, and wrote the word 'memories' on the board, and again drew an arrow to 'the unconscious'.

"And where do we get our intuitions from?" he asked. He wrote intuitions down on the bottom right, and sure enough, drew the arrow to point to the unconscious.

"What represses our memories when they are too painful for us to deal with?" he wrote *repressed memories* on the board with another arrow pointing to the unconscious.

"And where are our beliefs stored?" he wrote down beliefs on the lower left-hand side and drew another connector.

"And when we say that we use only 10% of our minds, where

is the other 90%?"

By the time he was done he had the inner circle of the unconscious surrounded by a number of individual items, including dreams, beliefs, mental illness, intuition, psychic phenomena, repressed memories, and on and on, all with lines linking them to central circle of the unconscious.

"When psychologists don't understand something, they say that it's done by the unconscious! But we have a different term for this catch-all. We call it the hidden worlds, not because we don't understand it, but because we *do understand* how these things work ... because we can observe what happens and it's not a dark, bubbling cauldron as Freud described it, but rather it's an orderly connection between you, your consciousness and the higher part of yourself. This happens through different levels of the aura up into the higher realms!

"That is partly what the Path of the Career Warrior is about, strengthening your connection with these other parts of yourself, so that you can observe what happens in the hidden worlds."

I had the sense that I shouldn't interrupt, so I kept listening.

"So, let's talk about your business success," he said, suddenly changing the subject.

I sat up and began describing the events of the past month, and how *Brainstorm Technologies* was now a well-known firm in the Lotus Notes community, and how we had sold enough of our products to get the company off the ground. He knew some of this from our phone conversations, but he particularly zoomed in on the aspect of my story that I hadn't given much thought to but which related directly to the discussion we had been having: my dreams.

I wanted to talk more about the business aspects of what had been going on, but he assured me that we would be doing this over the coming months, so he wanted to focus in on my dream in which my friend Mario had shown up from Florida. Of particular interest was how he actually showed up within a few days of the dream, and then convinced us that we should go to the trade show that was happening *in Florida*. The trade show had been a critical part in our company's early success and for many years after that, we would point to that trade show as a very important starting point in the company's history.

After listening to me silently, he started teaching again.

"Freud wasn't incorrect with his analysis of dreams, he was simply limited. He focused on interpreting the elements of the dream, which is not a bad way to do things at all. He just didn't fully understand the impact of the hidden worlds on what he called the 'unconscious'. Jung was a bit closer to how things really are — he paid attention to connections that others ignored, simply because they couldn't see them!"

"Are you saying that a dream cannot be interpreted?"

"I'm saying that you can break down a dream into various elements. Some of those elements are meaningful and some aren't. The key to interpretation is with you, not some dream dictionary! Of course, a dream is a collection of your wishes, fears, anxieties, physical condition, and all of that ... but that's not all. There is another level of meaningfulness that dreams have that you have to be able to recognize. When this happens, you've found another clue."

"What do you mean by *meaningful*? And I don't understand what these clues are leading up to," I asked, unsure where Ramaswami was going.

"Okay, let me start from the beginning and lay it all on the table for you plainly." A flicker of smile flashed across his face. "So that you won't get confused..."

"Where these clues are leading up to is the most important part of any meditative or spiritual practice: *to you*. When I say that there are messages from the hidden worlds, I'm not saying that there are messages from a cold, impersonal reality that you cannot see. They are messages specifically tailored...to you...from you!"

I thought I was beginning to understand. "So then you're saying that these messages are things that we're not ready to admit to ourselves consciously, and so they come to us in dreams...?"

"No, no no! You've still got it all wrong." He walked up to the blackboard and grabbed another piece of chalk, as if he was going to draw another picture. He hesitated for a second, and then just pointed the elements that were already there.

"I teach that there are clues all around us. These clues are really messages from the hidden worlds, and they reveal to us more about our destiny, our purpose in any given situation, and in our life. If we heed these messages, we are likely to get in touch with a higher part of ourselves and be aligned with what we are supposed to be doing here."

"Does that mean that following these clues will help me to be more successful in business?"

He smiled, and I knew the answer that was coming: "Yes, and no. It means that you will learn what you are supposed to learn from your business. That learning might come in the form of uncontrollable success, it might come in the form of indeterminate failure, or it might come in the form of continued struggle and hard work. But when you are aligned, you start to feel a purpose. You start to feel that what you are doing goes beyond what you are physically doing ... as if you're a part of something higher."

He paused. "Getting in touch with that something higher is what meditation is all about."

I was about to ask him another question when he held up his hands.

"The most direct message from the hidden worlds usually comes as a voice in our heads or as an insight. However, most people are too dense to get these messages in a way that makes us act, mostly because of all the mental clutter we have and our inability to distinguish between an insight, premonition, hunch, worry, psychic impression, or random thought-form.

"So, the next best place for these messages to come to us is through our dreams. Not all dreams have meaningful messages, but many of them do. When the message is particularly clear and you are awake in the dream, and you know what this message is about, these are referred to as *dreams of clarity*.

"They usually have either a symbolic or a literal meaning that directly impacts what is going on in your life. Your dream of Mario coming from Florida was undoubtedly a dream with a message in it, even though you didn't recognize the message at the time."

I was about to jump in when he raised his hand again, silencing me. "A dream of clarity can be a premonition of a future event, it can be a solution to a problem you've been slaving over that your *unconscious,* as the psychologists like to say, has solved. It could be a memory of a past life, or could allow you to have a connection to someone or something in the hidden worlds.

"Did you watch *Made in Heaven?*" he asked. I told him that I had watched it, and found it to be both interesting and sad at the same time. He didn't agree with my assessment that the film was sad, but acknowledged it definitely had a 'tone'.

"Do you remember when he came back and he kept getting signals about his destiny?"

I nodded.

"Those were messages from the hidden worlds. "Do you remember when she wrote the book about her friend Mike that no one else could see but her? That was also a memory of the hidden worlds."

"Are you saying that the hidden worlds are *heaven?*" I exclaimed.

He thought this was the funniest thing I had ever said and started laughing uncontrollably. He finally stopped laughing.

"Well, yes," he responded, as if he was talking to a five-year old. "You can think of it as heaven, but remember in the movie, when Timothy Hutton got to heaven, it wasn't really like the simplified concept that we have here, now was it?"

I didn't want to get into a theological discussion with him so I didn't say anything.

He continued. "Now, what was perhaps the *most important message* from the hidden worlds that Timothy Hutton's character received in this movie?"

I was silent and thought back to the movie. I couldn't think of it.

He raised his eyebrows. "It relates to his purpose and his contribution in this life? And it relates to what we've been talking about here…" he pointed to the board.

He waited patiently but I couldn't think of it. Then I saw 'dreams' written on the board and it came to me. "His song … he heard the tune for the song in a dream and he couldn't ignore it. Eventually, creating the song was his ticket to success in this life!" I replied.

Ramaswami nodded. "Yes, that's it. But it's not so much that it was a key to his success as it was part of his personal destiny! That's what I would call his unique *Warrior's Path.*"

I thought I was beginning to understand. Ramaswami had cleverly used a movie to convey to me concepts that I wouldn't have ordinarily been willing to accept with my rational mind.

"Now so far, we have talked about messages that are kind of 'in our heads'. The next type of message that you receive comes in the form of places, things and people around you, which evoke certain thoughts in your mind.

"Earlier, you had a particular reaction to seeing the Hyatt that reminded you of Mexico and the ancient pyramids they had built there. That was an example of an event in the physical world sparking something inside you, sparking a feeling. That *feeling* is a message from some part of you that you should pay attention to. Whenever it occurs, with people, places, or things, it is the key to developing your intuition."

"How do you know when a message is meaningful versus simply a coincidence or meaningless?" I asked.

"Again, the rule in the hidden worlds is no different than the rules of the physical world. If something repeats itself, it's probably significant. If you have a feeling once, and you never have it again, it may be unique, it may be interesting, but it's probably not a significant message. It's more of a one-off!

"These clues help us to recognize something about ourselves. Remember the analogy of life as one large treasure hunt. The obstacle to finding the treasure is ... you. And the treasure that you're hunting for is ... you!

"The clues help us to recognize our own patterns, and they help us to get in touch with the spiritual parts of us. That is part of the unfolding of awareness that begins with sitting quietly in meditation. That is what the Path of the Career Warrior is about."

I had been holding my comments back and was ready to unleash them, when suddenly I found that they had somehow abandoned me as I sat silently thinking about what he had just told me. The dream that happened before our Florida trip was quite interesting, I had to admit.

After a few minutes, though, I instinctively got back into practical mode and didn't see how I could use dreams to my benefit while starting a company. I told him so.

"The key is for you to write down interesting clues, whether they are in your dreams, in your thoughts, or in the world around you. When you start to do that, you start to see patterns, you start to distinguish between the *inner signals,* or feelings, that a certain type of clue evokes in you. You start to see a kind of precognition in your messages that you had never noticed before. It wasn't that it wasn't happening before, it was that you didn't recognize or mark it as such."

He seemed to be in serious mood now and ended our meeting.

I agreed to "keep writing down clues". I didn't have any more dreams of clarity for a while (that I recognized, anyway), but as we got our business going, I started to notice a repeating "signal" about our business.

I had several encounters with experienced entrepreneurs over the next few weeks and each one of them told me that the product that we had, while a good one, wasn't enough to build a multi-million dollar business on. "It's only a 500K market maximum," several of them said.

One of them was an experienced entrepreneur named Mark K., who had started a company called Edge Research. "You don't really want to be in this market," he said. "It's only a 500K maximum market. If I were you, I'd want to be doing something else."

The fact that I heard this several times led me to believe that it was probably true, and each time it had evoked a peculiar sensation inside of me, prompting me to write these down as "clues" about a direction I might want to take the company in.

Soon, taking a cue from these clues, I decided it was time to hire some developers who could maintain our current product while Mitch and I started working on our next product. After all, we didn't want to be bogged down in a market that was only 500K; we wanted to build a multi-million dollar company!

CHAPTER SUMMARY
MESSAGES FROM THE HIDDEN WORLDS

Clues can be sparked by anything in the world around you, and are messages that are meant to guide you.
Clues usually begin with some feeling being sparked inside you by something in the outside world (an external *trigger*). It could be a person, a phrase, even a building; the important thing is to recognize the feelings that come when your intuition is being nudged.

A clue is a message that is tailored to you. Two people being in the presence of the same trigger won't get the same feelings. One might ignore the trigger completely, while another person might find a profound message in the trigger. That's how clues work – they are highly personalized.

There are at least seven different types of clues and each of these is a different type of message from the hidden worlds.
It's too easy to dismiss these as the "unconscious" at work. What does the unconscious mean, really? Clues are really "unconscious" or "semi-conscious" messages from the hidden worlds. Here are some very important types of clues:

1. *Direct messages.* Sometimes (though not often), we get messages or clues directly – as either verbal instructions or a strong sense of knowing what to do next. I have woken up and heard what seemed to be a voice giving me specific directions to take in my business. Similarly, a *knowing* is something that pops into your head unexpectedly and you just know that it's the right answer. It's hard to separate this from other forms of intuition, but it's the *certainty* that comes with this type of message that's important. Usually our ability to get these messages is distorted, and so we have to interpret the clues we get; not so with direct messages – they tell us exactly what to do.

2. *Dreams.* Dreams are a way for our unconscious mind to assemble messages to us in metaphor and story. Although a dream can seem incoherent after we wake up, when we're in the dream, everything seems coherent.

Not all dreams are messages; some are just recycling our fears and wishes. Now and then, we'll receive a *dream of clarity*. Dreams are such a complicated and important topic that we'll spend a whole chapter on them later in the book.

3. *Bodily sensations*. One of the most reliable forms of clues is a reaction you have in your body in response to a person, place, phrase, or thing. Each of us has bodily sensations that is our body's way of warning us not to do something, or pulling us toward something. For example, clenching in the stomach is usually a clue that something is going on that's not pleasant. A warm glow in the forehead or third eye is one that I have often which tells me I'm on the right track. You might also experience sweating of hands and feet, queasiness in the belly, or strength in the gut. Like other clues, bodily sensations are highly personalized and you have to pay attention to what each sensation means for you.

4. *Funny feelings or a sense of déjà vu*. Sometimes you feel like you're in a surreal setting, or you have that most famous of funny feelings – déjà vu – like you've seen something or been somewhere before. As in this chapter, where the Mexican pyramid-shaped hotel building seemed to invoke a feeling in me of something ancient yet futuristic, an external trigger evokes funny or surreal feelings.

5. *Hunches*. A hunch is like a little voice whispering to you. You have a sense that something might be a certain way, but you aren't completely sure where it's coming from. Most intuition comes in the form of hunches. A "hunch" is also an acceptable way to describe why you want to move in a certain direction in the business world. The most successful entrepreneurs learn to follow their gut, about people, products, and markets. No one will complain if you say "My gut is telling me..." or "I have a hunch..." However, you may get strange looks if you say "I saw this in a dream..."

6. *Errant phrase*. An important type of clue that's often overlooked is a phrase that catches our attention in a

busy setting. It could be a phrase on a billboard, the title of a book in a library, a sentence or article title in a newspaper, or a snippet of an overheard conversation. Suppose you keep overhearing "Italy" in conversations, and then you notice an Italian restaurant where you never noticed one before, and then you are in the bookstore and you see an unusual book on Italy that catches your eye. A few years ago, a friend told me she kept seeing the phrase "Not all those who wander are lost." She saw it on a bumper sticker, and then saw it written somewhere else. I told her it was from *The Lord of the Rings* but she didn't know this – she wasn't even a fan of fantasy! Nevertheless, she was going through troubled times in her career and this message was very reassuring to her. An unexpected place to look for clues in the form of errant phrases is in your email, particularly when you're receiving spam. Just scan your inbox and see if any phrase or expression catches your eye. For example, I once saw an email that had the subject "my investors ruined my company." The email itself was some kind of spam, but the phrase caught my eye and turned out to have some meaning for me at the time.

7. *Synchronicity and coincidence.* Synchronicity is a term coined by Carl Jung that is an almost perfect example of what we call "clues". A synchronicity is when an inner event or thought unexpectedly matches an outer event. Some consider these mere coincidences, but others (like Ramaswami) consider there to be no coincidences. The connection between the inner and the outer is what makes a synchronicity significant. It is also what makes you notice that synchronicity is happening. Jung gives a famous example of this by French writer Deschamps. He was given some plum pudding by a Monsieur Fontgibu. Ten years later, in Paris, he noticed Plum Pudding on the menu (an external trigger) and suddenly had a craving for plum pudding (an inner sensation). He then remembered the incident with Fontgibu, who was fanatical about plum pudding (a memory invoked by this

craving). He then ordered plum pudding and was told that the last dish had already been served to another customer. He looked over and it turned out to be the same Monsieur Fontgibu! But a synchronicity doesn't have to be this coincidental or dramatic to be significant. You could be thinking about a particular actor that you haven't thought about in a while, and a movie comes on that night with that actor in it. Follow the clue. What's in that movie that might be interesting or important for you to know now? You're thinking about someone you haven't seen in years and you get an email or phone call from them. To unlock the clue, ask yourself: What does this person represent to you in your life?

Remember the two most important aspects of messages from the hidden worlds: if it's unusual, or if it repeats, it's probably a clue!

Where are these clues leading? To You.

To quote Ramaswami from this chapter: "Where these clues are leading up to is the most important part of any meditative or spiritual practice: to you. When I say that there are messages from the hidden worlds, I'm not saying that these are messages from a cold, impersonal reality that you cannot see; rather, they are messages specifically tailored ... to you ... from you!"

By saying they're leading to "you", Ramaswami is talking about a more expanded definition of you than you experience on a daily basis. In fact, the goal of all Yoga and meditation is to eventually drop the veils that get in the way of seeing reality as it is, and seeing yourself as you are, not as you have been led to believe you are by the challenges, hardships, pain, and pleasures of this life.

Clues may or may not help you be more successful in business. But they will help you to be more successful in your life.

When asked if following clues will make my business more successful, Ramaswami replied rather vaguely: "Yes, and no. It means that you will learn what you are supposed to learn from your business. That learning might come in the form of uncontrollable success or it might come in the form of indeterminate failure, or it might come in the form of continued struggle and hard work. But when you are aligned, you start to feel a purpose ... you start to feel that what you are doing goes beyond what you are physically doing. It is as if you're a part of something higher."

Getting aligned with "something higher", on a daily basis, is what walking the Path of the Career Warrior is all about. This alignment produces energy and more synchronicity, which helps you to find and advance on your own Warrior's Path.

10 THE NEXT BIG THING
FEBRUARY, 1994

That winter, Brainstorm officially moved out of our apartment
and into our first office space, about 1,500 square feet on the
fourth floor of an old building in East Cambridge, not far from
where I had first worked for DiVA Corporation and Lotus. The
space had been previously occupied by a law firm.

The corner office, which we decided would be mine, had a
floor that was raised higher than the other offices. When I asked
the landlord about this, she said it was because the entire
building was built on an unstable base, and slowly one corner of
the building was sinking an inch every few years. In order to
keep the floor level, the previous lawyer had put in the raised
platform.

This made me more than a bit nervous about moving into this
building, but the price was right, just $10 per square foot per
year, so we decided to stay. Our first employee was an admin
person to help us keep things organized in the office, to act as
our "receptionist", and to fill all the orders we were receiving for
our first product.

I had heard from several people very knowledgeable in our
industry that our single product didn't have enough of a market
to build a *big* business. Taking this message to be a *clue*, I
decided that the answer was that this was a good time to start on
another product, and this was perhaps a good time to raise a bit

of financing. The financing would let us hire some developers so that we didn't have to do all of the work ourselves, freeing me and Mitch up to start working on our next product, which I had already dreamed up.

This idea appealed to me greatly, as I liked to design and build new products; it was the most interesting aspect of the business, as far as I was concerned. I didn't like to be "bogged down" with the details of maintaining a product. Rather, I much preferred to be building new products.

I told Ramaswami about this in late January and he asked what we were going to do with the funds from the new financing. "We can hire some developers and start working on our second product," I replied matter-of-factly.

"Second product?" he asked, sounding slightly concerned. "What about the first product? You just released it last month!"

"Oh yes, we want to add some cool new features, but everyone's telling me that it's not enough to build a *big* company on, and I want to start on the next big thing in our space!" I replied.

"Next Big Thing??!!" he remarked, now clearly alarmed. Then he was silent for a few minutes. I knew that on the other end of the phone, he had closed his eyes and was contemplating what he called my "energetic patterns", which, after so many months, I was no closer to understanding than during our first meeting.

He made me agree to meet him at a specific address on Prospect street in Cambridge at a specific time the next morning. He said that it was time I finally learned a few things about my "energetic patterns" and how they could impact my business endeavors.

The next morning, I found that the specific address was a very old, almost dilapidated building with an orange awning hanging over wall-length windows. The windows and walls were covered with Chinese writing. From the pictures on the door, and what I saw inside, it was clear that this was a martial arts studio.

One thing I found amusing, though, was that the martial arts studio was next to a laundromat, both of which had the same décor and seemed to be owned by the same person. I chuckled at the thought of practicing karate while you waited for your laundry to dry.

Inside, I found Ramaswami sitting on the floor off to the right in a cross-legged position. There were several old Chinese men who were walking slowly around the room. At six-foot plus, with blond hair, he would ordinarily look out of place in the company of elderly Chinese men. But the fact that he was wearing his typical double-breasted suit (though he had taken his shoes off) made him stand out even more.

He motioned for me to come sit down next to him, which I did, after taking off my shoes. We sat quietly watching these men who looked much too old to be doing martial arts. One of them looked almost like a hunchback, and another one looked like he was too chubby to do any serious martial arts. Yet another was so skinny that I thought I could knock him down with a nudge.

The men walked slowly around into a formation, with the skinny one, who was probably the eldest, at the front. The others lined up behind him. He bent his legs and started to move his hand slowly up from the middle of his abdomen until his entire arm was extended on one side. Then slowly he brought it back. It looked like watching a dance in slow motion.

"What are they doing?" I whispered to Ramaswami, not quite sure what type of martial art, if any, they were practicing.

"T'ai Chi," he replied and motioned for me to watch. I suddenly recognized it from footage that I had seen on TV of parks in China where old men would gather to practice this 'slowest' of martial arts.

I watched as the men, who had seemed so clumsy and old, slowly increased the radius of motion of their arms and became more and more graceful as they moved in unison. It seemed like they were submerged in water from the pace at which they moved their hands.

I watched in fascination for the next 15 minutes and saw an amazing transformation before my eyes. They no longer seemed like the old men who had started the exercise. The hunchback was no longer hunched, the man with the belly seemed to have strong, powerful movements, and somehow the skinny man seemed well-grounded and unshakeable. This continued for a while and then suddenly Ramaswami got up and motioned for me to follow him. We left the martial arts studio and went into the laundromat. It was empty, except for an elderly Chinese woman in the back.

"I have something very important to speak with you about today," he said, as he motioned for me to sit in one of the orange plastic chairs that are most often found in laundromats.

"These gentlemen have been practicing T'ai Chi for quite some time now. Many, many years as a matter-of-fact. That is why they are very good at what they do. You saw the transformation that occurred in them. Let me assure you that they are experts at this particular martial art."

I asked him how it was possible that T'ai Chi could be an effective martial art, despite its slow movements. He told me that it was because of energy, which the Chinese called *chi*, not because of the movements themselves. Each movement, he explained, helps to increase the flow of *chi* throughout the body. This flow of energy was critical to helping them regain their physical vitality, and more importantly, to stop any foe that might come in their way.

I was doubtful. I had certainly heard of such stories before, but although the motions seemed to help their health, I couldn't see them deflecting a really experienced practitioner of a traditional 'hard' martial art like Karate or Tae Kwon Do.

Ramaswami laughed and told me that one day he would take me to an exhibition match, but that wasn't really the point for today's lesson.

I waited.

"To get to their level of mastery, they had to work for many, many years, becoming not just good at what they did, but masters of their art. Now, what would have happened if after the first year, they had abandoned the T'ai Chi and started learning Tae Kwon Do?"

I remained silent, wondering where he was going.

"That's right, they wouldn't have become nearly as good at T'ai Chi. And let's say, that after the second year, they abandoned Tae Kwon Doe and then started learning Aikido. And so on and so forth ... what would happen then?"

"I guess they'd become jacks-of-all-trades, masters of none!"

"Exactly! The reason I wanted to go over this with you is that you have a pattern that could be very destructive for you in the business world over the long run."

"Which is?" I asked, totally missing the point of his analogy.

"Can you think of a time in your life when you felt like you were doing too many things?" he asked.

I thought about it for a second and then recalled my experiences during my senior year of college. I had been the chairman of the class gift committee, which was in charge of getting a gift for MIT from our class. I had also taken a large number of classes in order to make progress on my double major, which included both Computer Science and Management. I was also working on an innovative thesis idea at the MIT Media Lab. And I had started a small high-tech mutual fund to make investments in all of these areas. On top of that, I had spent a significant amount of time entering a business plan competition, where Mitch and I originally had come up with the name *Brainstorm Technologies*.

"Okay, that's very good. Now, what was the result of doing all those things?" he asked, and I got the sense that he honestly wanted to know the answer, rather than asking the question to lead me down some path.

"Well," I said, recalling that time. "It was one of the most exciting times of my college career. My thesis went well and I got an A. The business plan competition went okay: we made it to the finals, but didn't win any money. The high tech mutual fund became too much of a burden and so we dropped it, the class gift committee became too much for me to handle so I had to drop it, and I ended up not finishing the double major because it would have taken me another semester to complete it ... and I wanted to get out in the work world," I replied.

"Aha! That's it. Now, let me ask you a question ... were there any other times when this kind of thing has happened to you?"

"What kind of thing?" I asked, still not seeing what he was getting at.

"Where you were doing too many things and had to drop some?"

"Oh, certainly," I answered. "It happened in high school, and even this summer when both Mitch and I were working on a consulting project and we were thinking of starting the company."

"Good, well that's it. Three times makes a pattern." He replied.

"Huh?"

"If something happens once it's probably a fluke or an isolated event. If it happens twice, it's probably interesting. If it happens three times, you've stumbled onto a pattern."

I didn't say anything. "But I had good reasons for becoming involved in all of those things. I was interested in all of them!"

"Yes, but your interest in *all* of them led *some* of them to suffer, didn't it?"

"I guess so," I acknowledge grudgingly, not really wanting to admit that he had found a pattern in my life.

"The problem, my friend," he said, leaning back on a washing machine and folding his arms while looking at me, "is that you are a talented young man."

"Why is that a problem?" I answered, surprised that he had given me a compliment, which he rarely did. "Isn't that a good thing?"

"It's a problem because things tend to come easily to those who are talented. And that, in turn, leads to certain destructive patterns."

"Easy? Things don't come easy to me. I have to work on them just like everyone else," I replied, now clearly becoming defensive.

"Let's see…" he tapped his chin a few times. "Didn't you once tell me that you graduated near the top of your class in high school?" he asked.

"Yes, that's true. I was the first person from my high school to go to MIT," I said with some pride. My ego was in full swing.

"Well, if you're so smart, kid, then why didn't you graduate *at* the top, *instead* of near the top?" he asked

"Because I didn't want to bother, I didn't really work all that hard." I replied, telling the truth. I remembered when a friend of mine had written a note on my high school yearbook, *"I wish I could not do any homework and be one of the top 10 in the class."* I told him about the note.

Secretly, though, Ramaswami had hit a bit of a sore spot for me. I had been very competitive in those days, and probably could have graduated at the top of the class if I had worked harder.

"Aha!" he said. "And has that happened anywhere else...?"

"Has what happened...?" I asked, more than a bit annoyed, as my ego was no longer feeling inflated.

"Have you been able to *'cruise through things'* easily anywhere else in your life?"

"Well, I guess at MIT."

"At MIT?" he suddenly became very animated. "You cruised through MIT? Isn't that supposed to be one of the most rigorous technical universities in the country...? In the world...? Did you get straight A's?"

"No," I replied. In fact, I had ended up with a B+ average, but again had done so with the least amount of effort of anyone I knew. I was usually off participating in some extra-curricular activities or reading some interesting books rather than doing my homework.

"Well, isn't that interesting..." he asked, stroking his chin for effect.

"Are you saying that I shouldn't have done all those extra-curricular activities, that I should just have concentrated on my studies and focused on getting straight A's?" I was dumbfounded.

"No, no, no!" he was now walking around in little circle slamming his hand on the washing machine, causing the Chinese woman in the back to give us a dirty look.

"I'm saying that you are used to having your career or school or profession come relatively easy ... and that has led you in a certain direction, like starting your company."

"Wait a minute!" I jumped up from the orange plastic chair. Now he had gone too far, I told him. "We worked extremely hard for several months to get our company off the ground. That was hard work!" I told him. "We worked probably non-stop for eight weeks, seven days a week, day and night, without much of a break to get our first product built."

"Oh, you worked hard, definitely, but it wasn't that hard.

Two months? Listen, I've worked with software entrepreneurs all over and sometimes it takes them a year before they get their first product done. And after it's done, they have a difficult time finding customers for it. It's the same pattern you've had all your life: it's come relatively easily to you, and so as a result, you think it's always going to be this easy."

"Huh?" I was genuinely confused and couldn't seem to grasp what he was saying.

"Let me use an analogy," he continued. "You're like the guy who studies T'ai Chi for the first year, becomes good at it, and then decides it was so easy that you'll now go and learn Tae Kwon Doe the next year. Again, you end up doing relatively well at it. And then, you decide that you're going to learn Aikido... but at the end of three years, you will end up being a less effective martial artist than the person who wasn't as quick as you were to learn any one of these arts, but realized that he would have to work really hard for years before mastering any aspect of it."

I didn't know what to say. Part of me felt like he was attacking me personally, but I see now that he was sincerely trying to make me see a pattern in my life that I didn't really want to admit to.

I scratched my head and didn't say anything.

"Are you saying, then," I finally started, making the connection to what was happening in the business world, "that we shouldn't work on a second product at Brainstorm?"

"I'm not saying that you shouldn't work on another product... I am saying that you should first make sure you understand how your first product is going to become a well-maintained product. Learn the first product well, understand what the plans are for the next few versions, what customers want from it, and how you are going to keep it as a cutting-edge product. You can do this by bringing in outside resources – that's okay. Your first product, which has been successful, should become a foundation that you build on, not something you abandon as you go on to your *next big idea*."

"But don't you agree that our first product might only be a half-million dollar a year market idea?" I asked him, echoing what others in our industry had told me.

"I don't disagree, but as you are the only player in this market space at present, why can't you get a really good percentage of that half-million dollars this year? Didn't you say that Lotus Notes was growing at 100% per year?"

"Actually, even faster than that," I replied.

"Then, there's no reason you can't do more than half a million next year, as the total market will have grown, if you really are the only product in this space."

It was something I hadn't thought of.

"I'm not saying don't raise some private money," he continued. "I am saying, don't go off building the second product until you have a good sense of how you're going to maintain your first product. You only have two people in the company right now capable of building a product and you guys know how to do it inside and out. Just hiring more developers and throwing the first product to them isn't the only answer."

"Wait a minute," I said again, incredulous at what I was hearing. "That flies in the face of everything I've heard about building a company. I thought that we are supposed to move into management so that we're not doing all the day-to-day work anymore! You're saying we should continue to be the ones to build the product? That doesn't seem right."

"No, once again, you're misinterpreting what I'm saying. Hire the developers, but work closely with them for a number of months until you are confident that they are producing the same high quality of the product that you are. If you want to move into management, that's okay. You certainly have a lot to learn, but don't do it by simply tossing away the thing you're good at: building the product.

"Look: entrepreneurs become one of two types of managers when they move from doing the work themselves to hiring someone else: either they become micro-managers or they become totally hands-off managers. Either extreme can be dangerous, but that's not the main lesson for today.

"Today, I want you to keep in mind that you want to build on a stable platform. Sometimes it takes years to build a stable platform, sometimes it only takes months. But to take the product that you guys know and to simply toss it off to some new developers, while you run like hell to do the next big thing shows a lack of understanding of how companies are built."

I sat and listened intently and started to soak it all in. Finally, after so many months, I felt that he was finally giving me some practical advice on building a business rather than going on and on about "energy." Still, I wasn't sure that his practical advice was correct. I explained to him that I thought the "clues" I was receiving from my environment were hints that I should start working on the next big thing.

"They certainly were clues, and it's good that you recognized them as such. But they are more clues that were aimed at helping you to recognize one of your patterns in life that could be devastating for you in your career. You're a Star Trek fan, right?"

I nodded.

"Well, Mr. Spock would always say to Doctor McCoy: *Your passions will be your undoing, doctor.*" As he said this, he imitated Mr. Spock's raised eyebrow, which I found quite amusing.

"Well, the number one reason why business fail is not because of the market or because they don't have enough money. The number one reason is that entrepreneurs are fickle and often make decisions very unconsciously. The number one reason businesses fail are stupid decisions. I like to say to most entrepreneurs, in the tone of Spock: *Your patterns will be your undoing,* unless ..."

"Unless what?" I asked.

"Unless you recognize them and don't react immediately the way you normally would. Look, lots of self-help gurus will tell you that you can change just like that." He snapped his fingers. "And yes, you *can* change, but it's not anywhere near as easy as it looks to change your ingrained habits, thoughts, beliefs, or patterns. That's why there's constantly a self-help industry."

"But if you can't change your patterns...?" I speculated, but Ramaswami interrupted me.

"Oh no, you can change them. But the first step is to recognize that you have this pattern. The second step is to realize that a pattern in your life comes about because of the decisions that you make unconsciously. In the words of the Buddha, *that which is subject to arising is subject to cessation.*"

"What does that mean? How does it relate to changing your patterns?" I asked.

"Meditation teaches us to recognize our thoughts and not to let them take hold of us unconsciously. Spontaneous thoughts arise based upon what is stored in our auras: our habitual thought forms, our habitual emotional states, and our life patterns, even our karmic patterns. If you recognize these thoughts and tendencies, you can stop them before they take you too far in any one direction. You can then learn to make decisions that compensate for your patterns and eventually release the energetic pattern."

I thought about what he was saying, and suddenly realized that I was getting late for a meeting back at the office.

"I'm not saying that you shouldn't do more than one thing… that is one of your natural habits, and because you've been relatively successful at most things you've tried, you think it's really easy. However, sometimes it's actually better to not be so talented, and to have to work harder over a longer period of time to make something happen.

"I'm just saying, be sure that you lay a solid foundation for this first product. Don't just leave it behind and move on to the next thing, or the same thing that happened in college will happen here: you'll be doing too many things, you won't be doing any of them extremely well, which is the key to developing a core competency over time. Then what happens?"

I didn't answer, so he continued: "Your reputation in the marketplace becomes skewed, things fall apart, and you have to get back to basics!

"So why bother leaving the basics in the first place?" he concluded.

I promised him I would give this some thought, but was really late for a meeting and had to get back to the office.

Later that month, I would decide, partly on his advice, and partly because of how our first product was taking off, to wait before we started on our next product. However, wallowing in the success of this second product, I would soon forget Ramaswami's admonitions about my patterns. I would lead my company to initial success with other products and services, laying the seeds for a disastrous situation. This was the direct result of my ability to succeed quickly in one area and then moving on as quickly as possible to the next area ... but all of that came later. Right now, we had a renewed focus on our first product.

In the next few weeks, I would also discover that one of the clues I had latched onto had a hidden significance. Mark K., who had started Edge Research and told us the market was very small, was actually building a competitive product! Now it made sense why he didn't want us to be in the market. It wasn't so much that the market was too small; it was that he didn't want any competition in this small but growing market!

CHAPTER SUMMARY
THE NEXT BIG THING

When a clue isn't a clue: learn to recognize External Patterns.

In this chapter, I told Ramaswami about how I had heard that the market for our first product was only $500K, a very small market for multiple companies to pursue and thrive in. Of course, I decided that this clue was pointing me in the direction of creating another product. The problem was that I didn't distinguish between what the clue was trying to tell me and my own recurring External Patterns.

My pattern was to jump into something head first for a little while, then get tired of it and move on to the "Next Big Thing." This had happened to me before several times.

The lesson here is *not* that you should keep working on a product or business even if the market is too small. But rather, when you feel compelled to make a change, try to understand if it simply your recurring pattern, or actually a good choice for the business itself. In this case, a second product was actually a good idea, but my tendency for jumping into the next thing without taking care of the first thing was what Ramaswami was warning me about.

An External Pattern is something that has happened to you in your life multiple times. Usually it's a result of an internal Energetic Pattern, which is what meditation helps us to recognize. If you can recognize the internal and external patterns, you can compensate for them, and eventually master them in your life and your career.

In this case, it might seem that recognizing clues and recognizing patterns work *against* each other. But when you learn to see that the clue here isn't just a clue. Our energetic patterns warp how we interpret and act on clues, how we make decisions, and as a result we end up getting results that repeat themselves in the world around us — i.e. our External Patterns.

Like Clues, External Patterns are repetitive.

There's an old saying that if something repeats three times, then it's a pattern. If something happens once, by itself it may or may not be that interesting. If it happens again, then you have repetition and you should pay attention. If it happens three times, then it's definitely a pattern.

In this context, I am referring to a chain of events in our personal life or work life that that repeats itself, with only slight variation. In business it could mean, as in my case, doing too many projects at once. It could mean sticking to something stubbornly even if it's not working out until you are forced to abandon it (a completely different kind of pattern). It could mean trusting people too quickly, and then having them turn around and betray you. Or it could mean the opposite. Each person is unique and has their own unique External Patterns.

I knew an entrepreneur who was very good at getting new, accomplished former entrepreneurs or executives to join the board of advisors of his company. At first, there was almost always a great relationship between them. When he was on good terms with his new advisors, he would bad-mouth his existing advisors to this new person, give them only limited information to base their advice on, and they would inevitably give him advice that agreed with what he wanted to do. The entrepreneur would trust that new advisor and take his advice on almost every major decision, telling his other advisors why this person was correct in their thinking but the old advisors were not. Then, inevitably, when one of those decisions didn't pan out, the relationship would sour. He would start bad-mouthing the new advisor to the rest of his advisors, and start blaming that guy for his own bad decisions. Then, he would find a new advisor and the same pattern would play out over the course of many months. I didn't realize it was a pattern until it had happened several times.

This is a nearly perfect example of an External Pattern that was caused by an internal Energetic Pattern. What was incredibly frustrating was that he had no idea that this was his Pattern — he didn't have enough self-awareness to recognize what was going on, even though it happened again and again.

Patterns occur in personal relationships just as much (if not more) than with work. We all know a certain young woman, or young man, who seems to somehow always get involved in the same *kinds* of relationships, even though they are with different people. While each relationship is different, in this case, they all follow a similar pattern — usually from euphoria to disillusionment in an almost predictable destructive arc. A little awareness of one's own patterns can help break the pattern by acting more consciously and less impulsively at critical times as the pattern unfolds.

External Patterns are usually caused by our Energetic Pattern.

In the context of the Career Warrior, each of us has an Energetic Pattern that is unique to us: it is the sum of our personality, wishes and desires, fears, compulsions, and even our karma from one or more lifetimes.

Where does this pattern live? Some would say that this pattern lives in our auras or our energy bodies. Others say that patterns actually show up in our bodies — as tension and knots in our bodies. Yet others say they exist in our minds and our beliefs.

According to ancient Yogic and Buddhist traditions, these are all correct statements.

In Yoga, each of us is composed of multiple sheaths called *kosas*, which could be likened to the aura or energy bodies (emotional body, mental body, astral body) in western esoteric teachings.

As we go through one or more lives, these sheaths get *samskaras*, or imperfections in them based upon our thinking, our reactions, our fears, hopes, disappointments, and desires. Taken as a whole, these numerous small distortions shape our energy field into a very unique Energetic Pattern. This Energetic Pattern not only influences what we do, but has an impact on our health and well-being, which is a whole separate but related discussion.

Yoga and meditation are ways to let these *samskaras* go, to release them from our bodies and our energy fields, and to gradually undo our warped Energetic Patterns. The densest sheath is our physical body, but it is surrounded by our emotional and mental bodies This is why breathing and other Yogic exercises actually have an emotional and mental impact in addition to normally recognized physical benefits.

With awareness, we can start to change our patterns.

Since we all have free will, External Patterns which repeat themselves are the result of hundreds, if not thousands of individual decisions along the way. These decisions are impacted by the way we think and feel in the moment, which is a result of our internal Energetic Pattern at any given time.

Patterns don't last forever. Sometimes they last through some number of years in our lives and then we find that we have changed and that pattern is no longer present, or no longer relevant. It just disappeared by itself. As the Buddha said: "That which is capable of arising is capable of cessation." In other words, that which we create, we also have the ability to un-create. Meditation and Yoga can help us to not just see but to clear up some of these distortions in our energy and perceptual fields.

By recognizing our Patterns, we can navigate more clearly. We can simply apply a counterweight to our normal pattern, which helps us to "balance out" and "see things clearly." If you usually make decisions too quickly, take a deep breath, remember the stillness of meditation, and decide to wait before making a decision. On the other hand, your pattern may be that you wait too long and don't decide quickly enough. When your pattern tells you to do nothing, take a deep breath, remember the stillness within meditation, and act like a Samurai warrior. Make a decision. It almost doesn't matter which one.

11 FISH JUMPING IN THE BOAT
MARCH-APRIL, 1994

The phone calls continued to come in fast and furious over the next few months as copies of our first product were literally flying off the shelves. There was no question that we had a "hit" on our hands.

With relatively little effort, we were able to get all of the major computer industry magazines (*ComputerWorld, InfoWorld, Information Week, Network World, Communications Week,* and *Computer Reseller News*) to write articles about us. More importantly, these articles resulted in a steady stream of potential customers who would call us, which meant we rarely had to go out and find customers. We became "mini-celebrities" within our target market.

We had always assumed that as the company became more successful, the amount of effort we'd have to put in would go down. But exactly the opposite was happening — although the company was becoming very well-known, the amount of work was increasing, not decreasing!

Mitch and I were still talking to potential customers (trying to get new sales) and existing customers (providing technical support) during the day, and working well into the night to improve the product.

Our development work at night was incorporating enhancement requests from customers and adding functionality to the product. I had decided, partly on Ramaswami's advice, that before we started working on another product, we really needed to beef up the current product and make sure it was "stable and maintainable."

After the experience with Mark K. and the competition from his company, Edge Research, I wanted to add some functionality that would "leapfrog" them, landing us another "hit" with our target market. That wouldn't give them much time to catch up, since they were still getting their first version fully working.

One cold February night, after we had finished our programming tasks for the evening, I brought up the new feature to Mitch and suggested that we start on it right away.

"But that's extremely difficult to create, it'll take us a few months to build just that one feature!" objected Mitch. "And we have plenty of other bugs and features that we need to address." He was for simply making the product more stable before moving on to doing something new.

"Yes, it will take a few months, but think of what it will do for us strategically. The fact that it's hard to build this feature is what makes it interesting! If it was easy, then Edge could do it as well as we could and it wouldn't be worthwhile!"

Although I hadn't realized it at the time, it was my old pattern of wanting to move on to the "next big thing" rather than concentrating on what was at hand. This time, though, the pattern was being applied in a constructive way to leapfrog our competitor.

We reached a solid compromise that we believed was in the interest of stabilizing the product, while fulfilling my need to do something "new and cool." Until we could bring in some employees, Mitch would work on stabilizing the product, which would be our 1.5 release, and I would start working on the "new and cool" feature for our 2.0 release.

"Great," I said, tired from a long day. I glanced at the clock. It was 1:30 a.m. "I'm going home to get some sleep." As I looked out the window, though, I changed my mind. A snowstorm was rampant.

I groaned as I realized that the phone calls would start at 8:30

a.m., from prospects, customers, and others asking us about business partnerships. Like most computer programmers (and college students), we considered 8:30 to be "absurdly early." Unfortunately, there was no way for us to change the rest of the business world, so we had to start thinking about how to work in it. We decided it was time for us to bring on some employees.

Ever the pragmatist, Mitch pointed out that we didn't have much cash to pay people very much. "We can raise some money from people we know," I suggested, immediately rejuvenated by the idea of doing something new. "I can write up a business plan and we can get some people to put money into the company. Since we already have a product and some customers, it shouldn't be too hard to show them the potential of the company!"

"How much do you think we need?" asked Mitch.

"I have no idea," I replied. "Why don't you do a quick spreadsheet? I'm going to start on writing the business plan tonight."

It didn't strike us that our lightning-quick process of making decisions in the middle of the night was in any way odd for a software start-up. I booted up my computer again and started on an outline for the plan while the snowstorm raged.

The next day, Mitch had come up with a figure that we would use for "cash flow" purposes. Though the business was moving along and we were selling products, it could be 30, 60, or even 90 days before we got payment from a major company. And in addition to hiring some employees to help with the Herculean amount of work that was piling up, we needed to buy (really buy this time rather than buy-and-return) additional computers, phone equipment, and more.

"$50,000 should be enough," he said confidently and showed me his spreadsheet. We both looked at the spreadsheet – which was very basic. If we hired two people, paid them each $3,000 per month (well below market rate), then after six months it would add up to $36,000. The other $16,000 would help us buy computers and other needed equipment.

We didn't realize that this was an absurdly simplistic (and incorrect) way of doing cash flow projections. But we didn't really know much about cash flow projections, income statements, or balance sheets, so it seemed as good of a number as any. In fact, I didn't think I had even seen that much money in one bank account before.

I told Ramaswami what we were doing. "Why $50,000?" he asked.

I explained how we had gotten to the number. It would ensure that we didn't run out of cash for a while and pay for the things we thought we needed.

He smiled and asked about an operating budget – where we filled out our expected revenue and expected expense budget over a period of time, then used some assumptions to calculate cash flow requirements. The concept of a true operating budget hadn't really occurred to us.

I promised Ramaswami that I would do a detailed budget to think about how much we needed, but as was often the case in those early, days, I got too distracted. *We have two potential funding sources already: Mitch's parents, and the parents a friend of mine from MIT – so why bother spending too much time on that, especially with all of the other things we had to do?* I thought.

I quickly wrote up a document describing our business. I didn't want to call it a "business plan" because it wasn't very long, so I settled on "prospectus", which sounded very "official" to me. It basically outlined the market for linking together Lotus and Microsoft products, touted the publicity and articles we had gotten in industry magazines like *Computer World,* and outlined our strategy for adding multiple products over time.

Both of our initial investors, Mitch's parents and the parents of another friend, were investing more because of their belief in us than in the actual business plan and numbers, and they quickly agreed to invest $25,000 each, which gave us the cash flow we needed. It was time to start hiring some employees.

First we approached a developer named Bob, who I had known at Lotus. Bob was a very experienced developer; in fact, they called him a *principal software engineer*, which sounded to me like a programmer who had a lot of experience. He was what we considered *"older and wiser",* as he looked like he was in his

30's.

We met with him at a local restaurant in the mall one evening. He had heard about what we were doing and was intrigued and wanted to know more. We explained to him what was happening with our product ("Ingenious!" he said when we told him how simple our product concept was but how it solved a very complex problem), which companies had bought it ("Impressive!" he said when we mentioned some of our customers, who were among the best-known corporations in the financial, manufacturing, and publishing industries), and what kind of help we needed, ("No problem!" he said as I described that we needed a C++ programmer who was familiar with Lotus Notes and Microsoft Visual Basic).

So far so good, I thought. We had just finished our dinner and the waiter came over. "Desserts?" We all looked at each other, to see if anyone else would make the first move to order dessert. When no one spoke, I jumped in, "I'll have some hot tea." Both Mitch and Bob ordered some coffee and dessert.

After our dishes were taken away, we could see that Bob was seriously intrigued by our idea. "How much could you pay?" He asked, looking at Mitch. Mitch looked at me to answer.

"Hmm..." I said. "Well, we have $3,000 per month in our budget," I answered, trying to sound confident and business-like.

He almost spilled his coffee as he answered: "$3,000? But that's only $36K annualized!"

"Yeah, but we're going to give stock options in addition to the salary. If this thing goes right, then you could come out a millionaire!" I said. Mitch was quietly observing Bob's reactions.

"But I make $70K now as it is at Lotus!" he said. "That would be a 50% pay cut." He could see that both Mitch and I were a little uneasy and that we really didn't have more than 3K to pay someone per month. He took a deep breath, and resumed his *older and wiser* tone that we had seen earlier.

"Listen, guys, I really respect what you're doing. It's exciting." He took another sip of his coffee. "If I wasn't about to get married and invest in a house, I'd probably join you guys for the stock. But right now, I have cash flow issues as well and couldn't possibly join for that amount."

He could see that were disappointed. "They key is that you guys need to find someone who is single, doesn't have a mortgage, and really values stock options more than he values cash. I might know of some people. I'll recommend them to you."

The check came. Bob, realizing that we were probably paying ourselves very little, took the check and treated us. The meeting ended amicably and he honestly seemed to want to help us out, even though he wasn't in a financial position to join us.

We decided that it would be best to follow his advice and approach people who were single, could live on a low salary, and who wouldn't be offended by our low offer.

The first of these was Kirk, a friend of Mitch's, who was 28 at the time (again, *older and wiser,* we thought). Kirk understood what we were trying to do, was articulate, and could handle a lot of the initial sales and technical support issues that came up during the day. More importantly, having been in the work force for a few years more than us, Kirk had been used to getting up early and coming into the office in the morning.

"Hmm…" said Kirk, as we sat at a Pizzeria Uno's in Porter Square in Cambridge. "Will you guys really be able to pay me? Do you have the money?" Kirk had been involved in a couple of startups in the past, including his own. None of the startups had made enough money to support him – so he was worried that we wouldn't even be able to come up with the $3K per month to pay him. The most recent one, which he did part time, had brought in $20,000 worth of sales in the previous year.

I smiled, beaming with pride, and explained: "Well, we brought in $20,000 worth of sales just last month."

Kirk looked at Mitch, as if to see if I was serious. Mitch nodded.

Kirk found this surprising, given the low price point of the product. "It seems too easy," he said.

"The catch," I explained, parroting what others had told me, "is that it's only a $500K market, which means that we won't be able to build a huge company off of this one product alone."

"That means," continued Mitch, "that we're going to have to build additional products to grow. But if we do that, we could grow big in a hurry."

Kirk was impressed with what we had done, but not too impressed with the salary that we offered to pay him. We agreed to give him a certain number of shares and showed him how he could become a millionaire if things went really well with the company. He said he'd think about it. Though he seemed skeptical about the "millionaire in a few years concept," he genuinely liked what we were doing and was getting very bored with his current position. He wanted to do something new and exciting, and he trusted Mitch from having worked with him in the past. He called us the next day and tentatively accepted our offer.

At the same time, I hadn't given up my notion of the "next big thing." Expansion was on our mind, and I decided that if we weren't going to start on the next product right away, we could at least start a consulting group to make more money from the customers of our first product, VBLink. It was a development tool, which meant that anyone who bought it would have to use it to develop an actual application.

We had just started to get requests from our customers to help them build full-blown applications using our software product. One company, an Israeli document management company, asked if we could use our product to build a link between their Oracle database and their Notes databases.

"Of course we can!" I said, speaking before thinking.

"Well how long will it take and how much will it cost?" asked the customer, whose name was Eddie. Eddie had a thick Israeli accent, but seemed like a straightforward guy who liked our product and company.

"Hmm..." I answered, trying to think fast. The reality was that I didn't know how long it would take us to build it. The conversation with Kirk was on my mind, and how we were selling $20,000 of software a month. That seemed like a lot of money, so I figured that something less than that would be good.

"It'll take a few weeks," I answered, sounding confident. "That'll cost about ... $15,000," I said. There were a few moments of silence on the phone. I wasn't sure if I had quoted a number too high.

"If that's too much," I continued nervously, "we could limit the scope and I can give you a better idea."

I heard him sighing on the other end of the phone. "Well, if that's what it costs, then it's okay. Let's do it. When can you start?"

I looked at my long to-do list and realized that there was no way we could start on it anytime soon, unless we hired another developer. "In a few weeks," I said and my mind began to race with how we could build a consulting team in the company to handle requests like this one. $15,000 seemed like a lot of money for one small project, I thought.

Ramaswami and others warned us that building a consulting company was very different from building a product company. "You don't want to get too distracted from your core business of building products," he warned me, but to no avail.

For help on this front, we turned to Irfan, my older brother by nearly two years. He was 25 at the time and had been working for Andersen Consulting in Detroit for a few years (also *"older and wiser"*, we thought). We also thought that his extra years in the work world, especially at a professional consulting company like Andersen (which was perhaps the best-known IT consulting firm at that time) would be perfect. He could do the consulting project that I had just boasted we could do, and he could take over building of our as yet non-existent consulting group.

"I'm not sure," said Irfan. "It sounds a bit risky." He explained that he had been thinking about a career change, and he was flirting with the idea of going to Wall Street to become an investment banker.

I explained that high tech entrepreneurship was where the real money was. He could be a millionaire in a few years if this worked out. He didn't seem convinced.

Then I shifted tracks. "Those Wall Street firms work you like a dog," I said. He laughed and pointed out that we were having this conversation at 11 at night; so joining us didn't exactly sound like it would be a cakewalk.

"Sure, but there's a difference," I answered. "Here at Brainstorm, you can be a partner, you can be one of the guys in charge. If you joined a Wall Street firm, or even stayed at Andersen, you'd be the low man on the totem pole for years and years."

This argument seemed to have some appeal; he liked the thought of being one of the "guys in charge". But after a few conversations, he was still hemming and hawing, viewing it as a "risky proposition." I had promised Eddie that we would start the consulting project "in a few weeks" so I was getting anxious too.

Finally, I explained to him that he had 'nothing to lose.' If the company didn't work out, he gained valuable operating experience, which would help him to land a job on Wall Street or anywhere else making at least $100K. And if it did work out and if things went really well, he too would be a millionaire along with the rest of us!

Much to my surprise, this approach of showing how there really wasn't much risk in joining us worked well. I would use it many times in the next few years as we recruited an interesting cast of characters around us.

Kirk and Irfan decided to join our start-up around the same time. For years, there would be a debate over who was actually the third co-founder, the first of them to actually start or the first of them to accept our offer.

Kirk took over many daily responsibilities of talking with and selling prospects, and supporting existing customers, which freed us up to focus on the next version of the product, and to do more marketing, which we realized was drawing customers to us.

Irfan started with the consulting project and became our third key man in the company, staying up late with us as we built out the product, and helping us put some structure and controls around our product development, including the concept of having an "independent" QA organization. With four of us in the company, plus our admin/receptionist/office-manager, we felt we were rapidly becoming a "real company."

A few days later, Ramaswami and I sat down to have lunch at a seafood restaurant near his office. We were in Kendall Square, the heart of the Cambridge high tech community. From the restaurant, we could look out at Memorial Drive and the Charles River.

It reminded me a bit of my first meeting with him almost a year ago, although this time there were no sailboats. It was now the beginning of March, and the river was still mostly frozen.

We began to discuss my rapidly evolving company, Brainstorm Technologies.

"What is your sales cycle?" he asked.

I had to admit that I wasn't really sure what a 'sales cycle' was.

"One of the most important measurements of any business, particularly in the computer industry, is the cost and timetable of acquiring new customers. The sales cycle is how long it takes from the time that you first make contact with a potential customer to the time that they buy."

I told him that I still didn't understand what he meant.

"Here's an analogy. Imagine you're going fishing and you put the bait out. The sales cycle is how long it takes you, on average, to catch a fish." I had been fishing only once in my life and explained that I still had no idea what he was talking about.

I explained to him that customers usually called us, and if they needed our product, they would usually buy it right there and then. Sometimes, they needed to go ask their supervisor if it was okay to buy the product. In those cases, they usually came back the next day and bought it.

He suggested that with such a short cycle, we might want to raise the price and see if it affected our sales cycle or number of sales. If the sales cycle didn't get any longer – we could easily double our revenue from the same number of sales. It would mean that our product was priced too low. If it affected the sales cycle and if all of our prospects began to delay their purchasing decision, or decide not to buy, then the new price would be high. It was a well-known technique he referred to as "turning up the heat until someone screams".

I agreed to try this technique of "turning up the heat." We would use it to raise the price of the product successfully to $795, which made it one of the most expensive objects for Visual Basic available in those days.

Then suddenly Ramaswami laughed.

"What's so funny?"

"Well, I think you guys take the cake for the shortest sales cycle I've seen in a while!" He laughed again. "It's as if you're going fishing, and the fish are jumping in the boat!"

He thought this was extremely funny. I didn't really see the humor in it. Years later, as I became involved in other businesses and finally realized that it wasn't normal to have the "fish jump in the boat", I understood why he thought this was so unusual. Most other businesses had to go out, find the fish, and then lure them in with bait before they caught anything.

CHAPTER SUMMARY
FISH JUMPING IN THE BOAT

Learn to ride your Energetic Pattern, not be mastered by it.
In this chapter, we see the first instance of making a conscious decision to apply an Energetic Pattern in a constructive way. Our patterns are not chosen consciously or logically. They are habits and tendencies and impulses we've picked up in this life (and perhaps in other lifetimes if the mystics are to be believed).

They have incredible power and contain our individual strengths as well as our weaknesses. You can make conscious decisions that channel a pattern in a particular way. In this case, I was able to use my pattern of wanting to work on the next big thing to work on a feature for our existing product, which would leapfrog our competition. The impulse to do something fun and new was still there – I just chose to apply it to an existing product.

There is an old Chinese proverb that applies to Energetic Patterns: "If you ignore the dragon, it will eat you. If you try to confront the dragon, it will overpower you. If you ride the dragon, you will take advantage of its might and power."

Everyone has an agenda. It's usually behind the scenes.
In a previous chapter, I mentioned a gentleman named Mark K, founder of Edge Research, who had tried to discourage us from attacking our initial target market because it was only "$500K," a very small market by most software standards.

However, we failed to ask what his agenda was in telling us this. It turned out that Edge Research became our only competition in this market, and the relationship would get even more complicated as the story goes on.

When you start a business, particularly one that becomes well known in its industry, people will appear out of the woodwork. From investors to advisors to employees to business partners to adversaries, everyone has an agenda. It's important to try to be conscious what each person's agenda is. That doesn't mean that you shouldn't trust new people, just protect yourself in the case where their agenda is different from yours.

Bringing in trusted people: should you or shouldn't you?

There's an ongoing debate about whether you should start companies with family members or close friends. You'll see that in our case, I started this company with my roommate (Mitch), then we brought in one of his close friends (Kirk), and my brother (Irfan).

When working with business partners, the most important thing is to align expectations. If one partner wants to build a company quickly and sell it, and another wants to run it for the rest of their lives, that's a mismatch of expectations. If, on the other hand, all partners are on the same page, then you have alignment. Working with people you know has the benefit of avoiding surprises and as a result, you know that you can (generally) trust these people in your business. But if things don't go well and you have to let a close friend or relative go, things can get awkward fast, and sour your relationship.

Understand your sales cycle to build a repeatable business.

Understanding how you get your customers, how long it takes for the "fish" to bite, and how much each one costs you is an essential part of building a repeatable business model. When we started Brainstorm, we knew nothing about sales cycles. In fact, our sales cycle was almost nonexistent (people would just call us and order the product), which led to the realization that our customers were "fish jumping in the boat"!

Eventually, though, every business has to understand its sales process so it can plan effectively. Otherwise you'll just be guessing and, as we'll see in future chapters, that's a dangerous game to play.

It worked out okay for us at this early stage because our source of marketing was press, which cost us very little. In an Internet or mobile app business, you might spend large amounts of money advertising to find customers, and you have to track exactly how much it costs per new customer – that is your customer acquisition cost.

12 THE HUNGRY DESERT
JUNE, 1994

"Are you going to the desert with Ramaswami?" asked James. We were having lunch at the food court in the CambridgeSide Galleria mall, the same mall where he had taught me about energy almost a year earlier.

It was a late lunch, so we missed most of the bustle of the lunch-crowd. True to form, we were sitting in a "high energy" spot, as James called it. There weren't too many people around, and we were right next to the windows, with both trees and water visible.

I had heard about the upcoming desert trip, but wasn't sure if I'd be able to go. "Tell me again about the significance of going to the desert?" I asked.

"The desert, the desert," James began, half-singing as he shifted forward in his chair and played with his fork.

"The *Energy of the Desert* is pure ... the *Energy of the Desert* is where most religious and spiritual insights come from. Jesus literally went to the desert, you know, and so did Moses. And Mohammed used to go into the desert to be alone and fast for 30 days each year. Even Buddha, who sat under a Bodhi tree and became enlightened, went into the desert *metaphorically*, even though he didn't physically go to a desert: he went to be alone and meditate by removing himself from the *opulence* of the world..." As he said *opulence*, he waved his hand around as if pointing out the mall and everything around us.

He suddenly stopped talking, inserted his fork into his

chicken teriyaki, and started eating ravenously.

It was early June and in a few weeks, on the summer solstice, the longest day and shortest night of the year, Ramaswami was planning a desert trip, which was a special kind of vacation to a power spot in the remote desert.

I began to think about my dilemma. I wanted to go to the desert with Ramaswami and some of his students, but I had several key constraints: time and money.

First, the business was really in motion and every day was critical. We were working six or seven days a week and taking several days off in the middle of the week wouldn't be looked at too kindly by my business partners, I thought. Second, we hadn't really been paying ourselves much, and it would cost a good amount of money to fly to Los Angeles and drive out to the desert and stay there for a few days.

"The summer solstice and the winter solstices are important times ... it's a great time to be in a power spot ... you'll really feel the energy," James said between bites of food.

As James and I spoke about the desert trip, I recalled a conversation with Ramaswami about power spots only a few weeks ago, when he had announced the upcoming desert trip. Ramaswami took a number of his newer students, including myself, for a walk to Walden Pond, which he claimed was also a power spot.

Walden Pond, where Thoreau lived and wrote the classic naturalist work *Walden*, was crawling with tourists on that sunny May afternoon. Although I had never read *Walden*, I was familiar with some of his more famous quotes ("most men lead lives of quiet desperation") and the general story: Thoreau, a protégé of Ralph Waldo Emerson, was a talented writer and speaker who could have been a leader of men. Instead, he chose instead to live alone in nature. He took almost no money, built his own house, and lived with the animals through snow, rain, and many quiet days, chronicling his "life in the woods" in the now famous book.

That afternoon, as we reached Walden Pond, I tried to imagine what it must have been like for him to be there many decades ago: before the tourists arrived, before the nearby road was built, before there was any air conditioning or heat. I suddenly felt a hunger swell up in me: a hunger to be alone in nature with the sound of the wind and the animals. Like most of my contemporaries, I had always lived and worked in cities or in suburbia. I had been camping once, but that was about the extent of my time spent in nature. I resolved to go buy a copy of *Walden.*

"Certain *power spots* naturally draw people. It's inevitable," Ramaswami said as he led a group of us around the Pond's main trail. I had been thinking about Thoreau and hadn't heard the beginning of his walking lecture.

"What determines a power spot?" he asked rhetorically. "For an occultist and a student of esoteric teachings, the important element is *Energy.* Places have an energy all their own. And people are often drawn to, or sometimes repelled by, that energy. That's what we seek. Certain kinds of *energetic signatures* that exist at physical places like this one, but in the hidden worlds."

I had a ton of questions that I wanted to ask, but the brisk pace of the walk made it difficult, and I was near the back of the group.

"There are energy lines in the Earth ... you are naturally inclined to follow them if you walk without thinking, and let yourself go. Washington, D.C., you know, was built by Freemasons, and they laid out many of the streets and the capital according to their knowledge of energy lines, which the Masons called *ley lines..."*

He suddenly became quiet and seemed to be concentrating on his steps as we climbed up and then down a small hill. We walked quietly along the trail, and halfway around the pond, opposite the area where we had started the walk, Ramaswami veered off the main path and led us into the woods. We came to a clearing and we all sat down to meditate.

"If you can, whenever you are in a pleasant *power spot,* sit down and meditate," he said in a very serious mode, his eyes were already half-closed, as if he was looking within.

"How do we know when we're in a pleasant power spot?" I asked, now close enough to start my usual barrage of questions.

He opened his eyes and looked to see who had asked the question. He chuckled when he saw it was me. "Well, Mr. MIT,

I suppose you'd like an electronic device that would tell you when a power spot is pleasant or not? An *energy detection device* perhaps?" He found this very amusing and started laughing out loud as he said an *energy detection device,* as if he'd just made a big joke.

I thought about it for a moment. *An energy detection device would be nice,* I thought, not realizing that he was jesting. *It could validate all of this stuff that Ramaswami and his students believe so fervently in.* Before I could answer, though, he suddenly shifted back to his serious, meditative mode, with his eyes half-closed. He spoke loud enough for all of us to hear.

"The truth is, that all of you already have an *energy detection device.* It's called your brain ... well not exactly ... it's more like your body ... let's call it your body-mind ... it can feel energy..." He suddenly opened his eyes and looked out at another student, a fellow named Steve, who was known within the group for being as paranoid as often as I was skeptical.

"Have you ever been in a place," he asked, looking at Steve but directing the question to all of us, "where you didn't feel quite comfortable?"

He paused to let the question sink in. Then: "Where your body was telling you that you shouldn't be there? It could be your hair standing on end, or it could be just a feeling inside of discomfort, or a stomachache or queasiness, or a different type of feeling altogether? And when you left that place the feeling inexplicably went away? Hmm...?"

Steve nodded and was about to describe a specific place where he felt paranoid when Ramaswami jumped in again. "There you go," he said, as if Steve had already answered and turning his attention back to me.

"You see, you already have an energy detection device ... it doesn't detect *power spots* specifically, but it can if you stop thinking and let yourself go. If you do, you'll start to notice what it is sensing. What it does is detect how well your current energy matches with the energy of the place you're at.

"The key to becoming a Career Warrior is to develop your *awareness* of the hidden worlds. This starts by becoming aware of *energy.* The *energy of places* is important, as is the *energy of times.* And at an important time of power like the summer solstice, it's a great idea to be in a place of power..."

He was silent and seemed to be viewing scenes in his mind's eye that were more interesting than what we saw around us. He had a content smile on his face, but we could tell that his mind was elsewhere.

"The most intense power spots are in the desert. In this continent, they're in the American southwest. That's because the raw energy is still there — it's not as populated as the rest of the country.

"But *power spots* can have unexpected effects on you at different *times*, which is why you have to be careful. This is why you need to be *aware of what's happening in the hidden worlds.* There are many places in the desert that if you go at one point in your life, you'll feel an unexplainable desire to get the hell out of there because you're not wanted.

"At other times, you might go to the same place and feel drawn to it and spend days or even weeks there! What you feel is actually the match between your energy with the energy of the place.

"The *power spots* exist independently of this feeling ... they just are. But your *feeling* is the key to whether you should be in a given power spot or not!"

The glaze left his eyes and we could tell that he was suddenly back with us in the clearing.

"Even though the Path of the Career Warrior is about applying these principles in your life and at work, sometimes getting *out of your life,* by going to a *place of power,* can help you to develop the right perspective to take back into your life!"

As he spoke, I had an odd experience. I was looking up at the sky, and suddenly noticed thousands of little specks of light fluttering around. It was as if each speck was there for a fraction of a second and then suddenly disappeared. There were thousands, if not millions of them. I thought I was looking at some kind of collection of biological organisms in the sky.

I tried to return my attention to what Ramaswami was saying. He continued to talk about the desert, and explained that there was a desert trip coming up at the Summer Solstice and spoke about the importance of being 'energetically clean' for the trip.

I couldn't concentrate on what he was saying. I looked back

at the sky and didn't notice anything at first. And then, all of a sudden I saw the specks again. Each individual speck seemed to be acting on its own; it would show up, fly around erratically, and then disappear. As I expanded my vision, though, I noticed that there was an overall pattern in the sky being produced. They made what looked like waves of energy that were vibrating back and forth across the sky. I could not only see but also *feel* these waves of energy washing over my body. I began to wonder if these waves were waves of energy that defined a *power spot*. I was so enchanted by this pattern of waves that I missed the rest of what Ramaswami said.

My thoughts returned to the present, as I sat with James in the food court and we finished our lunch. I wanted to talk about the practicalities of a desert trip.

"How do you guys pay for all of this?" I asked, referring to the trips that he was constantly taking with Ramaswami. Every quarter, on the solstice or the equinox, it seemed that they made a trip somewhere.

He smiled and explained that's why they were all computer contractors, who got paid good hourly rates, so that they would have money left over to travel frequently, often on spiritual trips.

I explained my financial situation – we hadn't been paying ourselves much at Brainstorm. After taxes, rent, and car payments, there wasn't much left over for travel.

He started laughing.

I didn't think this was a polite thing to do, as I was genuinely interested in going on the desert trip but didn't know if I could afford it.

"Oh, don't worry about the money," he said, brushing aside my concerns. "If you set your *intent* to go, and it's appropriate for you to go, then you'll find a way..."

"Do you mean that I should borrow the money from someone?" I had always been averse to being in debt and was shocked that he would suggest such a thing.

"Maybe, maybe not. I'm just saying that if your *intent* is right, and you don't worry about it too much, either the money will show up or an alternative will be presented to you. I've seen funny things happen when someone sets their *intent* on going on a spiritual trip – particularly a desert trip!"

"What do you mean by funny things?" I asked, but he wasn't paying attention. James had finished his chicken teriyaki but seemed like he was still hungry and he was now scouting out the different restaurants in the food court to decide what else he should have.

Something caught his eye and he held up his hand to me: "I'll be right back, I'm going to go grab some more food."

I sighed and saw that it was difficult to get James focused on a particular conversation for too long. He walked to *Au Bon Pain* and bought an almond cheese croissant.

"Now," he said, taking a bite out of the croissant and talking with his mouth half-full, "If you're going to go on the desert trip, you have to treat it as a serious endeavor. Did you get Ramaswami's instructions?" I hadn't.

He pulled out an instruction sheet from his bag and handed it to me. "This is my only copy, so why don't you make a copy at work and get it back to me, okay?"

"But," I started, "I'm not so sure that I'll even be going on this trip."

"That's okay. I didn't know if I'd be going on my first desert trip either. Swami tells us that either the desert calls you and you go, or it doesn't and you don't. That's it. There's no need to worry about it too much!"

I was about to protest that I didn't know if the desert was calling me or not, when he suddenly got up again. "No time to argue or worry, both of which I know you like to do. I have to get back to work ... make a copy of the instructions and give me back the original, okay?" And then he was suddenly gone, leaving me at the mall alone wondering what he meant by 'setting my intent.'

Instead of going back to work, I meditated on the trip to the desert and as I did so, breathing in and our very slowly, my anxiety melted away. I wasn't sure if I was going to go, or how, but I suddenly felt better about it. I felt refreshed, as if I had just woken up after a good, restful, sleep and went back to work. I put the instructions for the desert trip in my bag and promptly forgot about them.

A couple of days later I got an unexpected call from Steve. "Hey, did you hear about the Continental airfare?" he asked.

"Continental airfare? No, I haven't heard about it." I was in my office and it was a Monday morning. I was only half-awake and trying to get into the work I had to do that day.

"Continental had a misprint in the Boston Globe yesterday. They printed a non-stop round-trip ticket to Los Angeles for $99? It was supposed to be for at least $399!"

I was too groggy to grasp the significance. "So?" I said.

"So? Remember the desert trip? It's near Los Angeles, next week! I just called and they said it was a misprint, but when I complained to the manager – he said they had to honor the misprint. If you call today, you can get cheap tickets to LA!"

I suddenly woke up. I hadn't thought about the desert trip much since my lunch with James a few days ago. "$99, that's not bad," I replied. "What about a hotel?"

"I found this place in the Borrego Springs that's really cheap — it's called Whispering Sands. We can share a room. The rooms are only $49 total. I'm also renting a car so we can share that with a few other people."

I took a slow, long, deep breath. All of a sudden, it seemed as if the planets had just aligned and the desert was 'calling me'. I called and got the cheap tickets and made arrangements to share a hotel room. The financial problem was solved but I also had the issue of work that would be missed.

I remembered the 'instructions for the desert trip' that I had gotten from James and pulled it out.

"*A desert trip is an important energetic event. It's important that you make the appropriate preparations.*" The paper listed a number of items that I should have with me – a flashlight, a little mattress to sit and lie on while meditating in the desert, plenty of water, etc. It also had some practical do's and don'ts while in the desert. Finally, it had a set of instructions on what to do *before* the trip.

"It's important to tie up energetic loose ends. What will come up when you meditate in the desert is what you bring with you, emotionally and energetically. It's important that you don't have outstanding bills, emotional issues, or work-related obligations that will pull at you while we are in the desert. Try to tie these 'loose ends' up as much as possible before the trip so that you can be fully present while in the desert."

I thought about loose ends that I might have – particularly related to work. I was working on writing code for a new module of the product, and was in the process of interviewing and hiring a new developer. I also was writing an article for a magazine about our product, and finally, I was preparing to present at a conference coming up in a few weeks. All of these things, I reasoned, could be energetic 'loose ends' that could pull on me when I was out in the desert.

I worked frantically over the next few days to finish up the module, write the article, make the developer an offer, and finish the first draft of my presentation. At first, Mitch and Irfan were skeptical that I would be gone for almost a whole week on such short notice. We had all been working so intensely that the subject of vacations hadn't really come up. I had assumed that with the amount of work to be done in the company, none of us really had the luxury of going on vacation, so I wasn't sure how to state my case.

I explained to them the status of the items I was working on, and explained that I needed some time away to 're-energize.' To my surprise, they both came around very quickly.

"The reality is that in a start-up, there's no good time to go on a vacation, so you might as well just go whenever you want to go... the work will still be here when you get back," said Mitch.

"If we all keep working like this without a break, we're going to be burned out pretty soon," agreed Irfan, who then brought up a vacation he wanted to take later that year.

With my business partners in sync, I was finally all set to go to the desert. The loose ends had been taken care of. Except one. Ramaswami had given all of us one movie assignment, which he said would prepare us for the desert: to watch *The Last Temptation of Christ*. I had expected a desert movie like *Lawrence of Arabia*. Even though I had lived in Saudi Arabia, I had never seen that movie and wanted to see it.

"You can watch that too if you want. But it's important to watch *The Last Temptation*."

I asked why we had to watch such a controversial and

Christian movie. He laughed. "Don't worry about all that controversy. The part that's most important about this movie for you right now is not the scene of Jesus sleeping with the women! The important part for you now is when Jesus goes out into the desert, to be alone. That's what I want you to concentrate on ..."

I agreed and rented the video the evening before our departure, taking the night off from work, and watching it alone. It seemed to do a good job of setting the appropriate tone for the trip.

We arrived in Borrego Springs, a small town near the Anza Borrego desert south of San Diego, and the desert was different than I had imagined it. When I was ten years old, my family had lived in Riyadh, the capital of Saudi Arabia, for a year. We drove across the desert to Mecca once, and though I don't remember much of the trip, I remember the vast landscapes of open desert. I remember the two-lane paved highway in the middle of endless miles of sand dunes. For some reason, that's what I had imaged this desert would be like, too.

But this desert, in the American Southwest, was nothing like the Arabian desert. The best way I can describe it is that it was more ... *harsh*. There were no gently rolling sand dunes. The sand was not very deep and was full of small pebbles and larger rocks. There were small bushes every few feet and it was difficult to walk in a straight line because you had to avoid them.

The flat area was surrounded by rugged hills. Shades of brown stretched out in all directions: the brown of the sand, the darker brown of the bushes, and the even darker brown of the boulders. And we had to keep an eye out for rattlesnakes.

Still, there was something otherworldly about the hills. I couldn't describe why, but being there was exhilarating. There was a warm desert gale that was constantly blowing. It reminded me of the hot winds that I had experienced in Arabia as a kid. The desert gales seemed to be washing through everything and everyone energetically, keeping the place pure.

Borrego Springs wasn't much of a town. Rather, it seemed to be a small collection of buildings around a single rotary. There were four roads coming out from the rotary. Two of them were local roads that very quickly lost their pavement and became dirt roads. The other two represented the "main highway," if it could be called a highway at all. It was really just a two-lane paved road.

I decided to walk from our hotel to this 'downtown' area. It was hot, over 100 degrees, but the dry heat didn't seem to affect me as much as the humidity we had in the Boston summers. I walked to the rotary, which was large enough to have a little park area built into it. I sat down with my back to a tree, enjoying the little shade it offered, and began to write in my notebook. It had been months since I had written much and I began to write about my feelings about being in the desert.

That evening and the following evening, on the summer solstice, we went on a hike into the Anza Borrego desert. For a time, we entered an alternate reality of unending desert gales under bright shining stars. I had never seen so many stars in my life. Living in the city for so long, I had forgotten how breathtaking the starry night sky, with the Milky Way winding through it, could be. As I meditated, I felt myself floating free among these stars.

The next few days were spent in this fashion. The hot days were spent lounging in Borrego Springs recording my experiences in my notebook. At night, we hiked out to a remote *power spot* in the desert and meditated. The energy of the desert got more intense each night. I felt what Ramaswami would call an 'auric cleansing' process happening. It was as if the gale allowed the things in my aura that I wasn't overly attached to simply 'wash away.'

The sun shone brightly through the little window as I pulled up the shade. I looked at my watch. It was 8 a.m. and I had just come back on a red-eye from Los Angeles to Boston. The flight was appropriately named, as I could feel the redness building up in my eyes. Still, I was unusually energetic for having been in an airplane all night.

I sat near the window and watched the skyscrapers of Boston come into view. I realized that I had been literally and metaphorically 'away' from civilization for a few days, and it was strange to be back.

As the plane circled the city getting ready for touchdown, I began to reflect on things below. The cars were all lined up in traffic jams as the masses were on their way to work, ready to begin the daily grind. I remembered Thoreau and his quote about 'quiet desperation.' I felt that I had just had my own little taste of *Walden*: going out in the woods (or in my case, the desert) to live deliberately, if only for a few days.

As I walked to the baggage claim, I could feel the civilized world seeping back in slowly. But as I closed my eyes and took a deep breath, I sensed a feeling in my torso that was calm, energetic, and detached. Ramaswami would have said that I sensed a certain *energy* in my body. It was definitely there, but it wasn't concentrated on just one spot – it seemed to be all over my torso. It had the effect of a 'numbness' or 'coat of protection' around me that seemed to dull the effects of civilization on me. As I grabbed my bag, I felt like I was in a dream.

I debated whether I should go to work, and decided not to. I'd rather take it easy. It suddenly occurred to me that it was breakfast time. I stopped at a little shop and looked at the various muffins and bagels that were arrayed there. For some reason, the energy in my body seemed incompatible with the food that I saw, and I couldn't bring myself to eat anything. I got some water and started drinking.

Three days later, I was starting to become concerned. I hadn't eaten anything since I'd been back in Boston. Lots of water and orange juice seemed natural, but the food I saw somehow seemed incompatible with the energy in my body and I couldn't bring myself to eat.

I wasn't even hungry. Normally, I never missed a meal and snacked *often* in between meals. And now I hadn't eaten in three days. I got in touch with Ramaswami, who was not back in Boston yet, via email to see if he had any suggestions.

"I haven't eaten since coming back from the desert. I'm not sure if this is normal or not – I've never had three days before in my life where I haven't eaten. What should I do?"

He replied later that day with a few questions.

"Before I answer the question about 'is it normal', I need to know how you feel. The Desert can bring out many things – usually it brings out issues. How did you feel when you got back from the desert trip? Were you lightheaded from not having eaten? Are you having stomach problems that are preventing you from eating? Are you craving any certain kinds of foods?"

I explained that none of these were true. I just wasn't hungry. It wasn't that I wasn't feeling well — nor was it that I had a ton of energy to dispense — it was rather this unexplainable energy inside of me. I meditated to see if it would help me to see what was happening. In the middle of the meditation, I 'looked' down (mentally) to see this energy in my torso. It appeared to be like a diffuse star or ball of energy that had the color of the sun. I wrote all that I could about the energy and explained that I was drinking lots of water, and sometimes drank juice, but that was the extent of it.

That evening I got the reply,

"Dear Riz.

Not to worry – as far as I can tell, you are experiencing an energetic phenomenon, not a physical one.

Many practitioners of Chi Kung in China also experience this state — which they call biku — where they fill themselves up with an energy that makes food unnecessary for a period of time, because their body relies on the energy. Different people react differently to the energy of the desert - this is how your body reacted – by picking up some of the energy of the desert and bringing it back with you.

A person can go 'biku' for a day or for months on end. The key is to listen to the wisdom of your body. If you are feeling weak, or lightheaded, then eat. If you are feeling hungry, then eat. If you are not feeling hungry, then don't eat. Don't force yourself to eat because of cultural norms. However, be sure to drink plenty of water as your body needs it. The juice is also a good idea – try orange juice, cranberry juice, and apple juice in particular. The biku effect, if you're like others who work in our western society, will wear off of its own accord.

I'm still in the San Diego area and won't be back for some time. Good luck and I'll see you when I'm back."

Several days later, after five days of not eating, I walked by a grocery store and had a craving for an apple. I went in and bought one and ate it. That was my meal for that day. Over the next week, I slowly started craving food again, a little bit more each time, and I noticed the energy of the desert, which I had captured in my torso, was getting dimmer and dimmer.

By the end of my second week back, I couldn't sense it anymore, and was back to eating normally. Slowly, my attention had come back to the world. Once again, I focused most of my attention back on building the company, Brainstorm Technologies. The energy of the desert had faded.

CHAPTER SUMMARY
THE HUNGRY DESERT

It is important to find Places of Power using your built-in Energy Detection System.

The Career Warrior thinks about energy all the time, and not just in relation to the human body. If you go to certain places, you will notice that the energy in these places is stronger than the energy in many other places. These are Places of Power.

There are two types of Power Places: Natural and Man-Made. Natural Power Places usually are at the intersection of lines of energy that were referred to as *ley* lines in ancient times, or the result of some natural structure like a mountain, ridge, or valley. Man-Made Power Places exist because a certain number of people have been thinking the same kinds of thoughts in that place for a long time. Sometimes, a Power Place is a combination of these two types. Whatever the cause, it's important to be able to tap into the feeling of a place and to determine if it's a power spot for you.

A Power Place can induce positive or negative feelings in your built-in Energy Detection System, which is really your body. The question to ask yourself is: how do I feel in this location? Some Power Places have bad energy and make you feel like leaving right away. It's not that it's "bad" by nature, but it is incompatible with where you are right now. Others are very healing and you find yourself wanting to stay there for an extended time.

Take a Warrior's Trip to a Power Place by getting away from your daily life for a few days.

Places of Power which are remote and that have had few people in them over the years have a purer energy, and it is worth visiting those places on trips specifically intended for this purpose as a kind of energetic pilgrimage. The purpose of a Warrior's Trip is to commune with the energy of a place, get perspective on your life, and open up to your spiritual self.

You don't have to have a guide, or do an all-night desert trip like the one described in this chapter. You can do a Warrior's Trip staying at a seedy budget motel in the desert, or at a five-star resort — the important thing is your intent and your state of mind.

Of course, during the trip, you will want to leave the resort (or the motel) to find the Place of Power and use your intuition once you get there to locate specific Power Spots. Since energy is gradated, it's possible to find a Power Spot in almost any part of the world, but certain places rank relatively higher for a Warrior's Trip. It's more about setting your intent and following certain protocols to turn an ordinary trip into a visionary one.

Everyone needs time away from their daily lives to refresh. For most people, it's about seeing the sites, drinking at a resort with friends, hanging out in the pool or scuba diving. For the Career Warrior, a Warrior's Trip to a Place of Power is an important spiritual journey, no less holy than say, a trip to Mecca or Jerusalem or Bethlehem or Benares.

Remember, the hidden worlds leave clues in the physical world, and there is no better clue than the inherent energy of a place.

Two places that are particularly powerful and cleansing for the aura and are good for Warrior's Trips are the Desert and the Ocean. The warm desert gale and the cool ocean breeze are great for cleansing your auric field, and getting perspective on your life and work. Sometimes, it's critical to get this perspective, or just to renew. There are numerous desert places in the American Southwest, like Sedona, Arizona, (a great one that is very accessible, though it's gotten more crowded over the years). As for the Ocean, some of the Hawaiian islands are among the best places in the U.S. for this type of trip, but there are numerous places on all coasts that are not too crowded.

Find a Power Spot in a Place of Power

Of course just being in the Desert or near the Ocean isn't enough. You have to find a specific spot that is higher energy than the norm in that area. This can be an occult task of the highest order. A place like Sedona has many "energy vortices" – buttes and valleys that have been identified and have been written about in local guides. More powerful than following some instruction in a book (or a tour guide) is to find a spot that you are led to through your own intuition. Once again: follow the *clues*.

As an example, while I was working on the second edition of this book, I was vacationing in Hawaii. Driving around the island, my companion and I were led to a certain resort location (which was not where we were staying). After walking around the edge of this resort area, I noticed a particular patch of rocky coastline that called to me which was a little cumbersome to get to.

Following my intuition, I went there alone (remember *clues* are very individual). I ended up discovering an incredible Power Spot. How did I know it was a Power Spot? For one thing, I could feel the energy – it was unmistakable. How did I find it? I followed the clues. When the surf splashed up against the rocks, every now and then I would see, just for an instant, a rainbow. Since a rainbow had appeared to me in a dream the night before, I took it as a clue and followed these rainbows to see where they would lead.

It turns out that there had been a Native ceremony performed in that exact spot not too long before and remnants of the ceremony were still there. Off to the side, there was even a plaque that this was a sacred spot to the Hawaiians traditionally and they discouraged outsiders from going there. I didn't feel like I was trespassing, though, since the Power Spot had called me there. I didn't have to stay long – I soaked in the energy (and whatever messages it had for me), and then was on my way.

Some Protocols and Suggestions for Warrior's Trips:

I won't call these rules – they are rather suggestions for preparing for and taking a Warrior's Trip:

1. Set your intention beforehand that this will be a spiritual trip.
2. Take time and energy away from your daily life.
3. Try to clean up loose ends before you go.
4. Try to go during a natural Time of Power (equinoxes and solstices are great times).
5. Bring along books about Yoga, meditation, shamanism, or other spiritual journeys on your trip. These will help you to stay in the right mindset.
6. A Warrior's Trip is not about socializing or partying,

though you can certainly go with like-minded people.

7. Be sure to meditate or tune into the energy and environment. Pay particular attention to how you feel about a place during the day, at twilight/dawn, and at night.

8. Follow the *clues* to find Power Spots.

9. Keep a journal and write down what insights come to you during your trip,

10. Notice how your energy has changed when you first come back to the World.

13 ACTING VS. SINGING
JULY, 1994

"Issues? What issues?" I asked. "I would think that not eating for a week is an issue, wouldn't you?"

"No, not really," he replied calmly. "Not if you were *biku*. Don't worry. There are many strange things that will happen to you on the meditative path, the path of *energy*, that will seem odd and inexplicable to our friends in *respectable* western society." He looked around and pointed to the restaurant around us.

Ramaswami and I had just finished lunch at the Ritz-Carlton near the Boston Commons. The Commons is Boston's version of a nicer, gentler Central Park. It's a large park area in the heart of Boston, surrounded by buildings on all sides. There are a number of small ponds and geese, and walking there during the day is a great way to relieve stress.

Ramaswami had just finished grilling me with questions regarding my physical health. This was a few weeks after the desert trip. I was now eating regularly again, after studying my aura for a few minutes, he seemed to be satisfied that there was no real abnormality to my experience of not eating for a few days. Now he wanted to talk about *issues*.

"It could be any kind of issue," he said. "I lived in LA for many years, and everyone has a therapist out there," he continued, laughing. "We're used to dealing with our *issues!*"

I didn't find this funny at all. In my view of the world, therapists were for people who had problems, not for normal, dedicated, ambitious people like me. I was shocked to hear that he had a therapist!

He continued without missing a beat: "It could be a personal issue, like with a significant other, or a physical issue, or a psychological issue, or even your favorite..." he smiled and paused before continuing, "...a career or job-related issue. A desert trip has a tendency to bring out one or more issues to the forefront of our lives, or our relationships, or our work.

"That's why I don't recommend *desert trips* too often. They can be hazardous to your relationships because they force you to deal with issues that you might otherwise have suppressed."

I thought about it for a few minutes as we walked into the park. He mentioned that he had to be at a meeting downtown in a little while and couldn't stay. Meanwhile, he wanted me to keep him informed if any particular 'issue' seemed to rear its ugly head more than once.

"Remember," he concluded, "to look for clues. Clues can come from all directions, and if they repeat, they are probably important."

I wasn't comfortable talking about *personal* issues, so I immediately shifted the conversation away from me personally and started talking about the company. "One issue that seems to be coming up again and again in the company is the tradeoff between consulting vs. products."

"Oh?" he asked, suddenly very interested.

"I want us to start a consulting group," I continued. "That's what we brought Irfan into the company for, but we also have this issue of building the next product."

"That's a complicated business issue," he said matter-of-factly, "that really requires looking at your goals for the business. I can't spend too much more time on it now, but it is worth a more in-depth conversation with me, and some introspection on your own. As we meditate, we begin to see that the world around us is really a mirror for our own *issues, beliefs,* and even our *karma.* This is one example of an *internal issue* manifesting in the world around us!"

I quickly locked onto a single word that he had just said. "Karma?" I asked incredulous. Of course I had heard the term, and took it to mean 'having done something in your past life that comes back to bite you.'

"Think of it this way," he continued, his tone still matter-of-fact and refusing to acknowledge my incredulity. "This issue, because it keeps coming up, reveals an issue within yourself. That's what I want you to think about ... not just the external issue, but its counterpart: your *internal issue*. This issue could come from this lifetime or could come from a previous lifetime," he finished.

I told him emphatically that I didn't believe in past-lives and this seemed like a ridiculous topic to talk about when analyzing a serious 'business' issue. "Are you telling me I'm going to come back as a goat?" I laughed disdainfully.

He smiled. "My, my, touchy, aren't we? It's true that most of the Judeo-Christian religions no longer believe in past lives," he said, again pointing to the people around us. I assumed this meant that most of them were Christians. "But just because the people around you don't believe in something doesn't mean that it doesn't exist!"

He could see that I wasn't buying it. "I suppose next you're going to tell me that Aliens from Atlantis are going to land here!" I said, chuckling and shaking my head dismissively.

Just then a young woman interrupted us. She looked like she was in her late twenties, a few years older than me, but definitely younger than Ramaswami. "Excuse me," she said, hesitatingly. "I ... I ..." she looked at Ramaswami and didn't know what to say. "I had to say hello..." and she bowed her head to him.

I was jarred out of my mocking tone and state of disbelief.

"Have we met?" he asked her, smiling and winking at me mischievously.

She stared at him for a moment, and then at me, and then back at him. "I ... think so...but I can't quite remember. I'm Alice," she said and extended her hand.

He shook it with a smile. He was enjoying this little exchange, while I watched with a furrowed brow, trying to figure out exactly what was going on.

"Let me rephrase that," he said, gently touching her arm, still smiling. "Have we met ... in this lifetime or a previous lifetime?"

She smiled, as if this made perfect sense to her, nodding. I began to wonder if he had staged this entire encounter.

He closed his eyes and seemed to be scanning her auric field, though I still had no idea how he did this with his eyes closed. She just stood there, smiling, as if she was basking in some kind of glow. I stood next to them, suddenly feeling like I was the one intruding, even though Ramaswami and I had been having lunch, and she had just shown up.

Finally, he opened his eyes, nodding. "Yes, yes, that's it. Do you meditate?" he asked her.

Alice answered slowly. "Well, I've tried to learn about it several times, but haven't been able to stick with it."

"Well, you're probably drawn to the hidden worlds, just like my young engineer friend here," he said, pointing to me and chuckling. "The fact is, Alice, you have studied meditation with me before, though not in this lifetime..."

She had a surprised but reverential look in her face. "That's why you felt drawn to say *hello* to me just now. Do you remember when or where it was that you studied with me?" he asked.

She closed her eyes for a moment. "I feel something, like someplace that I would recognize but can't quite place ... someplace near a canal with unbelievably large buildings nearby. It doesn't seem like a real place and it feels surreal, like some long-lost civilization."

"Like maybe..." he looked over at me with a glint in his eyes, "... like maybe ... Atlantis?"

She nodded and smiled as if this made perfect sense to her.

I couldn't believe what I was seeing or hearing. "This is ridiculous!" I protested. "You must have arranged this ... all of this ... how likely is it that she would walk up just when I said *Aliens from Atlantis*,"

She looked at me. "I definitely haven't met either of you before," and then added with a smug smile, "in this lifetime."

Ramaswami held up his hand as if to calm me down, and turned to her. "What you felt was a probably a *karmic* pull towards me. This isn't that unusual, it happens pretty often to me in large cities. If you like, you can come to my next meditation seminar." He introduced us. "This is Riz, he can tell you when the next seminar is ... I have to be off now."

He was now running late so I didn't have time to ask questions, but he promised that we would get together to look more 'deeply' into my issue related to consulting vs. products.

I was left standing there alone with Alice. We talked a little bit and I told her about my experiences thus far with Ramaswami, meditation, and some of my skepticism. To my relief, she said that she wasn't *sure* she believed in past lives or Atlantis either, but she just felt drawn to Ramaswami when she saw us talking and she had to come over and say hello. I didn't know what to make of the whole thing, but agreed to hook her up with someone like James who could teach her introductory meditation techniques.

Presently we parted and I turned my attention back to the issue that had come up, whether to build a consulting group or simply build new products. This was an important business issue for me. In fact, it would dominate the first few years of the life of Brainstorm Technologies.

We had just released version 2.0 of our product, VB/Link, to critical and customer acclaim. Once again, we were able to get all of the relevant industry magazines to write about us, including *Information Week, Communications Week, ComputerWorld,* and *InfoWorld*, and we were feeling good about the prospects of this new version. These articles helped us to look much bigger than we really were, but they had also provided the fuel for us to hire a few more people. I could honestly say that our first product, VB/Link was now in good hands as we had hired two developers just to focus on maintaining this product. We had spent the past few months mentoring them, and finally Mitch and I no longer had to do all the development work.

Now the dilemma was what to do next, especially with the free time that we had just created for ourselves.

One suggestion that I had, and felt drawn to, was to start a consulting group, as we had intended to do some time ago. The other suggestion was to build a second product, which we termed DataLink, which would link Lotus Notes into relational databases such as Oracle and SQL Server.

They both seemed like viable alternatives, but I felt inexplicably drawn to the consulting idea. When we had first started the company, I had been very against the idea of doing "consulting", partly because of Ramaswami's advice, and partly because of my own instincts. "A consulting company doesn't have as much value as a product company," I had been told, and I repeated this to Mitch at the time. In fact, consulting companies were generally valued at one times total sales, while a product company could easily be valued at three to five times total sales, which seemed like a more attractive situation.

However, as I looked at our expense and revenue model, it became clear that consulting could help tremendously with cash flow. While one copy of our product sold for $795, one consulting project could easily generate $20,000 per month per person, which could add up quickly. Given the economics of consulting vs. products, I had almost done an about-face from the early days of not wanting to do consulting. It was a debate that my business partners and I continued late one night.

"No way! There's no way we can do both ... at least not *well,*" said Irfan as he grabbed a nacho and dipped it in the guacamole. "With only Mitch and me doing development," he continued, "we can either build the next product, or we can do consulting, but there's no way we can do both!"

Irfan, Mitch, and I were sitting in the Pizzeria Uno's at Porter Square, at the end of one of our late nights at work. It was after midnight on a weekday, and this was one of the few restaurants still open in Cambridge.

"What if," I suggested, still trying to have it all, "Irfan does the next product, and Kirk does the consulting, and Mitch keeps helping to build the old product?"

Mitch objected right away. "Kirk has to do technical support and sales for our existing product! He can't do consulting!" He was right, of course. Kirk was the only one of us in the office before 10 or 11 a.m. (or noon some days), and he was quite busy handling both technical support and sales, which I helped him with when I could.

"And," continued Irfan, "if we're going to build a new product, Mitch will have to help with it. One person isn't enough to build a whole product! This product is more complicated than our first product, and it took both of you guys working full-time to build that."

"Hmm..." I nodded, and grabbed a nacho myself. This was actually a typical management meeting for us, "management by pizza". We would sit at a restaurant late at night, exploring an important business issue. Eventually, we would rule out items that were clearly impossible, and decide on a course of action before we had finished our pizza. It wasn't a very mature management style, but it worked quite well for us at the time.

"Your food's here," interrupted the waitress. *Just in time, I* thought, as I grabbed the last of the nachos. After the experience with the desert, my appetite had come back and I was back on my start-up diet of pizza and Coke.

We abandoned our management discussion for a moment and started talking about other topics. We talked about Kirk, who had said he was actually going on a date that night. Mitch looked at his watch and laughed. "I should call Kirk! If he answers then his date didn't go so well!"

"Enough about Kirk and his date," I said, getting us back to the issue at hand. "Let's see if we can make headway on this consulting vs. products issue."

"If we only do consulting," started Mitch, in between bites of his food, "then we're not building any real value in the company. Sure we'll get some cash, but at the end of the month, we won't have built any technology that we could sell."

I explained the difference in the numbers: $20,000 per month for consulting vs. $795 per each product.

"Yeah, but," continued Irfan. "if we spend the next few months building this product, we all think we can easily sell $1 million of this product in the next 12 months, which is much more valuable than just doing consulting work."

"You said so yourself," chimed in Mitch. "That we can't build value as quickly in a consulting company as we can with a product company."

"Hmm..." I said, chewing my food and trying to see if there was some way to maneuver around this argument. It seemed, again and again, that building the next product was a better idea than starting a consulting group. "So consulting is better short-term, but the product is better long-term, right?" I asked. They both agreed and the choice seemed clear for the moment: we would start on our next product.

Yet for some reason over the next few days, the consulting group idea kept bothering me. I decided I would ask Ramaswami about it. I knew that he too would recommend building a new product rather than starting a consulting group. He agreed to meet me for breakfast at an expensive place in Harvard Square.

"I agree that is the right choice logically. But why, then," I asked, "am I so intrigued by doing consulting? It seems that I can't stop thinking of it. Every few months, it comes up again. It's almost as if this is a clue, a message from the hidden worlds." I was trying to bring a spiritual element into the discussion and had begun to think of the business more in this way.

"It may be a clue. But it may not be the kind of clue you think it is," he said.

"Huh? What do you mean? There are different types of clues?"

"If I remember correctly," he started calmly, "before you started the company, you considered doing a consulting company, didn't you?"

I admitted that we had.

"And why did you decide not to do that?"

"Well, for one, product companies are worth more," I explained. He nodded. In fact, he was probably the one who had first told me about the difference in valuations between product companies and service companies.

"And..." I said, trailing off.

"Yes, and what??"

"Well, I was already doing contracting at the time, which is like consulting, and I thought it would be more fun and more interesting to build a product. It was something new."

He smiled but didn't say anything. He held up his hands as if to say: "Well, there you are!"

"What are you implying?" I asked.

"Let me give you an analogy," he started, putting down his

fork. "I'm from LA. There's an old saying in the entertainment industry: All actors want to be singers."

He nodded his head as if he'd made a profound point, picked up his fork and knife and started eating again.

I was confused. "Huh? I don't get it. What do actors wanting to be singers have to do with our consulting vs. products issue?"

His mouth was full when he mumbled something else about actors and singers.

"Huh?" I said again.

He sighed, as if I was being really dull and he had to spell everything out for me. "That's an important dynamic that we find in the entertainment industry."

"Like who?" I asked, not imagining that any big-name actors would want to be singers.

"That's not important. It's just a *saying*."

"Oh." I said, and sipped my orange juice. I still wasn't sure where he was going with this.

"But that's only part of the saying. The other part, which is very important to you, is this," and he paused for effect. I stopped drinking and paid full attention.

"All singers want to be actors."

He nodded again and resumed his breakfast.

"Huh? Wait a minute, I thought you said that all actors wanted to be singers? Now you're saying all singers want to be actors? So which is it?"

He nodded as he kept eating.

"That doesn't make any sense," I protested again.

"Oh yes, it does," he said. "It makes perfect sense, and it applies equally well to the software industry. The point is this: each thinks that life on the other side is somehow easier. It's as if the grass is always greener doing something else. This is a personality trait of people with energetic configurations like yours..."

I remained silent as I pondered what he was saying.

"When you were doing contracting, you wanted to build a product. Now that you've successfully built a product, you want to do consulting. Not because it's the best thing to do for the company, because it's *your energetic pattern* ..."

I was stunned as it all started to make sense.

"It is a clue. It's a clue that your underlying beliefs are influencing your patterns, and it's difficult, if not impossible to fight against a pattern, unless we change the underlying beliefs that formed that pattern."

He had now gone into a realm that I didn't understand.

"Most of these types of beliefs come from past lives. It's also a personality trait of Sagittarians ..." he said, smiling.

"What?" I said loudly. "Are you talking about *astrology* and *reincarnation* again?"

"Absolutely, my young engineering minded friend. Astrology, the Tarot, these are all ancient sciences that we don't at all understand anymore. We ridicule them and don't pay any attention to them and treat them as mythical structures. But like most mythical structures, there are kernels of truth in each of them. You can experience this kernel of truth yourself, if you open your mind."

Now I was flabbergasted. Patterns I could accept. Energy I could accept. But Astrology was *out of the question* for a scientific-minded individual like me. It was in the realm of 'fantasy' and past lives fell in the realm of 'religion.'

I told him that I didn't think *fantasy* and *religion* had anything to do with my company's core issue of deciding what to do next.

"Sure they do. Of course they do. Nothing happens in isolation. Everything is related. Remember Alice? Do you think that was a coincidence that she approached us, just at the time that we were having this discussion?"

I groaned. I did remember the situation with Alice. It was odd, I had to admit, but I just didn't know what to make of it. I guess there were millions of people in the world who believed in past lives in the east, so I had to grudgingly admit that it was *at least possible*, even if I had been brought up to believe that they didn't exist.

While it seemed an appropriate discussion for a theology class, I wasn't comfortable talking about it in a business context. I looked around the restaurant. It was a haven for "power breakfast" meetings, and venture capitalists and businesspersons in all industries, dressed in suits, surrounded us.

"So I think," I started, avoiding the astrology and past life issues, changing the subject, but paying attention to the patterns, "that this is a clue that I am being tested, right?"

He smiled. "It's a clue to help you recognize your pattern and see if you can transcend it…"

I sighed. "So, we'll do another product, because it will help keep focus in the company and seems like the least trouble of the two paths we could take."

"Well done," he said. "But you really should deal with the underlying belief system here."

"How do I do that?" I asked, not sure what he meant by underlying belief systems.

"You could do energy work, you could talk to someone, do Yoga or other inner work."

"Talk to someone? You mean like a therapist? No way!" I replied, and became quiet and finished my breakfast. I almost felt as if he had insulted me.

He laughed and was suddenly his usual cheery self. "Okay, okay, let's forget about that. Tell me a little about your new product."

I immediately became cheerful again as I described DataLink, which was to be our second product, and would leverage what we had learned with our first product. Though we might do a random consulting project here or there, I concluded, we would hold off on building a large "consulting group" for now so that we could focus in our next product.

CHAPTER SUMMARY
ACTING VS. SINGING

Every business has a critical choice or issue in its first few years.
In our case, we were in the Enterprise Software market (though we didn't even know to call it that at the time). In this market, a core issue is usually about whether to be a product company, or a consulting/services company.

Because enterprises are so different, they usually have custom requests surrounding any implementation, and these can be very lucrative opportunities. In fact, IT departments are often willing to pay much more for services than they are on software – anywhere from two, or in our case ten times as much for services. This creates an existential dilemma: did we want to be a service company or a product company? This wasn't a purely academic issue. These two types of companies are structured very differently, are viewed by investors differently, and are valued differently. Also, it takes very different skill sets to run a service company (which is all about managing people and billable hours and skill sets) than to run a software product company (which is about the technology and features and distribution).

Each business faces its own decision like this, which is relevant to its specific market. Years later, as I was running a mobile game startup, we had similar issues come up: did we want to create games or just publish them? They both represent different parts of the value chain. A developer's core skills are in building games and content; a publisher's core skills are usually in marketing and distributing games. In TV terms, did we want to be the TV channel or the producer of a TV show?

There is no right answer to this kind of core issue, but to be successful as a startup you usually have to choose one business model or the other. And if you choose one and it's not going well (or even if it's going moderately well), then you might want to consider pivoting to the other one. Either way, you'll have to make a choice. Like they say in Hollywood, all actors want to be singers and all singers want to be actors.

The critical issue that your business faces is most likely directly related to your unique Energetic Pattern.

In this chapter, the issue of "acting vs. singing", which occurs for most businesses in some form, was particularly heightened by my own Energetic Pattern of wanting to move on to the Next Big Thing. In every industry and in almost every career, there is "another face" of that career where the grass always seems greener to someone with my particular energetic configuration.

As I said in the chapter: "I understand this to be the logical choice, to focus on products, but then why am I so intrigued by wanting to do consulting?" It was as if I was drawn to this other form of our business like a moth to a flame.

This feeling of intrigue is enough to make it a *clue*. This clue, however, wasn't pointing in a specific direction that I should go; rather, it was clearly pointing to my Energetic Pattern. Someone with a different Energetic Pattern might not be drawn so inexplicably to the "grass is always greener" aspect of this problem.

Our businesses (and our careers) are a result of the choices we make in response to the environment, and the way we make these decisions is very much based on our Energetic Patterns.

Just because you or I don't believe in past lives, or Aliens, or the Lost Continent of Atlantis, or even Nirvana, doesn't mean that they don't exist.

In this chapter, just as I was about to ridicule the idea of past lives, simply because I was brought up in a culture that didn't believe in them, a chance occurrence made me re-evaluate. This was a perfect example of a synchronicity. Ramaswami and I were just discussing and thinking about past lives and Atlantis, when an apparently random external coincidence related exactly to what we were talking about occurred. Most synchronicities aren't so dramatic – there is simply some relation between an inner event/thought to an outer event.

This synchronicity was a *clue* that I was being too closed-minded based on my own personal history and cultural and scientific background. The same might apply to the idea of God, Angels, Atlantis, UFO's or even Aliens. As Shakespeare wrote, "There are more things, Horatio, in heaven and earth, than dreamed about in your philosophy." If that were written today, we'd replace the word philosophy with "science."

Like the head of the US Patent Office who resigned in the early 1900's because "there was very little left to invent", we assume that the state of science at any given point of time (i.e. like today) is 90% of the way there. In other words, we almost understand everything and there's just a little bit left on our current course. But *time* proves that to be an erroneous conclusion as the years march on and entirely new fields of science and technology are discovered.

As a Career Warrior, the best thing to do when confronted with ideas that our society has pre-conceptions about is to keep an open mind, and let the evidence speak for itself. This was in fact, what the Buddha taught — that we should withhold judgment on many things and only believe or not believe it when we have direct experience of it.

14 TIMES OF POWER
OCTOBER, 1994

"So I take it you think that Astrology is a bunch of complete hogwash?" asked Ramaswami, as a woman with a black cloak passed us by. She had a symbol on her cloak, a pentagram, that was easily associated with witchcraft, and for those of us uninitiated, something sinister.

Ramaswami had just explained to me that the pentagram was not a satanic symbol by any means, but the upside-down pentagram had been adopted by a rogue group of "Satanists", which had given it a bad rap. A pentagram right side up, like the one on this woman's cloak, was indicative of the five elements: earth, air, fire, water, and spirit.

Wicca (or witchcraft as it is more commonly known) was actually a very 'holistic' religion that respected nature, he explained, and had little to do with "Satan', which was essentially a Judeo-Christian concept.

It was a natural fit, he continued, that a burgeoning student of energy and meditation like me should be interested in Wicca. Somehow the idea of studying 'witchcraft' didn't seem particularly appealing to me, nor did I see how it was relevant to the "Path of the Career Warrior."

Somehow the conversation had shifted to Astrology, which I had vehemently denounced as being simply "old wives tales" in front of him more than once in the past, echoing the views of major scientists of our day, including Carl Sagan and others.

We were in Salem, Massachusetts, on a brisk October

afternoon. The leaves had begun to turn brilliant colors and were falling from proud trees, a sign that the New England autumn was in full swing. It was quite crowded in Salem that afternoon – the fall was the busiest season for this famous seaside town. Much of the town had been redone to restore some of the "historic quaintness" that New England towns are famous for but many have lost.

"Of course I think it's a bunch of hogwash!" I answered. I had to admit that I was quite disappointed in him for believing in such 'silly' things. "I don't believe that the sun, moon, planets, and the stars have anything to do with our behavior here on earth!"

He listened patiently and nodded.

"Hmm..." he said in a mockingly-thoughtful tone, and we continued walking along the red line in the sidewalk.

The red line indicated that we were walking along the 'freedom trail', a mark for tourists in New England that was meant to link historic sites. The original "freedom trail" was in downtown Boston, and meant to mark Paul Revere's ride at the beginning of the Revolutionary War. It was soon expanded to include other historic landmarks. Salem was nowhere near these sites in downtown Boston, but the red line in the sidewalk had been expanded to mean 'this will take any tourist with money to good tourist locations in New England.'

We walked along it and noticed the Witch Museum, which had wax replicas of many of the events of the famous Salem witch trials of the seventeenth century. As I had never been, Ramaswami changed the subject and we went into the museum. The show was quite dramatic, and I was struck by how carried away everyone in the town had gotten in order for such a tragedy to happen. Dozens of innocent people were hanged because they were misunderstood and because of the preoccupation in Puritan society with 'Satan' and 'witchcraft.'

"It was a strange time," he remarked after we had left the museum, "with belief in superstition and witches and *ghosts!*" As he said ghosts he used the same disdainful tone that I had used when saying astrology. He chuckled and suddenly became serious again.

"It wasn't the belief in these things that was odd," he replied.

"We've believed in ghosts for a very long time ... and it's easy to verify that spirits do actually exist in the hidden worlds. But it was rather that the consciousness here got carried away! The group consciousness had such an astrological configuration at this particular time, in this particular place, which made it ideal for them to..."

"Yeah right," I said, interrupting him as we entered the Hawthorne hotel restaurant for tea. The Hawthorne is a well-known historic hotel just across the street from the Witch Museum that was named for one of the most famous sons of Salem, novelist Nathaniel Hawthorne. "There you go with that astrology stuff again..."

He laughed. "You don't have to believe in astrology to understand that there are 'times of power', just like there are 'places of power'. You didn't believe in those before either, did you?"

I understood what Ramaswami and others called 'places of power'– areas where multiple 'ley lines' or 'power lines' intersected, resulting in a higher energetic vibration in that place. These places attracted or repelled certain kinds of people. Although I was a bit skeptical at first, I had to admit that it was possible, because this idea could easily be based on the earth's magnetic field. More importantly, I had begun to be more aware of 'how I felt' in different places, becoming more aware of the 'aura' of the place. The desert trip in the summer had reinforced this concept and I was now very open to it.

"Is Salem a *power spot*?" I asked.

"Yes, and no. It has a very powerful energy, but that energy has changed for the positive as more and more real Wiccans have moved here. Recently, it's become more of a tourist destination, which always softens the energy of a place. You might think of it as a soft *power spot*!"

Few subjects are held in as much contempt by modern science as astrology, I explained to him. Though I wasn't officially a scientist, my engineer's training led me to at least want to follow a quasi-scientific argument when dealing with the hidden worlds.

I went on to explain why I thought astrology was based on ridiculous assumptions, and how it was simply a classification scheme that was meaningless because all it took into account was the month that the person was born in. "There are millions of people born each month, are you telling me they're all the same? You might as well believe that the full moon causes people to turn into werewolves!" I finished my argument with a hint of haughtiness that would have made my fellow MIT alumni proud.

Ramaswami just smiled, with a twinkle in his eye and nodded.

A waitress came by and we were about to order, when I noticed Ramaswami close his eyes and gaze at the waitress. I ordered, and she put her hand on her hip while she waited for him to come out of his 'trance.'

He suddenly opened his eyes and smiled. He ordered, and then said to the waitress, "Excuse me – didn't you work at the hospital?"

She got a confused look about her, then smiled. "Yes, I did. How did you know? I used to be a nurse! But it's been years since I was..."

He dodged her question and followed up with another one. "As a nurse, I was wondering if you wouldn't mind answering a question for my young engineer friend here..." he pointed to me.

I tried to look innocent as she looked over and studied me.

"Is there a particular time of the month that the emergency room is busier than usual?" he asked.

She laughed. "*You betcha.* Every time there's a full moon, we get all kinds of crazies. There may not be werewolves in the world, but I tell you, there's plenty of loonies, and they all seem to come out at the time of the full moon."

We chatted for a few minutes, and she gave examples of how the number of patients and the types of emergencies swelled during full moons. "I wouldn't have believed it if I hadn't seen it myself!" she replied, putting her hand on her hip again and shaking her head. "But you can count on it, like clockwork."

"Now," Ramaswami turned to me after she had left, "you could ask any nurse in a big city that same question and they'll tell you that during the full moon – no illusion – real evidence that the number of cases goes up. Every time."

"How did you know she was a nurse?" I asked. "Have you seen her in a hospital around here?"

"No, I wasn't really at the hospital. She had the kind of auric configuration of someone who's spent a lot of time in hospitals, so I thought she might be a nurse. That was simply a message from the universe — a confirmation of the message I'm trying to get across to you — about *times of power*."

I was confused and showed it, so he felt compelled to explain what he meant. "The Universe brought us a nurse just when we needed her! Quite a coincidence, eh?"

I was fascinated by this topic of his knowing that she had been a nurse and wanted to explore it further, but Ramaswami wanted to stick to the "moon and stars."

"Okay, so what if there are additional visits to the emergency room during a full moon?" I asked.

"Well, you just got done telling me that the moon and stars couldn't have an effect on human behavior, but here's a concrete example of how it does."

I thought about this as our waitress delivered my tea and his coffee. "The moon affects the tides," I explained, "through a gravitational influence. Maybe even a magnetic one," I answered, not entirely sure of my answer.

"Aha! Magnets again!" he laughed. "I'm beginning to think everything is a magnet, isn't it?" he smiled.

"Similarly," I continued. "It's not at all inconceivable that the moon can affect certain individual's fluids, inside their body, or their magnetic field. These chemical changes could result in changes in behavior ... mental instability ... explaining how or why the cases of injury and emergency room visitors go up." I smiled, quite proud of how my 'quasi-scientific explanation' fit together.

"Magnetic fields?" he laughed as he nibbled on a muffin. "You mean their auras, right?"

"Yes, fine, their auras," I replied. "The moon is close enough that it can actually have an effect, BUT – that doesn't prove astrology has any basis whatsoever!" I was adamant on this point. The stars and the planets, I explained were too far away to have any impact. The concept of astrology was based on planetary configurations when a person was born, and I found this totally unacceptable.

"The ancient *science* of astrology is actually a much more complex science than you think it is. It's not a simple classification of people into twelve categories. That's just what you see in the *horoscope* section of the paper. That's pure entertainment and has very little to do with real astrology, which has to do with the psychological makeup of a person. Remember, the hidden worlds leave clues, and everything is related. The ancient art or science of astrology is to look for those clues in the wide world. In their case, they looked up at the heavens at the time and place of your birth to reveal what might be happening behind the scenes."

I had been scowling at him, thinking of more arguments as to why astrology was a bunch of hogwash.

"Okay ... okay," he laughed and took a sip of his coffee. "Let's not worry about astrology right now. In fact, let's assume that it's a bunch of hogwash..."

I breathed a sigh of relief. I had no problem *assuming* it was a bunch of hogwash, I actually *believed* that it was.

"Are you going to have an anniversary party for Brainstorm this year?" he asked.

"I'm not sure..." I replied.

"This is an important time for the company, isn't it?" he continued.

"Well, yes it is, we are going on our one-year anniversary, and we have just released our second product, DataLink."

"I would go further ... and say that that not only is this an important time for the company, it's important for you personally, wouldn't you agree?"

"I'm not sure I follow...?" I was confused again and unsure where he was going.

"This is a *time of power* for you – early October, isn't it?"

"A *time of power*?" Now I was confused again.

"A *time of power*," he started explaining, "is a time that is particularly conducive to a particular individual, or even a group of individuals. This time, the first few weeks in October, is a time of power for you. Your energetic configuration reacts very well to the change in season, partly because you like change. You should celebrate it!"

"My birthday isn't for a few months..." I replied, thinking that's what he was referring to.

"No, no, it's not about your birthday, it's about times of year that are conducive to your spiritual and professional development."

"I don't get it. What is so special about this time of year?" I didn't see where he was going at all.

"A *time of power* is like a *place of power,* only instead of being related to the axis of space, it's related to the axis of time! Your auric configuration reacts well to certain energies in certain places. Similarly, as the earth goes through the seasons, there is a different energy in the air, and you react to it differently!"

I was frowning again.

"It's not that the first two weeks of October are particularly special in and of themselves. It's that they're a *time of power* for you, at least at this point in your life."

I thought about it for a few minutes and didn't say anything.

"Okay, let's start with the obvious. Let's look for evidence," he said. "Is anything special happening for you these first few weeks of October this year?"

I answered that we just released our second product, DataLink, which was a big step forward for the company, this week.

"Aha, a major step for you and for the company, no?"

"Yes, but that doesn't automatically mean that this is a *time of power*," I replied, worried that this was sounding much too close to a 'horoscope' and that we were about to go down the rabbit-hole of astrology again.

"And, the development of this product was the resolution of a major issue you were struggling with — whether to be an *actor* or a *singer*, right?" I nodded. This was true. We had resolved our products vs. consulting issue earlier by deciding to stick with products for now.

"And a year ago, what were you doing?" he asked, not letting up.

I thought about it. I had to admit that it was in the first week of October a year ago, that I decided to start the company — marking a point of major professional and spiritual change for me. During the second week of October, we actually started working on our first product, officially launching the company in our living room.

"See," he replied, taking another sip of tea and looking smug. "At this point in your life, this is an important time for you. You should celebrate it!"

When I didn't put up a fuss, he continued. "And what were you doing two years ago the first week of October? Was it a time of professional or spiritual transition?" he asked.

"Two years ago..." I tried to remember. In fact, at the end of September two years earlier, I had quit my job while on an assignment in Europe. I traveled around for a few weeks and spent a lot of time writing and reflecting on life. It was then that I had decided that it would be good to be involved in a start-up. I had quit my job with a consulting company, and decided to return to the US and joined DiVA Corporation. Not only was it a time of career transition, but that decision had unknowingly led to my encounter with James at the meditation studio, which was next door to DiVA.

"That would qualify!" he said as he finished his coffee. "See, as I said, this is definitely a *time of power* for you! You can use the anniversary of Brainstorm as a reason to mark this time for your celebration. When you want to transition to something new, this is a good time for you..."

"But I don't want to transition to something new," I explained, "I'm happy running my company!"

He laughed. "I didn't say that you should leave your company! I said that if you want to do something new, this is a good time for you. This is a good time to start or to release a new product, for example. It's a *time of power* for you ... remember that!"

We had finished our coffee and tea, and left the restaurant to walk around, amidst many tourists and falling leaves, as I thought about this.

"The Path of the Career Warrior, my young skeptical friend, is about developing *awareness*. Eventually, we want to develop an awareness of the hidden worlds. This isn't so easy to do in a flash, so to help us we look to the world around us. What happens in the hidden worlds leaves clues all around us, in both our inner and outer lives. How do you find those clues? You become aware of patterns in your life.

"Awareness doesn't just happen, it has to be developed over time. The Career Warrior is particularly attuned to the *Energy of Places* and the *Energy of Times*. Examine your life, find out how you feel at different times — times of day, times of the month, times of the year. Is it easier to get things done at a certain time of year? When the Career Warrior develops an awareness of our feelings at different places and different times, we start to become aware of the hidden worlds in an intuitive way. Then, we can use this information to follow our own Warrior's Path."

I wasn't sure that I believed what he was saying about October being a *time of power* for me, and I definitely didn't put any credence in astrology, but I did have to admit that major transitions seemed to happen at that time of year for me. As I was only in the second year of my professional career, it was hard to validate his theory. It was also hard to refute it since each year I had a major transition going on at that time.

Later that week, I took all of our ten employees out to dinner, marking the first anniversary of Brainstorm's founding. We did it each subsequent year that I was CEO of the company, marking it as an important time for us. In later years, I would readily admit that the first or second week of October was a '*time of power*' for me, automatically making it a time of power for any company that I was involved in. After all, a company, I was learning, is really a reflection of the inner lives of the key people.

CHAPTER SUMMARY
TIMES OF POWER

A Time of Power is a time when the current flows with you rather than against you.

In this chapter, we discussed how a Career Warrior learns to develop more awareness of the hidden worlds by tuning into the Energy of Times. Are there certain times of day that are easier for you to get work done? Are there times of day when you are more creative? How about your coworkers and friends?

These questions have different answers, depending on who you ask. Ramaswami would say that people with different Energetic Patterns will find it easier to work late at night or early in the morning, for example.

Similarly, as the moon moves around the Earth in approximately a month, you'll find that certain times of the month make certain endeavors – career or spiritual or personal – easier or more difficult. Finally, you might even notice that certain times of year bring with them a whole set of feelings and issues and Energy that can impede or enhance your ability to get things done, and the flow of the seasons has to do with this.

It is also possible that you have entered, for some inexplicable reason, a Time of Power in your life. This is less structured than the natural, recurring times of power. For example, you might find that a particular Year becomes the Year of Living Dangerously for you, while other years are Years of Living Conservatively.

The key then is to learn to use your Energy Detection Device (i.e. your body) and clues in the world around you to uncover the Times of Power that work best for you.

There are natural Times of Power that you should be aware of.

As you'll recall, the *energy of places* is based very much on the natural world, and so it is with the *energy of times*. There are some times which are naturally more powerful than others. If you pay attention, you can use these times to get energy and support for goals in your life, or tune in more deeply into the hidden worlds.

Birthdays are very powerful times of year. Rather than

setting resolutions on New Year's Day, which never seem to work out for most people, I believe it's more powerful to set them on your birthday.

Certain times of day certainly make it easier to tap into the energy of a place. For example, twilight, a time of transition between day and night, is a great time to tune into the inherent energy of a place.

The four natural holidays in the year are the transitions between the seasons: the Spring and Autumn Equinoxes, and the Summer and Winter Solstices. These are literally times of transition when the days will start getting shorter or longer — the Solstices are the longest and shortest days of the year and the energy of change is at work. You'll notice that many religions have put their holidays to be around these natural holidays. Was Jesus really born on December 25? No one knows, but it's awfully close to the natural holiday of December 21.

The full moon is also a time of power in its own right. In some Eastern traditions, the full moon is considered a spiritual holiday, despite legends of werewolves and "loonies" in the West. The Buddha is said to have reached enlightenment on a full moon, and in countries like Sri Lanka, all full moons are considered holidays for this reason! In western traditions, every full moon has a name ("the harvest moon", etc.), each of which is good for a particular purpose.

Did the Buddha really achieve enlightenment on the full moon? No one knows for certain since it occurred over 4,000 years ago, but one thing we can be sure of is that the full moon is a natural *Time of Power*.

Part III:
The Warrior's Path

15 CLEANING UP AN ENERGETIC MESS
DECEMBER, 1994

"You have to understand that everything is related ... even this picture of a tree," Ramaswami remarked as we walked into my office and he saw the Ansel Adams picture on the wall. A college friend had given it to us when we moved into our new office space.

The sun had just set on this cold winter evening, and we could see the sky darkening from the wall-length windows in my office. Just a few days earlier there had been a snowstorm (one of many that winter), and the remnants of the storm were still piled up on the side of the roads. The company had grown to over 15 people, and we were now thinking about our next product.

This *time of power*, corresponding to the first few weeks of October for me, had in fact brought about a number of changes. We were now a two-product company and this doubled the amount of demands on our time. We had just moved into new office space, located just a few blocks from MIT, and had spent the last month settling in.

The new space was 5,000 square feet, quite a bit more than we needed. While the 15 of us had been cramped in our old space (which was only 1,500 square feet), we found that this space could easily accommodate three times as many people as we had. Luckily, we found a biotech company that sub-leased us the full 5,000 square feet, but only made us pay for the amount we needed.

Although the space itself was very large, it didn't take long for my office to become cluttered with all kinds of documents, files, books, and other materials. As the CEO of this still-small-but-very-rapidly-growing company, I found myself pulled in a dozen different directions at once. Sales needed my help in closing deals. Developers needed my help with the next release of our first product, VB/Link. Luckily, Irfan and Mitch handled the second product, DataLink, which left me free to deal with operational issues.

And there were a lot of operational issues. I had to worry about cash flow. We were trying to set up international distributors. We were coordinating several marketing programs simultaneously, including ads, mailings, and conferences. On top of all that, we were constantly looking to hire good people, and the free flow of resumes into my office only added to the clutter.

Ramaswami, as usual, was dressed immaculately in a designer double-breasted suit, and seemed completely in control of himself and his environment. I had just given him a tour of the new office space, hoping to impress him with our rapid growth. *The Boston Globe*, I explained as we walked back into my office, was thinking of writing an article on us as the profile of a successful Cambridge technology start-up.

He smiled and leaned back against the little round table at one side of my office. I typically used the table for informal meetings. "Congratulations!" he said, and then crossed his arms, staring at me.

I immediately thought that he was going to give me a compliment. Something like: *Wow, that's really impressive! Not everyone could have grown a company so quickly.* That was, of course, the reaction that I got from most people as I explained our successful first year in business. Somehow, I liked and even fed on the praise.

"Congratulations," he said again, pausing. "But ... don't let it go to your head ... there's still some very important lessons to be learned here.

"You are almost, but not quite, at the point where many rapid-growth businesses begin to feel the strain and fall apart. The key to understanding this is not in some business school book, but rather in understanding Energy."

"Energy?" I asked, becoming annoyed that he hadn't complimented our performance to date.

"Do you remember when I taught you that you could turn your work into meditation?" I remembered it, but hadn't thought much about it recently, I explained. I had been very busy building the company.

"Now that you have your own business, a successful but highly disorganized business, this becomes even more important..."

"Wait, what do you mean, *disorganized*?" I asked.

"Well, for starters, look around you." He pointed to the various piles of papers spread throughout my office. They were everywhere — on my desk, on the floor, on top of the file cabinet.

"How can you deduce," I said, a bit miffed that he wasn't reacting with the praise I was expecting, "that we have a disorganized business simply from the fact that my office is a mess?"

"Do you have projections for next month's sales?" he asked rapidly. I had to admit that I did not.

"What are your accounts receivables?" This I knew, because I had just reviewed them with our accountant.

"Do you know how many days outstanding they are?" he asked. I didn't.

"Can I see an org chart for the company?" he asked. I went up the whiteboard and started to draw one, but realized that there wasn't a clear one, except that Irfan, Mitch, myself and, to a lesser extent, Kirk, were in charge of everything.

As I attempted to draw the org chart I realized that maybe he was right. Having never seen an 'organized' company before, I didn't quite know how to judge if the company was 'disorganized.'

But it didn't seem logical to me that he could make that judgment simply from looking at the mess in my room. "After all, I could have a very clean room and still have a disorganized company," I replied.

"*As above, so below,*" he replied, repeating a favorite mantra of his regarding the hidden worlds.

I sighed. *He's probably right*, I thought as I sat down in my chair and decided to finish up a few emails before we left for our scheduled cup of coffee.

"It's an important principle, but sometimes I like to state it differently. You need to learn this if you are going to continue this rapid growth, because it has an impact on your life and everything in it."

I stopped sending emails and listened intently.

When he was sure he had my attention, he continued. *"What is true in the hidden worlds is also true all around us.*

"The Path of the Career Warrior is about, as I have said, the development of *awareness*. Awareness of what? Awareness of what is happening in the hidden worlds. And not just what is happening there, but the relationship between *here* and *there.*"

"As a Career Warrior, your job is to figure out how what you do here," he pointed to my messy desk, "and here," he pointed to his head, "affects what happens *over there* in the hidden worlds." He pointed out the window. "Even more important than that, though, is *perceiving* how what is happening in the hidden worlds *affects*, *influences*, even *creates* what is happening here — in our lives, in our relationships, and yes, even in our jobs and our career.

"As I've said before, this awareness doesn't just happen in an instant … it starts off as a hunch, as a clue to a greater treasure, then as we meditate, as we rearrange our lives based on these hunches, it opens up. We start with simple things and gradually build up our awareness."

I was listening attentively to his description when a question occurred to me.

"You know, I've never asked why you call it the Path of the Career Warrior?" I asked.

He laughed. "Ah, yes.. Well, there are several essential skills that the Career Warrior must learn to develop and then use in his or her own life. Some of these skills are adapted from Shamanic traditions to be used here, in the real world. And some are adapted from Tibetan Buddhism. I could have called it the Path of the Career Shaman, or even the Path of the Career Monk, but that seems a little out there for some people in the business world," he explained.

"But *Career Warrior* — it seems a little war-like, doesn't it?"

I asked, even though I had to agree that a year ago, I would probably not have been interested in a path called the Career Monk.

He laughed. "War-like? Yes, maybe. But being a Warrior isn't just about fighting — it's about a mindset, a frame of reference — a *way* of living that is different than an ordinary person."

I was listening but didn't say anything.

"In almost all societies in the past, there have been warrior sects, or *castes,* which were set apart from the ordinary citizens of that society. The was particularly true in the far east — China, Japan, etc. In Japan, you had the samurai, who were the foot-soldiers of the Shoguns. Yes, they were *soldiers*, who learned to *fight*, but even more important than that — they were warriors. Being a samurai was about adopting a certain frame of mind, with extreme discipline, that allowed them to reach a state of readiness where a fight could be won and a certain *one-ness* could be achieved."

"Do you mean it allowed them to fight better?" I mentioned a scene from the Seven Samurai, a film that I had seen in college and had loved.

"Yes, that's it. As I've said before, watching a movie, where an actor or actress totally embodies a frame of mind or a particular lesson is one of the best ways to internalize it in our society. There is an overlap between the monk and the samurai. Musashi, who was rumored to never have lost a battle, wrote the Book Of Five Rings about this mindset."

I had heard of this book in the context of the business world. It had gotten popular in the eighties and early nineties "Isn't that the book that many business people are reading? It's like learning to fight your competitor, right?" I thought I saw where he was going.

"Well, yes, and no. A samurai, a true warrior is preparing for battle. But if you examine their code of conduct you will see that what they were really doing was all about Energy — how to save it, how to store it, how to refine it, and how to unleash it at the appropriate time. So you might say that being a Warrior is as much about Energy as it is about sword-fighting. Speaking of movies, did you ever do the assignment I gave you to watch

Conan?"

Some time ago, he had given me the assignment of watching *Conan the Barbarian* — with Arnold Schwarzenegger and James Earl Jones, because I liked both action movies and fantasy films. I had, in fact, watched it.

"Well," he said, and put his hands out.

"Well, what?" I remarked.

"By now, you've gotten pretty good at finding nuggets within movies that tap into a certain state of mind. Was there anything in Conan which relates to what I'm talking about here — to being a warrior? Remember, a warrior requires discipline and refinement."

I thought back to the movie. Suddenly, I remembered a theme that ran through the violence in the movie. "The riddle of steel?" I asked, hesitatingly.

He smacked his thigh. "Yes! That's it." Suddenly he puffed up his face and started with his best James Earl Jones very famous voice (who incidentally had also done the voice of Darth Vader in the Star Wars movies): "Yes, the Riddle of Steel…you know it, boy?" He smiled and his face was contorted to the point where he *looked like* the James Earl Jones character. "Shall I tell you, boy?" He continued, quoting from the film. "What is stronger than steel is human flesh. What is the power of steel next to the hand that wields that steel?"

He switched back to his own voice and continued without missing a beat. "The skill, the training, the refinement, are all tied to Energy."

"But the Career Warrior hasn't been about fighting others," I remarked.

"Exactly. Those who liken business to war have overdone the analogy. Yes, there are competitors, and yes, you have to fight them. But business is much more than that. It is about your own personal growth. The business world is an arena that allows you to battle your inner demons. Those are the real enemies. The Career Warrior, like the samurai, is constantly struggling. The inner battle — the one against your patterns, your prejudices, your karma — is the real struggle. The battle against your competitors in the business world is only a by-product of this struggle."

"Hmm," I started, and nodded. I had to admit that unlike much of what he'd taught me, this made perfect sense to my logical mind, so far.

Ramaswami continued: "A warrior struggles…as don Juan used to say: *'A warrior is so named because he is constantly struggling against the forces that stand in the way of developing knowledge.'* I would say it's the forces that stand in the way of developing *awareness of the hidden worlds,* and our ability to *act on that awareness."*

"Who's don Juan?" I asked.

"Ah yes, I almost forgot. You have two assignments this month. The first is an energetic assignment — to clean up your room." He smiled and pointed all around. "I mean, your office," he laughed as if he had just made a big joke.

"The second is a mental assignment. Rather than keep giving you movie assignments, I'm going to start assigning esoteric books — not the easy, popular ones — you know, how to heal your life in seven steps, and get everything you want in seven days. The Path of the Career Warrior is much more subtle than that. Rather, I'm going to assign the ones that are tough to read but contain the most hidden wisdom. Your assignment is to start reading Castaneda."

"Who's Castaneda?" I asked, having never heard of him.

"You've never heard of him?" He snickered and shook his head. "You Gen-Xers — you guys are hopeless!"

He explained that Carlos Castaneda was an anthropology student who wrote about a series of visits to the Mexican desert that introduced him to a path of 'Sorcery'. He had met an old Yaqui sorcerer, named 'don Juan' who mentored him on this path, which was one of the first Shamanic paths that westerners had been exposed to en masse. The books were quite famous in the seventies, he explained, and Castaneda had even appeared on the cover of *Time* magazine as the godfather of the new age movement. Being a child of the eighties, rather than the seventies or sixties, though, I had never heard of Castaneda, let alone read any of his works.

"His first book, *The Teachings of don Juan,* is a bit of a waste, as it focuses on psychotropic drugs, which aren't necessary for our path of Shamanism. So I suggest you start with the second book, *A Separate Reality*, or even better, start with the third book, *Journey to Ixtlan,* where he discovers that it wasn't the drugs after all which were responsible for his mystical experiences." He chuckled and I could feel another Gen-X comment coming on.

"What are these books about?" I asked, deflecting the upcoming generational comments.

"Well, a lot of things. But most importantly, they're about *Energy*. And the three occult skills that don Juan teaches him: *Seeing, Stalking, and Dreaming.* Even though don Juan's Warrior lives in a totally different context than the Career Warrior, it's still instructional to be exposed to that particular view of the world. His terminology is particularly useful in describing *Energy.*

"I like to put these skills to use in the modern world, which means they have to be adapted. First of all, the Career Warrior develops the *perception of Energy.* Secondly, as you start to understand the relationships between the hidden worlds and the modern world, you are learning to *re-arrange or re-deploy* the energy in a meaningful way. You would be amazed at how much energy we waste ... it shows up in our auras and it saps our ability to either build a business, or to develop better perception.

"As you learn to re-arrange or re-deploy your energy, the real meaning of these skills becomes apparent. You can re-arrange your energy in the physical world, which is the skill of *stalking,* or better yet, in the dream world, which is the skill of *dreaming.* As you become proficient at these, you can do amazing things, amazing things ... you can't even imagine ... you can't even imagine!" He seemed to tune out for a few seconds, as if he were seeing images in his mind's eye. I remained silent as I didn't know what to say.

"We were scheduled to have some coffee, weren't we?" he suddenly said, as if waking up from a dream.

"Let's talk about this mess and the impact of *Energy* as we go out, which is your lesson for today. *Stalking* and *dreaming* we'll leave for another day."

He got up from the desk and started examining the writing on my white board. The board contained a jumble of writing from various 'ad hoc' meetings that I had with my people on a regular basis. I hadn't erased anything in a long time, and so it seemed almost like an incomprehensible set of scribbles on the board.

"How does this talk of *Energy* relate to the mess in my office?" I asked.

"What you need to be concerned with most is your state of mind." He smiled slightly and took on a deep, serious voice. *"First of all, your energetic configuration, which includes your state of mind, is affected by everything around you.* And what you have around you is a bit of a mess..."

I could sense a feeling of annoyance creeping up on me. Ramaswami was in the office of the CEO of one of the fastest growing high-tech companies in the Boston area, and he was basically telling me to 'clean my room.' It reminded me of the way that I used to get annoyed when my mother would tell me to do something. Sometimes, even though what she was saying made perfect sense, I couldn't bring myself to admit that I needed to be told by my mom to do something.

He continued. "But that's not all, the flip-side is also true: *Everything around you is affected by your energetic configuration, including your state of mind.*" He smugly pointed again to the piles of papers and this time included the white-board for effect.

We grabbed our jackets and walked out of the Brainstorm offices. I noticed that there were quite a few employees working hard at their computer terminals and this made me happy. I remarked that I liked it that they worked late hours without having to be told to do so.

The cold evening had a crispness in the air that helped to clear my mind. It served in stark contrast to my crowded office. We turned on Massachusetts Avenue and he asked if I knew a good coffee shop nearby. There were several, but I suggested that it might be interesting to walk to MIT, which was only a few blocks away. On our walk to campus, we passed many college students sporting backpacks. Many of them seemed to have their heads down and shoulders hunched up as they walked. We arrived at the coffee shop and sat down.

"Let's continue the one topic that is most important to a Career Warrior, as important as it is to a samurai, or to a Yaqui Sorcerer: *Energy.*

"Simply put, a messy desk is a sure sign that energy is being wasted in the hidden worlds. And if energy is being wasted, then we're being less effective than we could be in our business first, and second, in our quest to use meditation to develop higher awareness.

"Okay, so here goes. Our environment is a reflection of the state of our mind. But our state of mind is also a reflection of our environment. The natural conclusion is that by changing our environment, we can encourage a change in our state of mind. And vice versa."

I sipped my tea and remained silent, trying to construct a mental model of what he was saying.

"By cleaning up your desk, you are, of course, helping yourself get organized, but there are subtle energetic pulls that deprive you of the energy and focus needed to run a business and needed to develop perception of the higher worlds. So, you are not only cleaning up paper, you are cleaning up dozens of things that might be considered *energetic loose ends.*"

I continued sipping my tea.

"A *loose end* is a commonplace term that's very important in the study of the hidden worlds. We all have loose ends in our lives; things that we never followed up on; people who left us hanging, people that we've left hanging; little tasks that are awaiting our attention in our apartments. In our work, we have tasks that fell down the priority list because we never got to them; perhaps phone calls that were never returned, or phone calls that we're waiting for a call back from."

"Yes, but what do these things have to do with Energy?" I asked.

"Everything! You might think that these loose ends are nothing to worry about. But, I assure you, the weight that we sometimes feel on our shoulders when we have 'too much to do' is not simply a psychological concept. From an energetic perspective, these things are real tugs on your energy and they hold you back from having the clarity, focus, and daily energy you will need to be successful!

"Especially as an entrepreneur, you probably have tons of loose ends ... A loose end is like an energetic cord ... and energy can flow out of the cord ... draining our energy."

"Are you saying that I should be more organized?" I asked, not fully comprehending where he was going.

"Yes, but that's not all. It's important that you understand that every task left undone, especially if it deals with another person, is an energetic loose end ... You can nicely organize those loose ends, and have them *not be a drain*."

"Are you saying that certain tasks are loose ends which drain energy and certain others tasks aren't?" I asked, still confused.

"Yes, that's what I'm saying." He nodded his head and started to drink his coffee. "Have you ever felt overwhelmed with too much to do?" he asked. Of course, I often felt that way as an entrepreneur. "Well, when something has been hanging over your head for a long time, and you start to make progress on it, do you feel anything different?"

I began to think about a marketing project that we hadn't made a decision on for a long time. I explained to him that sometimes when a decision dragged out too long, and we finally made it, I felt lighter.

"Yes, yes, that's it!" he said enthusiastically. "You physically feel lighter! Relieved! It's not just a psychological thing, it's a loose end that is no longer pulling on you. From an occult perspective, you've loosened up an energetic pull, and it frees up energy for you to be able to enjoy life more or to simply focus on the remaining tasks.

"In order to tie up a loose end, you don't have to resolve it completely. As long as you make arrangements for resolving it, it won't weigh as much on you. At least not for a while. If, however, you let it drag on, there is a subtle pull on your energy. Can you think of some other examples where this is the case?"

I thought about it some more. I explained that I often let my bills pile up. Then when I paid them, I physically felt 'lighter.'

"Yes, yes, that's it! Each of those bills, individually, is a little energetic pull that you don't feel. When they pile up, they become energetic pulls that are strong, but you still may not notice. In fact, it is a fact of human nature that we don't notice pain if it happens gradually or subtly. It's only when the pain goes away, or in this case, the load of the bills goes away, that we notice a difference."

"What you are doing is what sorcerers call *intelligently redeploying your energy.* The energy is freed up. That's why I have my students clean up energetic loose ends before going to the desert."

I thought about the desert trip that I had taken earlier that year. Ramaswami was planning a desert trip on the winter solstice, but I had other plans and wouldn't be able to make it. I was going to comment on it but he started talking again before I could.

"There are both tangible benefits and occult benefits to tying up loose ends. The first tangible benefit is the way others perceive you. Rather than viewing you as a black hole, they know that if they present something to you, they'll get an answer one way or another rather than just letting it die out.

"Think of the times that you were waiting for someone to get back to you but they never did," he instructed.

I thought back and realized that I would get annoyed with the person who didn't call me back or didn't follow up, and would eventually take what that person said less seriously. But, I had to admit on the flip side, there were many people whose calls I didn't return and quite a few issues that I let slip to the back burner without ever resolving them.

"There's nothing wrong with putting a project or document or anything on the back burner," he explained. "But, if someone is waiting to hear about it, that's the problem. You can simply get back to them and say, *'we'd like to put this on the back burner for now.'* If you do this, it brings a sense of closure to things. Notice that it's still an open issue because it's on the back burner, but it's taken care of for now ... it's no longer an energetic drain on you *in the moment.*"

"This seems like rather simple and practical advice," I replied. "Follow up and you'll feel better."

"Sure it's simple. But it's also not often followed."

We had by now both finished our drinks. "What a lot of things you use the term *Energy* for," I said suddenly, as I became confused with all of these lessons on Energy. "How does this relate to the energy-enhancing breathing exercises you taught me last year?" I asked. "And how does it relate to the energy of the desert?"

He chuckled. "Energy comes in many different forms. At its core, on a much higher level, it's similar, but it's hard to see that from where you are. For our purposes, there is the energy of places, like the desert, which is how we recognize *places of power.*

"There is the energy of times, or *times of power.* There is also the energy of *situations*, which we haven't talked much about yet.

"Then, there is the *energy between people*, which has many gradations." He looked at an Asian couple who was walking by. "When you're involved with someone in a deep relationship, your energy and theirs start to merge — you start to take on the same posture, and the same energetic configuration. Look at that couple; you can sense the similarity of energy between them. Each one's energy has influenced the other's — now they even walk the same way."

I looked at the couple. At first I thought he was saying that because they were both Asian, but then I began to notice a particular hunching forward that they were both doing in sync. Though I couldn't see the energy, I could feel that they were together in some unseen way.

"Then, there is the *energy of our body.* We feel this energy all the time. The energy-enhancing breathing exercises I taught you last year were meant to increase your energy by bringing more energy in. But there is another way to increase our energy.

"By tying up or releasing loose ends, we are increasing our energy by reducing the *drains* on our energy. This is a powerful technique, which can be used to enhance your occult skills. There are many exercises that are great for increasing energy in this way."

We had both finished our coffee and tea, and got up to leave the coffee shop.

I was going to ask him what he meant by occult skills, but I suddenly had a disturbing thought. "Are these pulls cumulative?" I asked.

He chuckled. "Oh yes, definitely."

"That means that I have years of people that I haven't followed up on!" I was a little shocked at the consequences of this. I told him that I had many loose ends from previous years, many people I hadn't resolved issues with, and that it just seemed like too much work to deal with that many loose ends.

He chuckled louder. "Oh, yes, definitely! There are occult techniques that are practiced over many months that are designed just for that specific purpose ... to clean off energetic pulls from years past that are holding us back!"

"But how can you go through life and not get them to pile up?" I asked.

"Oh, it's very difficult, but it's based on what I'm telling you here today: clean up and organize your documents at work, create a long list of everything that you haven't followed up on, and make sure you periodically take care of these things. At the end of each day for the next month, simply tie up the loose ends. It might be as simple as sending someone an e-mail or it may require that you mentally release someone or forgive them for something, or that you call and speak to them."

It seemed like a daunting task to me.

"Oh, yes, it is. But it is one of the most powerful occult techniques available, the energy that it frees up is tremendous. There are entire schools of mysticism dedicated to doing this one technique. The effects can actually be perceived in the aura!"

I suddenly became preoccupied with thinking of the monumental task of tying up *all of my energetic loose ends*. It must have shown in my face.

"Don't think of it as a daunting task!" he slapped me on the shoulder. "And don't think of it as something that has to be done all at once! There is no urgency here ... this is the process of life! Clean up your loose ends one small step at a time. Focus on your loose ends at work for now. Think of it as a game...a long term game!

"It doesn't just happen with loose ends from this lifetime ... the more important the loose end, the longer it lasts; when it happens across lifetimes, it's called *karma*. But that's another lesson altogether. I have to go now to a late-night meeting. See you, and don't forget your two assignments."

I agreed to clean my room and try out reading some Castaneda.

That evening, I went back to the office. Most of the developers had left, though both Mitch and Irfan were still there. Around 10 p.m., they both stopped by my office to see what I was up to and found me sitting on the floor amidst piles of papers. I was organizing them into little 'follow-up' piles and was throwing a large number of them away.

"We're going to go grab some pizza. You wanna come?" asked Mitch.

I looked at the piles. I had made quite a bit of progress, but there was more left to do. "No, you guys go ahead—I'm going to clean up this energetic mess."

They both gave me a strange look. Pizza was my favorite food and I almost never turned down the opportunity to go out for it. They looked at each other to see if something was wrong. "Okay, okay, I'll come," I said, getting up from the mess for a bit.

I continued the next day and by the end of that weekend, I had a well-organized office and a 'long-term loose end list' for my business. It included resumes that needed to be followed up on, phone calls, documents, product ideas, financing issues, etc. Of course, there was a huge pile of garbage that didn't need to be followed up on that I threw away. The list was quite large and I simply made a little bit of progress on it each day.

That next week, though we were still the same company that we had been, I suddenly felt more in control of what was happening. My direct reports commented on how focused our meetings had become compared to what they had been. They assumed it was simply because I had cleaned my office. I definitely felt, though, the difference in my level of mental clarity as I started to take care of loose ends, one at a time— some that had been outstanding for awhile.

Over the next month, I saw this clarity have a tangible effect in my ability to focus in and solve problems when they arose in both my personal life and in the office. I felt lighter physically, which made me freer to take care of things. I also found that my concentration during meditation had increased significantly.

It tied to the earlier lessons that Ramaswami had taught me about the relationship between our work and our meditation. I had started on this path because I was interested in seeing how meditation could help me improve my work. What I didn't know was that my work could also be used to improve my awareness of the hidden worlds and the strength of my meditation.

This 'energetic cleanup' had two interesting results. First, my dreaming attention started to open up. And second, I felt energetically ready to push the company in a new direction that would change everything.

CHAPTER SUMMARY
CLEANING UP AN ENERGETIC MESS

What is true in the hidden worlds is also true all around us.

A Career Warrior's job is to figure out how what you do in the world (and what you do inside your head), affects what happens in the hidden worlds. Just as importantly, you have to figure out how what happens in the hidden worlds affects, influences, even *creates* what is happening here — in our lives, in our relationships, and yes, even in our jobs and careers.

The twin rules of energy apply here: Your Energetic Pattern, which includes your state of mind, is affected by everything around you. Everything around you, in turn, is affected by your Energetic Pattern, including your state of mind.

A task like cleaning up your desk (or room) is a great way to start cleaning up energetic loose ends.

This is actually a far more important lesson than just cleaning up your desk or your room. An energetic loose end occurs when something or someone is pulling at your attention, and that pull hasn't been resolved. It could be a follow-up to a phone call or meeting, or it could be something more substantive, such as a decision about your business or your life. Whatever form it takes, an energetic loose end has the ability to drain your energy. There are occultists who believe that these loose ends are very real and can be perceived as 'cords' in the hidden worlds.

The important point here is to understand how what we think and do, how we interact with the world, lingers on in some shape or form long after the event. You can take it even further — our energetic loose ends include not just unresolved connections with others, they also include unresolved feelings about ourselves, which are embedded in our energy fields and our bodies. These loose ends pull and prod our Energetic Pattern into a certain shape.

In Eastern traditions, karma is sometimes presented as something left over from previous lives. It is, more accurately, the law of cause and effect. One way to look at this is that everything we do, internal or external in life, the process of *living* itself, is a cause or an effect or both! In other words, living is about creating karma. An Enlightened Being is someone who, through their own meditation and self-actualization, has become free from the creation of new karma and has resolved all of their existing karma.

For the rest of us un-enlightened beings, it's important to start by cleaning up energetic loose ends as often as we can. Our whole life we've been creating them, and many believe that leftover loose ends from previous lives are a form of leftover *karma.*

Whatever the explanation, it is important to start going back in your life and career by cleaning up loose ends as much as possible. This is not just a theoretical thing, it will free up energy and you may actually feel the physical difference when you are free from so many energetic cords pulling on you from the past. This will free you up to make better choices and to intelligently redeploy your energy, which is being wasted by servicing existing loose ends.

The Path of the Career Warrior combines Western and Eastern esoteric teaching.

Yoga, meditation, and energy were the focus of many esoteric traditions in the East, ranging from Taoism to Buddhism. In the West, gnostic traditions emphasized personal experience over dogma. In the Americas, the esoteric practices of medicine men and shamans in Native tribes had similar beliefs.

The Warrior traditions were alive and well in places like feudal Japan, where the samurai placed a great deal of emphasis on mental and energetic training as well as technique – and often turned to Zen monks for guidance.

Tibetan Buddhism is one place where many esoteric traditions survived much longer than in other parts of the world, thanks to Tibet's remote nature. The diaspora that happened there with the Chinese invasion has had an unexpected benefit: Tibetan holy men, anxious about the survival of their hidden traditions, are spreading these teachings in English more than they ever had in the past.

The principles in the Career Warrior have been culled from similar elements from many of these traditions, making it a uniquely American path.

16 STALKING A MILLION DOLLARS
FEBRUARY, 1995

"We've decided to raise Venture Capital financing!" I said to Ramaswami, thinking he would be pleased, recalling the many conversations we had about the limits to how fast a company can grow on its own without a lot of outside financing.

The company was moving along very rapidly now. We had signed up distributors in other countries, including Japan, Australia, and several European countries. We had also surpassed $1 million in total revenues recently.

Our second product, Datalink, which bridged Lotus Notes with databases like Oracle, had been a big hit. I also had an idea for our next product, a bridge between Microsoft Office and Lotus Notes, which seemed to resonate well with every customer I brought it up to. I thought we were on to 'the next big thing;' this product idea had come to me in a dream as I was walking a tightrope between two giants — Lotus and Microsoft.

Oftentimes, our biggest issue would be cash flow. Though we would sell a good amount of product, it would take 30, 60, or sometimes 90 days before we got paid. Also, though we were still profitable, we were still paying ourselves very little in terms of salary, and we wanted to hire additional people. All of this pointed to the need for money from the outside to help grow the business.

Ramaswami and I had many conversations about the pluses and the minuses of raising financing from Venture Capital companies, who would invest millions of dollars in early stage, high-risk technology start-ups. If we were successful, they (the VCs) and we (the entrepreneurs) would both make millions of dollars in a relatively short period of time by taking the company public or selling it.

"Well done, you're in for an *interesting* time," he said with an odd smirk on his face. He asked us what our 'story' would be.

"What do you mean, our story?" I asked.

"Your pitch — the story that you're going to tell to the VCs?"

I had no idea what he was talking about, but I assumed he meant our business plan.

"We're building products that help companies integrate the Microsoft products with Lotus products," I said, explaining very honestly what our products did.

"Are they only Microsoft products?" he asked.

"No, not really. In some cases, we help companies integrate Oracle and Sybase products with Lotus Notes."

"Hmm ... okay ... that's the beginning of the story, but not the final story — it's too specific, too tied to specific companies' products. For VCs to be interested, you have to have the aura of being a company that will be the leader in a new, emerging market. Your story has to be broader, more generic."

"You can't sell generic products..." I responded, trying to show the experience I had built up over the past few years. "Customers want to buy something specific to solve their specific problems, not something generic."

"Yes, yes, of course!" He nodded and laughed at my statement. "That's true. But VCs want a business model that'll work in a market that's a sure bet. And so the way you pitch your story is very important."

"And it's not just the pitching of the story; the story itself has to make sense. You have to convince yourself that you're going to be a leader in this market, with or without the VCs."

"We are in a growing market," I explained. "Lotus Notes is a the first real groupware platform for collaboration. This is a growing market, more than doubling every year."

He nodded. "That's good. I like that. But the best way to show a business model is to show how other companies have been successful with similar business models. From an occult perspective, you're creating a *way of being,* an energetic pattern, and then you're *fitting into the energetic pattern.* It's what don Juan would call *stalking.*"

"What do you mean, *stalking?*" I asked. It sounded like an illegal activity.

He laughed. "No, it's not an illegal activity! If you have followed your assignments, you would have read some Castaneda and have a sense of what I'm talking about."

I nodded. I had read some of Castaneda's books as assignments from Ramaswami. Though they intrigued me, they seemed to confuse me more than they explained things, and I inevitably forgot most of what they said after reading them.

He sighed.

"You like assignments and mental constructs. Okay, I'll give you another assignment. Read *The Power of Silence,* also by Castaneda, which explains the art of *stalking.*"

I went off and read the book over the next few weeks. It described a series of exploits of Yaqui sorcerers obsessed with making each other perform ridiculous tasks, all in the name of *stalking.* Once I had finished the book, I called Ramaswami to catch up.

"Now do you understand *stalking?*" he asked.

I protested that I did not. I recalled an incident from Castaneda's book where the teacher made the student dress up like a woman to *'learn the art of stalking.'*

I protested to Ramaswami that this did not seem like a viable way to approach Venture Capitalists, which seemed to be a much more serious activity.

He chuckled. "Yes and no. Of course it's a more serious activity, but at its core, it's no different. Raising VC money is about playing a part — like an actor or an actress — the point of wearing the clothes of the opposite sex is to understand what they go through; to understand how your clothes, how the expectations of those around you, your environment, affect how you think you should behave. Most importantly, it gives you an intuitive sense of how you influence your environment, based upon the energy you put out."

He suddenly burst out laughing. "Don't worry, I won't make you go do that exercise! Though you might consider it someday. It's very instructive!" I didn't respond, as I had no intention of dressing up in drag to learn about the 'female point of view.'

"What does all this have to do with raising Venture Capital?" I asked, which was the topic at hand, or so I thought.

"The Career Warrior learns the art of *stalking* by studying the energy of different situations, different types of businesses, different managers, and using elements of those *energetic configurations* when they are relevant to the task at hand."

He could see that I hadn't quite understood what stalking was all about. "Okay ... let me give you an assignment that is a little more mainstream, but gets the point across nevertheless. Read the book called *Samurai Selling,* which touches on the same principles but explains it in the language of business and energy. Even a mainstream guy like you should be able to get that!"

I went and bought the book and read it quickly. It was a small book, which talked about the *ki* of salespeople who sell successfully. *Ki* was the term that was used in Japan for energy, though their definition of *energy* was much closer to Ramaswami's multi-purpose use of the word than to our modern scientific definition. The book showed how to prepare your *ki* for a sales encounter, using analogies and stories from the time of samurai in feudal Japan. He was correct — this book actually made sense to me and I believed that I understood it correctly.

"Acting, or *stalking*, as you've been calling it," I explained, recapping what I had learned from my reading assignments, "can be done superficially, with a set of techniques, or it can be done at the core, where you strengthen and transform your *ki* so that it results in the desired outcome."

"Well said," he answered. "This is part of the trick of *stalking*, to totally transform yourself into that which you are *stalking*. In the world of start-ups, only one out of dozens of companies get serious VC financing. To be that one, you have to do more than just talk like a VC company, you have to smell and walk like one. The best way to do this is not to act, but to *become* the kind of company that VCs would want to back."

I listened raptly. It was one of the few times when he was actually giving me relevant business advice. I didn't even mind that he was talking about "vital energy" or *ki*. It made sense to me.

"A VC wants to back a company that will grow to $50 million in sales within five years," he continued, explaining the world of venture capitalists to me. "That means that not only does the market have to be very large, but your strategy has to be *ambitious!*"

"$50 million?" I asked incredulously. I explained that we were just passing the $1 million mark in total sales, and it seemed like *a very big* stretch to get to $50 million in sales from where we were.

"Oh, don't worry," he laughed. "You have to show how, with enough financing from them, you could grow to that level. You don't actually have to grow to that level that quickly. Very few companies actually get there. The VC's place their bets and two or three out of ten make it to this level of sales, two or three get bought before they get there for a good amount of money, and two or three companies fail altogether. The money that they make from the companies that succeed more than covers the money lost in the companies that fail."

"So I have to show how we'll get to $50 million in sales, but I don't actually have to do it?" I asked. "It seems kind of dishonest."

"No, not exactly. That's not the right attitude. In order to have the right *ki*, you have to come up with a strategy and business model that you honestly *believe* will get you to that point. You can't simply be acting."

I was still skeptical.

"Basically, you have to show that the market for your company's products is *large enough*, and that your business model can *scale* ... That's what it means to adopt the *ki*, or the energetic configuration, of a VC-backed company."

The first step was to write a business plan and financial plan, he explained, that reasonably showed how that kind of growth could be achieved. "The difference between *stalking* and *acting*," he concluded, "is that while stalking, you actually *become* that which you stalk. It's an energetic transformation.

229

Is that a smart thing to do? Maybe, maybe not. It depends on your goals for the stalking. It depends on your *appropriateness,* if you remember the four Keys to Manifestation, the four points of the diamond that I told you about so long ago."

I remembered the diamond, but only vaguely. I was calculating in my head what the company would be worth if we had $50 million in total sales.

"Yes, that's true," he replied when I told him my calculations. "The company would easily be worth $100 million, if the company went public. And each of you — you and your partners — would easily be worth many millions of dollars. *If it works.* If it doesn't, well then you're in trouble, in fact you're out of business! This is what I call the *Endless Wheel of Financing,* which can be very risky."

Now I was struck. I always knew that I had wanted to start a company and eventually make a lot of money, but I had no idea how much money I could make. This seemed clearly like the road map to get us there. I was so struck that I didn't pay any attention to the warning he slipped in at the end about the *Endless Wheel of Financing,* though it would come to haunt me later.

I promised to go off and write the business plan, but I wasn't sure what he meant by business model. He explained that it was a description of how we make money that was more generic than our specific products.

I described our products again, in more generic terms this time – our products were middleware for the rapidly emerging groupware market. Taking his cue, I explained that Lotus Notes was only the first platform for doing collaboration in this growing market. Our products bridged the gap between this new platform and all the existing products out there.

He wasn't really listening. "Yes, yes, that's very nice," he said, yawning. "You need to get them excited."

"How do I do that?" I asked.

"By understanding what you're *stalking.*"

"Oh? And didn't we just say that I'll be stalking a VC-backed company?"

"What you really want to do is find a company that had VC

financing, that had a business model similar to yours that succeeded in a similar but different market. Better yet, if you can find *several* examples of those, and build a business model that mirrors theirs, you have a much better chance of success in raising your financing."

I nodded my head but couldn't think of any companies off-hand that we could stalk.

"If you do a good job at stalking them, you will eventually become like them — which is a successful venture-backed company that goes public. *But remember, you could also end up with nothing if things don't go exactly as expected.* That's a risk you have to be willing to take."

I went off and met with a few other advisors who were able to provide me with solid examples of companies that successfully built "suites of products" on top of a new, emerging platform. I wrote our business plan and perfected the story. More importantly, during this time the key management team members "bought into" this model — we agreed that with the appropriate financing, we could produce a suite of ten products, each selling $4 million a year, getting us to $40 million in five years. The other $10 million, I figured, could be from consulting. I then distilled our 20-page business plan into 20 slides, which became our *pitch* that I would give to potential investors.

Finally, we were ready to start the fundraising process. I did several test pitches. One was to Ramaswami.

I thought that he would be happy with us raising the money, given that he had helped me formulate the story. I also thought that he might want to invest as part of the financing. When I had first met Ramaswami, I had thought that he was a Venture Capitalist. Now I realized the distinction — he was an *angel investor,* who was a wealthy individual, rather than a full-blown Venture Capital fund.

"I might have been interested earlier, but my investments usually range from $50K to $200K," he explained. "Brainstorm is now at the stage where you need institutional investment — at least a million dollars' worth," he continued, "from a real Venture Capital fund. My investments are typically done at the early stages when I help co-found the company."

I was disappointed in that I had hoped he would become an investor in Brainstorm. "Isn't that why you were interested in helping me all this time?" I asked.

"Well, not really." He smiled. "My real interest in working with you wasn't — isn't — to invest money."

"Oh?" I asked. It hadn't occurred to me that he had been patiently showing me spiritual techniques for any reason other than to be a part of the successful company that I hoped to build.

"I've made plenty of money already. In fact, I'm liquidating all of my positions and will be going to the Himalayas soon to meditate, leaving all of this behind," he said, waving his arms around.

I was visiting him at his offices in Kendall Square. This was the same place where I had my original meeting with him. Only this time, the Charles River was frozen solid. The sky was beginning to turn red with the late afternoon sun. I suddenly had a feeling of coldness run down my spine as I glanced out at the empty river. I remembered the sailboats that had been there on that bright sunny day and felt their loss.

"You're leaving Boston?" I asked.

He smiled a knowing smile. "No, not just Boston. I'm leaving the country, to spend the rest of this incarnation meditating with my master in the Himalayas."

He hadn't talked much about *his* master, and I started to ask a flurry of questions. He smiled, but didn't answer any of them.

"So, don't you want to know the real reason I was interested in you?" he asked.

My mind went blank. If it wasn't because of my entrepreneurial bent, I couldn't imagine what it was.

"The real reason that I was interested in you," he began, "is because of your ability to communicate."

"Huh?" This was a surprise to me.

"Well, I'm leaving soon, and I need someone who has the right karmic and energetic patterns to continue on my work, to communicate some of what we've been talking about — business and spirituality — to the rest of the world."

"Me?" I was dumbfounded.

"Why do you think you entered all of those public speaking and writing competitions in high school and in college?" he asked. "It meant you were training yourself to be a *communicator*."

I had no idea where he was going with this conversation.

"These are karmic influences. Each of us is here to fulfill a task. To *contribute* something. And each of us is here to learn lessons. That is the essence of finding your own unique Warrior's Path. Yours is tied up with communication. You've been a writer and a speaker in many past lives — and at some point in this life, your attention will turn away from making money and starting companies, back to that. That's part of your Warrior's Task in this lifetime. I assume that when you do, you'll want to include what we've been talking about all this time!"

"Huh?" I said again. I felt like he had just whacked me with an invisible club. "Now wait a minute!" I sat down, regained my composure, and became a little more assertive.

"Once I have a successful company," I continued, "*after* I make millions of dollars, then I'll have no trouble writing and speaking about how to start and grow a company. I assume at that point I would know enough to actually write and speak about business topics. I admit I do like to write and to speak. *But...*"

"Yes, but what?" he asked with a childish smile on his face, as he put his hands on the table in front of him and crossed his fingers.

"But ... that's still years away, at the earliest!!" I said, hesitating. "And even then I don't think I'd want to be teaching Meditation. Meditation and Career Success? No ... that doesn't seem like something I'd be doing! That's way out there!" I pointed to the sky and the setting sun. "What will people in the business world think? What will venture capitalists think? They'll think I'm nuts. That I'm not a *respectable* businessman!"

He laughed and seemed to be having a grand old time with my growing discomfort.

"Okay, okay, let's forget about all that. I'm not leaving for a few months anyway. We'll talk about this again, I'm sure. Let's focus on the task at hand: *Stalking Your First Million Dollars*."

I straightened up and felt the energy in the room change. I focused in on the task of raising the money and was suddenly comfortable again. He said that he was going to pretend to be a VC and ask me two tough questions that I should be prepared for.

"How much consulting will your company do?" he asked.

"Ah ... well, we'll do some," I answered, fumbling. Actually, I wanted us to do a lot of consulting.

"That's the first issue you need to be careful of. Let's call it the *Consulting Issue* — you and I have discussed it before — remember *all actors want to be singers and vice versa?*"

I nodded.

"You want to be sure to tell them you'll be a product company. This is important, because consulting is a different business model, okay?"

I nodded slowly.

"Think of it this way — if you're auditioning for an acting job, you don't want to go in there and claim that you're going to be a great actor and a great singer! It does happen, but not often. If you say that, they'll think you're probably delusional. You should focus on one or the other —and I think your products are your strongest suit right now."

I nodded again and accepted this argument, at least for the VC presentations.

"And secondly, who will be the CEO of the company moving forward?" he asked.

"I ... will be the CEO for now," I said, unsure how to answer this sensitive question.

"Actually," I continued. "I have heard that VCs will want to hire their own CEO, and I'm all for hiring an experienced CEO," I said.

He nodded his head. "This is a most important issue ... you have to walk a tightrope, on the one hand, you have to show that you're a competent CEO yourself — and in fact the state of the company to date proves this." He smiled. I was too busy listening to realize that he had given me one of the few compliments I'd heard him dole out.

"But unlike most entrepreneurs, who are control-minded and power-hungry, you want to show them that you're open to hiring a new CEO, because you have never run a big organization before, if that is what's best for the company."

"How about this answer," I responded, adopting a serious tone. "For now, I plan to be the CEO, but I realize that as the company gets bigger, I may not be the most experienced person to lead the organization, so I'm open to bringing in a new CEO at the right time."

He paused for the longest time. Then suddenly declared with a smile: "I think you're ready to raise your first million dollars!"

CHAPTER SUMMARY
STALKING A MILLION DOLLARS

The Career Warrior is constantly learning to understand energy. Three occult skills are particularly interesting: Seeing, Stalking, and Dreaming.

Although these terms are borrowed from the teachings of don Juan to Carlos Castaneda, there isn't really a need to read to through his long (and sometimes confusing) works to get to the heart of what a Career Warrior needs to know. Essentially there are three skills of interest:

- *Seeing* is about perceiving *Energy* — knowing where and how it is flowing and how it is configured. Perceiving the energy of people, places, and times is a good start.
- *Stalking* is about re-deploying or re-arranging your energy to take on a different energetic configuration. Stalking is kind of like acting, and the best actors stalk their roles, just as a hunter might stalk his prey to understand it.
- *Dreaming* is about putting ordinary dreams to work, what the Tibetans would call using skillful means. Just as we introduced a kind of meditation at work, so dreams can be used to enhance perception, awareness, and to progress spiritually on the path.

Venture Capitalists invest in growth companies in growth markets.

When you are looking to grow a project and need investment and support, it's important to understand the motivations of your potential investors. At this point in the story, our company was too far along for angel investors (wealthy individuals, usually former entrepreneurs who invest in early stage companies), and was ready for Venture Capital. To know how to pitch to a VC, you have to understand how they think and how they work.

Stalking a VC-backed company means to make your company and your business plan akin in a very real way to the kind of high growth company that VCs are looking to invest in, hoping it will become the leader in a new emerging market.

The principles of VC investing haven't changed that much since the time of this story: The company must be going after a large enough market in which a substantial company could be created. The numbers vary during boom and bust cycles, but in general only a small number of companies are able to raise this kind of financing.

While VCs will give you lots of fuel for your rocket ship (i.e. cash to grow), the danger of going down the VC route is that many VC-backed companies fail because of the pressure that is put on them. They crash and burn because they spend the money in anticipation of future growth, which may or may not happen. A good ratio is that two to three out of ten investments will "make it big", two to three will fail completely, and two to three will get the VCs their money back.

The true art of stalking is about changing your ki, your energy, to that which you are stalking.

In our case, we wanted to grow from a small company with great prospects but limited funds into a substantial company that was doing $50+ million in annual sales (the target for VC-backed companies in those days; today the targets are much higher).

The principle here is the same that the best actors use to get into their roles and "become" their subjects. Some of the best actors stay in character during the breaks in between takes.

How do you find the energetic configuration you are trying to adopt? Find similar companies in other markets and look closely at their business models to find one that might apply in your target market. Simply *acting* like you are a company that can be really big isn't enough. You have to demonstrate that you are a company that can be really big and is getting market traction.

You also have to be in an industry and business model that VCs believe will scale rapidly and become extremely valuable. In those days, consulting companies were not generally backed by VCs, but product companies were. This again cut to the core issue of "acting vs. singing" that we were facing, and understanding what business models investors find attractive. A few years later, in the dotcom boom, this changed as everyone needed to take their businesses online, and many consulting companies were formed to help clients get there fast.

In an updated version of this dilemma, VCs used to not invest in game companies because it was a hit-driven business and hard to predict. This changed during the social gaming and mobile gaming booms, and VCs did many investments in gaming companies for awhile, and then this trend changed yet again. Stalking is about understanding the current trends, taking on the right energetic configuration, and riding them.

Your Warrior's Path is the unique combination of lessons you are here to learn and the contributions you are here to make.
In this chapter, though I was already on my way to becoming an experienced entrepreneur, Ramaswami revealed what he thought my own unique Warrior's Path was to be about — it had to do not just with business but with spirituality — including writing and communicating these ideas.

Many clues in our lives reveal what our life path should be — sometimes when you follow the clues, they lead in unexpected directions. Needless to say, at the time, as an MIT-trained engineer and emerging respected young businessman, I was mortified at the idea of talking about meditation, energy, synchronicity, clues, and the hidden worlds in the same vein as startups, venture capital, product roadmaps, sales cycles, and shareholder value.

Sometimes traveling down our own unique Warrior's Path is a bit scary. If it wasn't, there would be no lessons to learn from it. But even in those early days, the clues were pointing me in a broader direction than I was capable of grasping. This book came about partly because of the seeds planted about my Warrior's Path way back then by Ramaswami.

17 DREAMS OF CLARITY
MARCH, 1995

It was a conference ... similar to the ones that we had attended over the past few years. The conference was taking place at a hotel that was attached to an airport. I didn't question the scene of it as I walked along the red carpet with some colleagues. Someone pointed out a group of individuals standing next to a makeshift booth, alongside their luggage.

I went over to say hello. The leader of the group was Mark K. I hadn't seen or heard from Mark in at least six months. His company, Edge Research, was the only real competitor we had for our first product, VB/Link. At first, we weren't too worried about them as competitors, as customers we talked to clearly preferred our product over theirs.

We had a temporary scare, though, when his company was bought by Lotus. We were worried that with the backing he now had, he would be able to gain market share on us and potentially put us out of business. However, much to our surprise, the guys from Edge seemed to disappear after their acquisition and we hadn't heard from them in the last six months, so I was quite surprised to see him at this conference.

"How's business?" he asked me after I said hello.

"It seems to be going well, especially with our new product, DataLink," I answered, referencing our second product, which we had just come out with a few months earlier.

"Oh?" he said, smiling and pointing all around. "It seems like these conventions are all looking too familiar, aren't they?"

"Yeah," I replied. "After a while, you start to see the same people, again and again, don't you?"

We exchanged some additional small talk, and then I started to walk away. There was something about the conversation and the convention that wasn't quite right, but I couldn't think of what it was at the time.

I woke up the next morning and realized why the interaction was so strange – it was all in a dream. Although I often had dreams about work, they were usually a jumbled mix of work-related items; for some reason, this interaction with Mark K. was extremely vivid and it stayed with me through the first half of the workday. I started to think about his company, Edge, which was now a wholly owned subsidiary of Lotus.

What an odd thing that I would have a dream about them today, I thought to myself as I finished lunch, recalling that I hadn't heard a peep from them in at least six months. I quickly shrugged off the thought and returned to work.

Just as I came back to my desk, the phone rang. I answered, and to my surprise it was someone from the partner program at Lotus, a gentleman by the name of Peter K. We knew Peter because he had been heavily involved with companies like ours, particularly just before the Edge acquisition.

"…because Brainstorm is one of our key partners, we wanted to make sure to tell you before the general announcement was made."

"Oh?" I wasn't so sure I liked the tone of his voice. "Which announcement is that?"

"Well, we're coming out with a product in the Notes integration space. We wanted to warn you because it'll compete directly with your new product, DataLink."

I was a bit angry to hear this news. If Lotus came out with a competitor to DataLink, it would surely kill our market. The whole market for DataLink was based on the fact that it wasn't easy to move data from databases such as Oracle and Sybase into or out of Lotus Notes. Peter went on to describe how the new product would work and how it was going to become the standard way for companies to move data into and out of Lotus Notes, effectively reducing the market for third party products like DataLink.

I grumbled with him a bit, and he invited me to come in to

talk with their product managers so that we could find a positioning that would make DataLink work *with* their new product rather than competing against it.

As we finalized our plans to meet, a thought occurred to me. "Why haven't I heard about this before, if it's just about to be released?" I asked. It was an honest question. Normally, a company as large as Lotus couldn't keep a new product under wraps for very long.

"Oh, it's been developed by our subsidiary out of New Hampshire, Edge Research. Do you know those guys? Mark K. and company?"

I almost dropped the phone. I was about to tell him about my dream the previous night, in which Mark had appeared. As I started, I had to stop myself and remember how odd it would sound in the corporate world to be talking about dreams. Whenever I tried, I would often get a polite smile and then a quick change of subject. I decided not to mention it.

Later that week, I was dying to talk to someone about my odd dream experience and the coincidental appearance of Mark K. in both my dream and the real business world on the same day. I got in touch with Ramaswami to talk about it. He was traveling on the west coast and asked how the VC financing effort was going. I was speaking with several VCs about a possible investment and when I told him the names, he seemed to be satisfied.

"Okay, so tell me more about your dreams. As I told you, *clues* come to us in our dreams. Have you been writing down your dreams lately?"

I had to admit that I had not. I agreed to start doing so and we agreed to go over them when he returned.

"About your seemingly coincidental dream: You had a *dream of clarity*," he answered, after I explained my dream to him fully when he returned from the west coast.

He was not wearing his characteristic Armani suit. Rather, he had on a dark windbreaker with jeans and it was odd for me to see him in such casual attire. We were in Salem again, and near the water. The snow had started to melt but there was still a very cold ocean breeze coming in.

"A dream of clarity?" I asked, not knowing what he was talking about. I know that he had mentioned something similar to me once before, but I had forgotten all about it.

"Yes. Remember when I told you about *messages from the hidden worlds*? Well, the most common messages from the hidden worlds come in the dream state, because your conscious guard is down. Messages flow more easily that way."

I nodded, but didn't say anything, trying to grasp what this meant in the business world. "So ... that was a message from the hidden worlds, right?"

"So ... what do you think it was about?" he asked.

"I was hoping you could tell me!" I answered.

"*Interesting Reaction. But what does it mean*?" he asked in a comical voice and lifted his arms, palms up, and stared at me with a dumb smile.

At first I had no idea what he was doing. Then I realized that he must be quoting a book or a movie to see if I had seen it. "Hmm..." I thought about it for a second, and then had a flash of recognition. "Jack, the Pumpkin King, from *The Nightmare Before Christmas*."

He smiled and nodded his approval of my movie-scene recognition skills. The wind was coming in even more strongly and we started walking over to a café.

"I can't tell you what your dreams are about," he said. "Only you can know what your own dreams are about. It's up to you, kid." He said this in a tone that I knew wasn't quite true. He definitely had an idea what my dream was about, but wanted me to discover it on my own.

"Well, it was obviously about our competitor, Mark K., and his company, Edge Research," I started, explaining the nature of the dream and the nature of the phone call I had gotten from Lotus on that day.

"Well, yes, and no," he started. "Sometimes, you go to sleep and dream about work? Has that ever happened before?"

I nodded again, as I had dreamt about work many times. "That tends to happen when I'm going over something in my mind again and again, or am particularly stressed out, or have been working really hard."

"Yes, exactly, on the surface," he said and began walking around in an animated way. He suddenly stopped and pointed to some dirt. "That is the obvious meaning of the message. What is the hidden meaning of the message?" He swept aside the dirt with his foot so we could see what was underneath for effect.

I was silent. I had no idea what he was talking about.

"That was a signal to you that you are a *dreamer*," he answered.

I smiled in a confused way. He laughed, "Well, yes, you are a dreamer from the perspective of wanting to create things here on earth, but that's not what I'm talking about here, I mean a dreamer in the shamanic sense. It is part of your Warrior's Path."

"Do you mean like in don Juan?" I asked, referring to Carlos Castaneda's books, which I was still struggling to decipher.

"Yes, like don Juan, but not exactly. Most so-called primitive cultures have *dreaming* as a key part of their shamanic rituals. Almost every culture that has had deep spiritual connections has placed a high value on dreams. Even in Tibet, there is a whole science of Tibetan Dream Yoga as well."

We continued walking and found our way into a café. I recognized it as the café in the Hawthorne Hotel where we had eaten a few months back, when he had been talking about *times of power.*

"There are dreams, and then there are dreams, you know," he explained as he looked at the menu.

"Do you mean different kinds of dreams?"

"Exactly. There are little dreams, which are simply reflections of what you've been doing during the day or the week. They regurgitate all this. They often seem jumbled when you awake. These are what the Tibetans call *karmic dreams.* As you get more in touch with the hidden worlds, though, these dreams come less and less and you get big dreams, what I like to call *dreams of clarity.*"

I was listening attentively.

"Sometimes dreams of clarity have really obvious messages, as in your dream, and hidden messages, which your dream also had. The thing that often distinguishes a dream of clarity from an ordinary dream, in addition to its message, is the *quality of the dream.* It often makes an impression on you. You remember it, even if you didn't write it down. It's imprinted on you."

"Like my recent dream with Edge Research," I said.

"Exactly. The fact that you remembered it clearly was a clue that it was a dream of clarity. The fact that something from the dream appeared in your waking life the same day was another clue, that this was a dream of clarity. Often, a dream of clarity will have a precognitive element, as yours did. So, as I said, some dreams of clarity contain important messages that we need in this world." He stopped and pointed all around us.

"In other dreams of clarity, you can actually *travel* to other worlds."

Now I was lost. The waitress came over and we ordered. Part of me was worried that he was about to start talking about *past lives* and *astrology* again, two subjects I wanted to avoid in the middle of a crowded café.

"Just like Jack the Pumpkin King, in the *Nightmare Before Christmas*." He started laughing as the waitress left. "You know how Jack traveled up to Christmas-land? He went to the trees that led to the different worlds — Christmas-land, Halloween-town, Easter-town, etc. Dreaming is emphasized so much in so many cultures because dreams can actually be portals to other, non-physical worlds, if you can leave the stuff of this world, your energetic loose ends, behind. It's just like that clump of magical trees!"

I nodded but laughed at the thought of him using such a fun but silly movie as a serious example. "Ramaswami, that's *fiction*! It's a kids' movie!"

He laughed. "Oh? Is it really?" he said. And for a second I didn't realize where we were and everything around me looked strange. It was as if I was in a dream.

He saw my confused look and snapped his fingers a few times to bring me back to attention. "Okay let's talk scientifically, my young engineering friend. The development of the dreaming attention is similar to what modern science calls lucid dreaming, though the purposes and intent are not the same." I looked at him funny and started involuntarily chuckling.

"Lucid dreaming..." he paused, as if sensing a thought, then broke out in laughter. "No ... a *lucid* dream isn't the same as a *wet* dream!" Just as quickly he got serious again. "A lucid dream is when you are awake in the middle of a dream."

"Like a daydream?" I asked.

"No, it's an actual dream. Your body is actually asleep — in bed. Everything is the same as it is in normal dreams ... everything is the same *except you ... you know that it's all a dream* ... your mind is awake, just as it is awake now. Does that make sense?"

I had to admit that it didn't.

He shook his head in a sigh. "Okay, listen, normally in a dream, what do you look like?"

I had to admit that I wasn't sure what I looked like. I assumed that I looked like "me."

He smiled. "Yes, it is you ... and do you think in dreams? Do you have consciousness?"

This was a tough one. I didn't always remember my dreams. Sometimes in a dream I was afraid ... other times I was having fun ... many dreams just seemed to be a jumble of memories of people, places, and things.

"Well, I'll answer for you. The answer is yes. Yes, you do think in a dream — it's what we call your *dream consciousness*. But, normally, the dream consciousness is different than your normal everyday consciousness — your *waking consciousness*. Can you remember any of your dreams from last night?"

I had to admit that I could not.

"That's because you are no longer in touch with your dream consciousness. There is a wall between your waking consciousness and your dream consciousness ... when you wake up in the morning you can usually remember your dreams but as the day goes on, you quickly forget your dreams ... unless you write them down. The farther away you get from this wall, the harder it is to remember."

I brought up that I still remembered my odd dream about Edge Research.

"Yes, unless the dream makes an impression on you ... usually if a dream makes an impression, that means that it's a *dream of clarity* ... and contains some kind of message from the hidden worlds!"

"Similarly, your dreaming consciousness, which is on the

other side of the wall, *forgets* that there is a waking consciousness. You have forgotten that there is a physical *you* who is lying in bed sleeping. What happens is that your consciousness gets submerged in the dream — the dream seems real to the dream consciousness, but anything that's not there doesn't seem real. So the waking consciousness, which is on the other side of the wall, seems like it doesn't exist! You've forgotten about it!

"So how do you bridge the gap? The same way you would remember anything. By giving yourself a reminder. In the same way that you can remember your dreams if you write them down when you first wake up, so you can remember your waking consciousness by giving yourself a reminder just as you fall asleep."

"I remember reading something like this in Castaneda's books," I replied, happy that I had remembered something from his reading assignments.

"Yes. Don Juan taught Carlos a trick. He said that he could use something in his dreams as a '*memory cue*' to remind him. He used his hands … so the next time Carlos saw his hands in a dream, he would know that he was in a dream."

Ramaswami went on to explain that it wasn't the hands that were important. It could be any cue. Then he smiled and became silent.

We finished our meal, walked into a new age bookstore, and I bought a dream journal — which was really just an artfully crafted notebook. My assignment, he explained, was to put the dream journal near my bed, so that I could write down dreams as soon as I woke up. The more I wrote down my dreams and thought about them during the day, the more likely I was to bring waking consciousness closer to dreaming consciousness. It would also serve as a memory cue to try to *wake up* while in a dream.

"This is important," he explained, "because I'm going away soon. Since we just got the message that you're a dreamer, we have to do a crash course to awaken your dreaming attention. Once I leave, this will be the only way you can communicate with me."

That evening, I tried the to remember to look for my hands in my dreams, but was unsuccessful. I dozed into a comfortable slumber and when I awoke the next morning I had forgotten almost completely about the dreaming attention. As I got out of bed, I noticed the dreaming journal sitting there. I got it to write down my dreams but for some reason I couldn't remember what I had dreamed.

By the third night, I found that if I recalled my dreams while I was still lying in bed, consciously walking through the events of them, then I could get up and write them down. However, if I just jumped out of bed, the dreams would be 'washed out' of my short-term memory and I wouldn't be able to write anything.

My attempts to find my hands were not going well. I found that if I concentrated too much on my hands while falling asleep, I would wake up. This led to problems the next day at work as I hadn't gotten much sleep — I had spent much of the night trying to "go to sleep and be awake." If I didn't concentrate enough, then I would drift off into a normal, non-lucid dream.

The following week, we met for lunch at a pizza place in Harvard Square and discussed my attempts. "I trust you've been writing down your dreams?" he asked. I said that yes I had but explained my predicament.

"I think you're trying too hard; you're trying to wake up, rather than gently realizing that you're in a dream." He suggested this as he held up a slice of pizza for effect. I looked at it but didn't notice anything unusual about the pizza.

"How do you know that this isn't a dream right now?" He looked around and laughed. "If this was a dream, you would be in your dream consciousness, and you would have been engulfed by the dream world. How would you know, *with absolute certainty,* that it wasn't a dream?"

For a moment, doubt flickered in my mind as I looked around. *It could be a dream,* I thought to myself.

"Yes, that's it," he replied. "That's exactly the feeling you need to have, several times a day. If you do it often enough, your dreaming self will remember to do it during the dream-state."

"What about looking for my hands? Should I not do that

anymore?" I asked.

"Not if you want to get some sleep!" he laughed. "As I said, there is nothing special about the hands. It's simply a memory cue that you give to yourself. Not unlike reminding yourself to buy some milk at the supermarket when you leave for work in the morning. Later on in the day, if something or someone triggers the memory, you'll remember to go to the supermarket and buy some milk."

I wasn't as confident as he was that this would work.

"How will I know if it's a dream? If *this* is a dream?" I asked him.

"Does anything look amiss?" We looked at the lunch-eaters conversing all around us. It looked like a normal lunchtime. Ramaswami was wearing a suit, as usual, and I was dressed down, as usual.

"No." I replied.

"Then this may not be a dream ... but you can't be sure unless you do a concrete test."

"What's a concrete test?" I asked.

"The test depends. Think of something that you can do in the dream state that you can't do in the ordinary waking state. That becomes your concrete test."

I thought for a few minutes. I suddenly recalled a dream I had many years ago, when I had been in Japan. In the dream, I had been in a classroom, but suddenly got bored with the students all around me and decided to fly away. I literally let the weight out of my body and flew up into the clouds. It was exhilarating to be flying in the clouds — I stayed there for hours and woke up refreshed. The dream was so vivid that I remembered it many years later, particularly the feeling of floating amongst the clouds.

"Yes, that's perfect. It is a skill that your *dreaming body* has that your physical body doesn't. Go ahead and give it a try," he said, waving his hands as if he was waiting for me to do something.

"Huh?"

"Well, try your concrete test..."

"You want me to try to fly? Now? Here in Harvard Square?"

"Yes, that will tell you once and for all whether this is a

dream or not."

"Of course this isn't a dream!" I replied, getting angry.

He sat patiently munching on his food. He raised one of his eyebrows and said. "Fascinating!" It was an imitation of Mr. Spock from Star Trek that I immediately recognized. He held the face and said, "Are you *a hundred percent certain* that this isn't a dream??"

Suddenly, I wasn't so sure. Harvard Square took on a surreal quality about it. I let the weight slowly out of my body and expected to float above Ramaswami. For an instant I was looking down on the two of us, but then I was back in my seat.

The din of the restaurant was as real as could be. I hadn't gone anywhere.

"Okay," he replied, releasing his eyebrow. "You're correct. This isn't a dream." He paused for effect. "But it could have been. Remember to try that test at least a couple of times a day, even if it seems silly. Remind yourself to do it ... and at some point, when you're dreaming, you'll remember to do the test."

For the next few weeks, I sporadically reminded myself to check if I was in the middle of a dream. Oftentimes, this would happen in the middle of a meeting at the office. Luckily, I didn't have to reveal what I was doing to my employees or business associates. Several times, I thought that the situation might be a dream, but it failed the concrete flying test.

Then, one evening, I found myself walking around my apartment in the dark. It didn't seem unusual, but I remembered that I should constantly check whether I was in a dream. I stopped and looked around. Nothing seemed out of place, and I was going to skip the test, when I decided to go ahead and try it for the hell of it.

To my surprise, as I let the weight out of my body, I floated up and was hovering above my couch. This was a dream! And I knew it was a dream ... I was having a lucid dream! I floated out toward the window and could see the light of the moon outside. I tried to fly through the window but seemed to get 'stuck' so it was difficult to get out.

I backed up and then somehow suddenly found myself outside my apartment. I was flying! It was an incredible feeling of freedom as I hovered over the rooftops of Cambridge and found myself over the Charles River.

I swooped down very close to the river, skimming the surface in the darkness. It was an exhilarating feeling! Then I flew up in circles, getting higher with each circle. I looked over at the Boston side and noticed a city of odd-looking structures. There were minarets and many colored cone-like structures. They seemed to have odd writing on them. I flew over the structures and realized that this wasn't Boston – it was another city – in another time and place. There was a chill in the air.

Suddenly, I found myself back in my bedroom. I had woken up, and felt extremely refreshed. I looked over at the clock and saw that it was 3:00 in the morning. I was wide awake and remembered my dream experience vividly. I sat down at my desk to write down the experience. It was my first real experience of the "emergence of my dreaming attention."

I tried it again the next few nights but to no avail.

All of this happened in the middle of tremendous change in the company. Ramaswami was traveling a lot, and not having anyone to talk about it with, I soon became preoccupied with the *stalking* I was doing to try to bring a million dollars into the company in Venture Capital financing.

Soon, I found myself forgetting all about dream work and the dreaming attention — I was too busy turning all of my attention, my waking attention, to the business at hand.

CHAPTER SUMMARY
DREAMS OF CLARITY

Dreaming is an important part of life and can be put to use.

Numerically speaking, sleep, like work, takes up a big portion of our lives. The Career Warrior learns how to put the time we spend sleeping to use to use in his or her spiritual growth by turbocharging his or her dreams. Dreams can be put to use by:

1. understanding the types of dreams,
2. recognizing clues from our dreams, and
3. opening up and strengthening our dreaming attention

Mystics from all religious and spiritual traditions (priests, saints, shamans, medicine men, lamas, yogis, etc.) have always put an emphasis on dreams as a primary means of communication with the hidden worlds. Many great religious and political insights, scientific inventions (the periodic table, the sewing machine to name just a few), works of art (Salvador Dali's paintings for example), literature, and film have come from dreams. While I won't go into detail here there are so many examples that entire books have been written chronicling these experiences. Dreams are one of the most important type of *clue*.

Understanding the different kinds of dreams.

Ordinary dreams are usually just a creative (and sometimes jumbled and hard-to-follow) regurgitation of things we have seen during the day or in our lives. In ordinary dreams, our mind is burning off mental loose ends we have accumulated from the world or even from watching TV or reading a book (Tibetans call these *karmic traces*, and part of the purpose of dreaming is to tie up these trivial loose ends).

Dreams of clarity are different. In dreams of clarity, we move out of our ordinary expulsions of trivial karmic traces and move into something that has greater objective truth.

What kind of truth? It could be about some event that is happening in our lives, unknown to us, like the example in this chapter of the emergence of a competitor. It could involve a dead relative who is telling us something important about our family or loved ones. Or it could involve an important mental state that provides clarity on the nature of dreaming.

Ordinary dreams show how dreams are created based upon what happens to us in life. Dreams of clarity reveal that the world of dreaming is linked to the world of waking in unexpected ways.

EXERCISE: Write down clues from your dreams, especially those that are unusual, vivid, or repeat.

To begin looking into your dreams for clues, you might start by paying attention to specific locales within your dream. In the first dream in this chapter I used the example of a conference. This would be a locale for many interesting dreams about business for me in the years to come. It was a clue that this dream was about business and that it might contain an important clue to me.

Like other clues, a dream of clarity will make you feel something unusual — perhaps unusual clarity or an unusual feeling of surreal-ness or vividness in the dream. There may also be some unusual elements in the dream itself — i.e. someone you haven't thought about lately suddenly pops up. These are clues that you may be getting a clue in a *dream of clarity*.

Like other clues, you should write down dreams that seem to be pointing you in a particular direction for your work or career. I have had ideas for businesses, products, and books come to me in my dreams.

One of my favorite stories of inspiration coming from dreams is about how a B-movie special effects guy had an extremely vivid dream about robots emerging from a nuclear holocaust. His friend Gale encouraged him to write down the dream and to draw some of the images he had seen. Eventually she encouraged him to flesh out the story and write a screenplay based on this dream.

That screenplay ended up being *The Terminator*. The young man was James Cameron, who went on to become one of the most successful filmmakers of all time.

The emergence of the dreaming attention is an important part of waking up.

Many Buddhists use the metaphor of dreaming to describe how we all go through life, totally unaware that there is a greater part of ourselves, and a greater life "out there." Of course that is exactly what happens when we are in a dream. While dreaming, we forget that there is a part of us lying in bed that has a whole other rich life — the dream seems like reality when we are in it.

The process of waking up inside a dream (without physically waking up) is usually called lucid dreaming, and is a part of many esoteric traditions. Though today the term lucid dreaming is more of a psychological term describing a kind of dream, the Career Warrior sees that becoming lucid is an important part of using dreams as spiritual practice.

Some people don't even realize that lucid dreaming is possible, or that it's a learnable skill. The Tibetans tell us that if we can "wake up" while in a dream and realize that it is a dream, then why can't we do the same in ordinary reality? Why can't we wake up and remember that we are more than a physical being with a single life, just like Siddhartha did when he became the Buddha?

After his enlightenment, when he was asked who he was, Siddhartha simply said he was "Buddha" — i.e. he was "awake." This implied that the rest of us are asleep. He realized and actually saw that there was a greater reality that we weren't able to normally perceive. If you can "wake up" in your dreams, you are on the path to being able to "wake up" in the dreaming that is our physical reality.

EXERCISE: *To strengthen your dreaming attention, try a concrete test and remind yourself that you might be in a dream.*

Another way to refer to the process of becoming lucid in a dream is the "opening up your dreaming attention." Usually there is a wall between the dreaming attention and the waking attention — and memory of one fades as we move into the other. Just as we usually forget our dreams after we wake up and go about the business of our day, so we tend to consciously forget our waking life as we lay down and go to sleep.

One of the most effective techniques for opening up the dreaming attention is called a "lucidity test." This is something that you can do inside a dream that you cannot do in real life. The trick is that you have to remember to do this lucidity test in the dream — and given that most of us forget our waking life when we dream, this is no small feat.

The key to remembering the concrete "lucidity test" is to do it during the day when you are awake. In this chapter, I described how trying to fly was a sure-fire way for me to test whether I was in a dream or in physical reality. By doing this regularly throughout the day, you are training your mind to question reality. Just as the old "tying a piece of string on your finger" was meant to remind us of something, doing the lucidity test is a reminder that we put into our aura. If you do it intently during the day, your mind will remember to do it during the night — in the middle of a dream. This means that you do the lucidity test and, much to your surprise, it is successful, which means that you must be dreaming!

18 THE ENDLESS WHEEL
JUNE-OCTOBER 1995

"A million dollars! Wow!" Irfan, Mitch and I were sitting with our bank statement in front of us. It was a sunny afternoon in June, and our hunt for Venture Capital had been fruitful. We ended up getting a commitment for $2 million, of which the first million had just arrived in our company's bank account. Previously, our balance had rarely gone above $50,000, so we were quite surprised to see a seven-figure balance.

"Congratulations – that was good work!" Irfan said to me. They hadn't seen much of me over the past few months. I had been constantly meeting with venture capitalists, negotiating term sheets, and otherwise working on getting the financing complete.

"Now we can build a real company!" said Mitch.

Suddenly, I remembered a conversation with Ramaswami that had occurred not that long ago.

"Some entrepreneurs have a tendency to celebrate when they get their first Venture Capital financing..." he had said. "It's tempting with all of that money in the bank, to go out and have a party! To think that you've made it. But the reality is that you shouldn't celebrate. When you get that money is when the *real work begins.*"

When we had the conversation I had no idea what he meant by the *real work begins.* Over the next few months, as we would start building the organization, I would learn quickly. I wouldn't see much of Ramaswami, as he was traveling around the country putting his affairs in order for his imminent departure to the Himalayas.

Between June and October, we wasted no time in starting to 'build our organization.'

First, Mitch, who was in charge of marketing, came up with an aggressive marketing program, which included advertising, aggressive public relations, seminars, trade shows, analyst tours and hiring a marketing department. These all seemed like the "right" thing to do, now that we were no longer a small outfit with limited funds. Now we were one of the best-funded startups in our market-space and we had very aggressive growth plans. We needed to market ourselves and project the "image" of the successful company we wanted to become.

Then Irfan, who had been managing all of our product development, needed adequate resources to fund our three products, VBLink, DataLink, and OfficeLink. So far, we had been developing them haphazardly, with a few developers and with us pitching in to do development work late at night after our business meetings were done. To build a quality development organization, Irfan explained, he needed to have a couple of developers working on each product, and he needed to have a testing lab so that he could test out how well the products worked in different scenarios. He also needed a chief architect to ensure consistency between all of our development efforts, and a QA (Quality Assurance) manager to oversee the testing. This also seemed reasonable; I was painfully aware of how haphazardly our code had been written to date and our lack of testing.

We also needed to build a customer support organization for our very rapidly growing list of customers. Kirk had decided to leave the company, and our customer support was being neglected. We needed to hire a support manager and a couple of people to man the phones.

Finally, and most importantly, we needed to build a sales organization. Our business plan called for us to get to $50 million in sales within the next five years. To do this, we needed a very strong VP Sales and a real sales organization. We started hiring them too.

Within two months of the financing hitting our bank accounts, the size of the company had doubled.

Slowly, as the organization grew, a strange thing happened: I became bored with the nuts and bolts of managing everyone. I wanted to do something "new." After all, we needed to get to $50 million in revenues. This meant, according to our business plan (which we now took as gospel), having ten products with each selling $4 million worth, and another $10 million in consulting on top of that.

With this in mind, I asked Irfan to start developing a fourth product, ArchiveLink. Irfan wasn't too excited about doing this, because he said that we had a lot of existing code that was unstable, particularly in our third product, OfficeLink. We needed to shore up that code, he explained, before we started writing new code. But I reminded him of our plan and gave the go ahead to hire more developers to work on it.

I also began looking for smaller companies with interesting products who we might buy.

"Well, we have the cash," I explained. Between our million dollars in the bank, and another million dollars that we could call on, I figured that this might be a cost-effective way to get to the ten products that we needed.

The investment in marketing started paying off immediately, as more magazines and newspapers started writing articles about us. Not only were we the only reasonably financed small company in our market space, we had also become one of the "hot, growing" startups that everyone wanted a part of.

One day, just after the Boston Globe had done another article on us, I got a call.

"Hi Riz? It's George."

For a second, I didn't recognize the voice. Then I remembered: George had been at the consulting company that I worked at just after graduating from MIT. That consulting company had sent me to Europe on an assignment a couple of years ago. After leaving that company, I had ended up at DiVA

Corporation, which eventually led to my encounter with James, Ramaswami, and the Path of the Career Warrior.

"Hey, I was just reading the *Globe* and here was this article about some 24 year old whiz kid, and I said to my wife: wait-a-minute … this is about Riz! I hired him in his first job out of college!"

We had a good laugh and started reminiscing. It turned out that George had left that consulting company and was looking for the next thing to do. "Really?" I said, and as usual, I had an idea. This seemed an unmistakable "clue" to me – I had been wanting to start a consulting group for many months now, and here was a guy that I knew and trusted, who knew all about starting consulting groups, who happened to be available.

"Well, why don't you come in sometime and let's talk about a position here." George came by that evening, and I described our new "business model" to him, and told him about this emerging market that we're going after. He agreed to come aboard and build our consulting group. He started the next day.

As September came to an end, we were up to 35 people, and I was suddenly made aware of a lurking problem.

I was sitting with Art, my new Director of Finance, and he warned me that our sales for September were nowhere near the numbers I had put into our original business plan.

"That's okay," I said. "They'll pick up in the fourth quarter — plus I'm working on acquiring at least one new product and building our consulting group with George."

"That's fine. Except that I think maybe that our expense structure is growing faster than we should." We had lost $25,000 in August, which was per our business plan and didn't seem to be too big an issue. We had lost $50,000 in September, our biggest loss to date. This was a little more than the loss in our business plan. But it was only off by about $20,000 which didn't seem to be too big of a problem to me, given that we had just raised a million dollars and our investors had committed to putting in another million anytime we wanted.

Venture-backed companies, I explained to Art, were supposed to rack up losses as they hired the people who could take the company eventually to $50 million within five years.

"So you see, it's really an investment in our future," I finished.

"That's fine, but if the numbers don't pick up in October or November, then I think we might be in trouble. Our hiring plan calls for us to be 50 people by December, and we can't support that on our current revenue stream," he said.

I again pointed to our plan, which showed our revenue doubling by December.

"Well, okay," replied Art. "But I don't really see how that's going to happen."

"And another thing," he warned, "You're spending all your time with George building the consulting group and negotiating with people on buying their companies, I don't think you're spending enough time and attention to our core business of products. There are too many things going on here — it's becoming too political — with all of these departments and all of these vice presidents!"

I assured him that I would look into it at the appropriate time and prepared to leave his office. "And one more thing," he continued, catching me before I could leave. "We're going to run out of office space pretty soon, too!"

It was now the second week of October, and I was excited to see Ramaswami as I hadn't seen him in months. With all of the changes in the business, I had been very busy and he had been traveling.

We met near the MIT campus, just a few blocks from our offices. The leaves were starting to turn all shades of yellow, orange, brown, and red. I could feel the energy generated by the new college students who had just arrived on campus.

"So, how is your dreamwork going?" he asked.

"Dreamwork?" I had to admit that I hadn't been paying any attention to my dreams lately. I had been meditating, but not as regularly as I would have liked. Managing a growing organization had become an all-consuming task.

"Yes, in addition to meditation, I would say, that for you, *dreamwork* is the most important aspect of the Path of the Career Warrior."

"The most important aspect?" I asked, incredulous. "You haven't said that before. I thought that *dreaming* was just one skill out of many."

"Aha. Well, it is an important part for everyone who walks this path. But each person also has their natural strengths and weaknesses in terms of getting in touch with the hidden worlds. Yours happens to be *dreaming*. There are several main reasons why we focus on dreamwork in the Path of the Career Warrior.

"The first is that we can get insights in the dream state that we may not be able to make consciously. Each of us has an energy field, and this field is shaped by a collection of our physical, emotional, mental, and belief structures – our Energetic Pattern. It's very difficult with all of this stuff going on to sometimes get messages when they come to us. In the dreaming attention, we can get these messages more clearly by bypassing our conscious waking attention."

I had to admit that lately I hadn't been paying attention to "clues" or "messages from the hidden worlds", though I did have the intuition that bringing George aboard may have meant that the timing was right to finally start our consulting operation.

Ramaswami looked at me in a funny way as I said this. He took a deep breath and said, "Yes, well that is an issue, isn't it?" I suddenly knew he was referring to my old pattern of getting bored really fast, and wanting to move on to the 'next big thing.'

I explained to him that now that we were a VC-backed company, we had to move even faster and the only way I could think of to scale revenues in the way that we said we would in our business plan was to run like hell to build an entire suite of products and consulting.

"That fits you quite well, doesn't it?" he asked. "It's funny how your Energetic Pattern has created a reality that lets you … deal with your issues!"

I didn't know what he was talking about.

"Well, that scenario seems to fit your Energetic Patterns quite well, doesn't it? You like to do lots of different things, not be bogged down by too many details, and your current business plan of getting up to ten products, which got funded, gives you the opportunity to do something *new* every so often."

I did have to admit that it seemed like a reasonable fit, though I immediately started complaining about how big the company was becoming. "It's not as much fun to deal with all of these different vice presidents, and directors and what-nots," I complained. I then told him how much I had enjoyed the "old days" — when it was just Mitch, Irfan, myself and a few developers huddled around a table eating pizza. Although it had only been a few months since we raised our VC financing and started our expansion, it seemed that years had passed since those days. That old, bootstrapped company with great prospects but very little money, seemed like a distant memory.

Ramaswami was listening carefully.

"The second reason we do dreamwork," he continued after a few moments, "is that it helps us develop our *dream consciousness*. Now I'm referring to the lucid dreaming aspect of *dreams of clarity*. Why is it important to develop this? Because for one, you can use the dream state to explore places, and get in touch with people and beings who you can't communicate with regularly."

He paused as if he was letting this sink in. "Because you're a dreamer," he continued, "this can be an invaluable tool for you."

"But how can you say I'm a dreamer?" I protested. "I haven't even been remembering my dreams lately! I don't think I've had any *dreams of clarity* in many months."

"You may have ... you may have ..." he nodded his head while he was smiling. He changed his voice and started looking around: *"What ears or eyes do we lack that we cannot see or hear another world all around us?"* He looked at me and smiled.

I knew he was quoting from somewhere – I just couldn't place the quote. I thought about it for a minute, while he waited patiently.

"I give up. I can't seem to place it."

He smiled and gave me a clue, "Desert Planet ..."

"Desert planet? Of course, it's from the Orange Catholic Bible in *Dune*!" I replied, referring to one of my favorite science fiction novels.

"So," he continued. "Just because you don't remember it doesn't mean that it isn't happening. I say that you're a dreamer based upon your ability to awaken your dreaming attention, when you are meditating regularly and put your intent to it, which you haven't been doing lately.

"And that can come in handy, especially since you probably won't see me after today."

For some reason, though Ramaswami had been preparing me for the fact that he would be "leaving town", it hadn't really dawned on me until that moment that he would be leaving.

Since I usually only saw him only once a month, or only once every few months, it didn't seem that odd to me that he had been traveling. Suddenly, the impact of what he said finally hit me. *He would be gone. I may never see him or hear from him again.*

"Not unless you come to the Himalayas someday!" he said, with an understanding smile as if he had read my mind.

I didn't say anything. In that one moment I realized how important the Path of the Career Warrior had been in the early days of starting and growing my company. As the company had grown in the last few months, a growing sense of emptiness had been creeping up on me.

I thought that this feeling was being caused by the growing size of the organization. I realized that it was because I had lost touch with what had become an "energetic configuration" that I had when the company was very small and getting started. We were so focused on sales, budgets, profit and loss numbers, I felt that I had lost touch with the creative side of building a product and solving customer problems — the energetic configuration that had led me to start the company in the first place.

I realized that it also had to do with the increasing linkages of my work with principles in the spiritual worlds — *The Path of the Career Warrior*. Because Ramaswami hadn't been around, I hadn't been thinking about these linkages much recently. Now, I realized that they had added something to my work day as I constantly saw my daily work as 'Warrior's Tasks.' In the ensuing frenzy to build the company, I had lost touch with all of that. And my old pattern of wanting to do the 'next big thing' was in full force.

"Now, now, let's not get too nostalgic," he said as he noticed my mind wandering. "My point is that you can use *dreaming* as a way to contact me, or contact other sources of insight and wisdom, that you can't find in the world around us," he said, waving his hand at the restaurant.

"But the most important reason for developing the dreaming attention," he continued without missing a beat, "is that it helps us to understand the *nature of reality*."

I was still lost in thought. He noticed this and snapped his fingers a few times and waved his hand in front of my face.

"I know you're a dreamer who can journey out of body, but right now I want you to stay here, focus. That is important. Remember the very first thing that I taught you: though the path of the Career Warrior is about developing an awareness of the hidden worlds, that doesn't mean that you can go off whenever you want. To be effective in the world — to make *your unique contribution* — to find your Warrior's path, you need to be *here* during the day."

When I didn't respond, he kept on. "There's a time and place for journeying into the hidden worlds, and there's a time and place for focusing on what you're doing here, in the physical world."

I snapped back to attention and could suddenly hear the voice of the other people in the restaurant. I could feel the hardness of the chair that I was sitting on.

"Good. Now, do you know the difference between *a reason* and *a cause*?" he asked.

I didn't know the difference.

"Dreams help us to understand the *cause* and *effect* relationship between things in our waking lives and the hidden worlds. There is often a direct *cause-effect* relationship between these two."

He smiled and got a twinkle in his eye. "Though it's not always what you think!"

"Huh? I don't get it," I replied, trying to focus on what he was saying.

"Okay, let's take the example of the dream you had earlier this year, about your competitor – what was their name again?"

"Edge Research, which is a subsidiary of Lotus," I replied, remembering the dream that had come up on the morning before I got the call tell me that Lotus was announcing a new, competitive product, developed by none other than Edge Research.

"Yes, yes. The *cause* of that dream was straight forward –

though it requires believing in psychic phenomena. It appeared in your dreams be*cause* of the phone call you would get that same day."

I nodded my head. It was, in my opinion, a reasonable enough connection (as long as you ignored the precognitive element).

"Similarly, if you have been thinking about something all day, you may have a dream about it that night. That's a *cause-effect* relationship. It appears in the dream be*cause* you were thinking about it all day."

I nodded and agreed that this also seemed reasonable.

"Similarly if an alarm clock goes off, and you end up having a ringing in your dream ... the cause of the ringing showing up at that moment in the dream state, is the physical alarm clock which is going on in the waking world."

I had to admit that in all the time I had known him, I hadn't known him to be so logical. "Yes, even I can agree to that!" I replied.

"But what is the *reason* you had this particular dream *pre-cognitively*?"

"Huh?" I explained that I didn't think there was a difference between the cause and the reason.

"Oh, there is. Although the cause of a particular image or situation may be clear, the important thing is the *reason* why a dream of clarity appears at a particular point in our lives.

"The *reason* that dream appeared in your life was because you needed a signal. It was a convenient way for you to become aware of the nature of the connection between the waking state and dreaming state. It was a demonstration that the hidden worlds do exist — and it was a signal that you are a *dreamer*. It was also significant that this signal, this message from the hidden worlds, came to you about your business. It was a clear signal that if you choose to work on that aspect of yourself, you can develop it highly."

"Oh?" I asked, not sure where he was going, and definitely losing his train of logic.

"It was a dream of clarity not just because it was precognitive of what would happen that day. That would be a relatively uninspiring use of the hidden worlds — since there really wasn't any time for you to act based upon the dream. The only reason that makes sense is that it was a *message from the hidden worlds,* that *dreaming* in general, and *dreaming about work* specifically, is a key part of your Warrior's Path! That's why I know you're a *dreamer!*"

I wasn't so sure that's what the dream meant and started to protest again. He slammed his hand on the table hard. Everyone in the restaurant looked at us. "No time for arguments! That is in fact what it meant. It was a demonstration – a signal – from a part of you that you can't see to the part of you that remembers the dream!"

"Okay," I said, not wanting to get him overly animated as everyone was already looking at us. "So you're saying that my Warrior's Path is to become a *dreamer?* That seems like an odd Warrior's Path." I remembered his definition of Warrior's Path: *a blend of the unique lessons that we're here to learn, combined with the unique contribution that we're here to make to society as a whole.*

He laughed. The waitress had come over to see if everything was okay. We said that it was and I tried to grasp what he was saying, which I just couldn't seem to be able to do.

"No, no. I said that *dreaming* is a part of your path — it's not your actual Warrior's Path. Your *dreaming* will help you to find your path. The fact that your dream was about work is significant. The business world and the hidden worlds — you might say that these are both on your particular, unique, Warrior's Path."

"Oh?" I said, hiding the fact that I was uncomfortable with this line of conversation.

He sighed and shook his head. "Okay, let's get back to what you're comfortable with. Let's talk about your company. Tell me more about the events of the past few months at work and your current concerns?"

I told him the events again and the worries that our Director of Finance had that we would be racking up huge losses. I told him about all of our new departments, our vice presidents, our new products, and the new consulting group.

"Venture-backed companies always have losses, don't they?

It's an investment in the future." I replied, trying to look confident.

Ramaswami nodded his head, but his eyes seemed to have glazed over. I realized that he was looking at something in his mind's eye and was no longer seeing me, though his eyes were open and he seemed to be staring directly at me. I quietly ate my lunch for a few minutes until he "came back".

"Let me tell you about another concept," he started upon his return. "In Buddhism, we have a concept of the Endless Wheel. Each time you come back for a new life, you're going round the wheel again. When you finally reach enlightenment, when you reach *nirvana*, you can step off of that wheel and then you can choose your own destiny. You are no longer at the mercy of the wheel spinning round and round.

"Most people don't even realize they're on this wheel — they keep going round and round — again and again."

I had heard of the concept before, but saw it as part of the religious belief in reincarnation, which I wasn't sure I believed in. And I certainly didn't see its relevance to my business situation.

"Well, its relevance is by way of analogy. In the Venture Capital world, once you raise money, you build up an expense structure in anticipation of future sales. You don't know for certain if you're going to meet those sales numbers or not. In fact, very few venture capital backed companies actually do.

"So what happens? Inevitably you run short on cash much sooner than you thought you would. And so you have to go raise *another round of venture capital* – another few million dollars, let's say. And this cycle continues … again and again … until…"

"Until what?" I asked.

"Until you step off of the Endless Wheel of Financing."

"And how do we do that?"

"Either you become profitable – which you might say," he smiled, "is the *nirvana* of most businesses. Or you get acquired, which is a *nirvana* all its own, if you make enough money, or you get thrown off the wheel – which also happens fairly often."

"Get thrown off? What do you mean by that?"

He laughed. "It means you go out of business. It happens.

Often."

It was a sobering thought. One that I really hadn't considered before. In all the time that I had started and grown the business, the thought that we would go *out of business* if we didn't meet our numbers had never occurred to me. I had been raised on stories of business success – and had convinced myself that the possibility of failure didn't even exist.

"Well, we're far from that," I replied. "We've just missed our September numbers by a little bit, that's all. We'll pick it back up in the fourth quarter."

"Perhaps. Perhaps not. I'm not saying that you're going to go out of business — that's a morbid thought. I'm just saying that you have stepped on the Endless Wheel of Financing, and you need to think about how to keep that wheel spinning. That may be more money, or it may be running a profitable operation. Monitor the numbers and be aware. It's okay to run huge losses in the beginning of company, while you are still building your first product — but you guys are an operating businesses. You're not building your first product — you're building your *fourth product.*"

I thought about it. Somehow a part of me began to worry what might happen if things didn't go as expected over the next few months. But another part of me, the eternal optimist, couldn't accept that we had made any mistakes. It had never really known failure, and wouldn't even acknowledge this possibility.

"Now, let's say you start to run huge losses. The *cause* of the losses is clear – you didn't bring in enough sales and you spent too much money, correct?"

I had to admit that seemed like a reasonable definition of why a company would go out of business.

"But what is the *reason* it's happening to you, at this point in your life? Now think of your Warrior's Path."

"My Warrior's Path? I'm not sure I know what that is."

"Well, part of it, as I have said before, and why I've spent so much time with you, will be to use your communication skills and your business skills to help promote a message that meditation and career success are inter-related — that is part of your Warrior's Path."

Ramaswami had said this once before, but of course I hadn't paid any attention to it. I still found it difficult to see myself writing about "occult" and "weird" subjects like the hidden worlds. "I'm an engineer and an entrepreneur!" I protested. "I've meditated some, but that doesn't qualify me to go out and teach meditation or write about the hidden worlds!"

He smiled and didn't say anything.

"You must be joking!" I was getting worried that he actually expected me to teach and write about these subjects. "I have a business to build — that keeps me pretty busy, you know."

He nodded and smiled some more, but didn't say anything for a few moments. There was an awkward silence.

Suddenly he burst out laughing. "Okay, okay, let's forget about this. You can do it in your own sweet time. So, back to my question. What is the *reason* why this is happening at this time?"

I thought about it for a few moments as I finished eating my lunch. *Why would this particular situation appear at this time in my life?*

"My old pattern?" I finally responded.

"Yes, your old pattern! You need to learn to release the pattern and not give into it. Take a deep breath when you get the feeling that you want to start something new.

"Your old pattern isn't a negative thing in and of itself – it is what has helped you become successful at so young an age. It's part of who you are!

"But when you let it run amok, and certainly having this money at your disposal has let you do that — what happens? The business loses focus. Suddenly, you're doing too many things at once, and the quality of each of these things eventually suffers! Remember there is a time and a place for each new idea. That time may not be now!"

I listened but wasn't sure I understood.

"Sometimes, we get clues in the environment, in the world around us, and we are meant to follow them. This is often referred to as synchronicity – but it isn't always fun and games. Sometimes, we get clues because we are meant to see if we can *resist them.* It would be nice if everything just happened and worked out, but sometimes the clues are a *test,* to see if you've learned your lesson. Sometimes it is a test to see if we can release our instinctive patterns and find our true path."

We continued talking about my pattern and the many wheels that I had set in motion in the company. I wasn't sure that I totally believed that this would cause problems for me in the business world, though. The only way for me to have any fun in the business, I explained, was to start working on something new.

He smiled, as if he had heard all of this before. "We shall see... we shall see..." was all he said.

Our lunch finally came to an end. I had a meeting back at the office, and Ramaswami would soon be leaving for the Himalayas.

"After all," he said as we got up to leave, "this is a time of transition for you, isn't it?"

It suddenly occurred to me that this was the second week of October, one of my *times of power*. I chuckled as I realized that it hadn't occurred to me that my last meeting with Ramaswami was during this same time period.

"I'll see you again, but probably not like this," he said, pointing to the physical world all around us, and got in a cab. "Until then, remember what we talked about!" Then he was gone. And it was time for me to get back to work.

His last lesson was perhaps more important than I realized.

CHAPTER SUMMARY
THE ENDLESS WHEEL

Raising money for a new business feels like a cause for celebration – but remember, the real work starts now!

In this chapter, after we raised our first million dollars, we felt great! We felt like we had accomplished something — it was a validation of our business, our market, and our management of the company to date.

Today, this perception is heightened in the tech world in Silicon Valley, which has an eager "startup culture" that watches who's getting financed by whom. Those who get VC money pat themselves on the back and the press reports it as if it was a significant business event (X, started by engineers who left Google, just received $Y million from VC firm XYZ). If XYZ is a "top-tier" VC, or $Y is large, it's celebrated even more by the new startup paparazzi.

However, the problem is that a financing event, by itself, doesn't mark any actual progress in the business. Instead, it creates a bar or hurdle that the company must get over, defined by its valuation (i.e. the price at which investors are buying the company's stock). Basically, a valuation when you raise money is setting an expectation of what the company must sell for in the future to be considered "successful" — i.e. if it sells for ten times the valuation in your first round, that's considered a successful venture capital investment. If it sells for two times, that's not a good exit by VC standards. All of this is trying to anticipate how much the company will be worth *if it meets its optimistic projections.*

I have already pointed out that most companies do not make their projections. Some exceed their projections, but most take much longer to get to their projected level of sales. So a financing event is really setting some expectations for the company, and once the money is in the bank, your investors expect you to spend it to make the very rosy projections that were given to them during the sales pitch. This means that the real work of building a company is just beginning!

Beware of the Endless Wheel of Financing.

In building a company, the argument usually goes like this: spend lots of money in preparation for extreme growth. But this can be dangerous as the company will start to generate large losses each month as it invests in marketing, hiring, and infrastructure. If the sales don't ramp as quickly as you expect (which is often the case), you're going to run out of money and then ... you need to raise even more money!

This is the Endless Wheel of Financing. To get off the Endless Wheel, you need to make the company profitable or sell it — neither of which are that easy once you've started on this merry-go-round. In the tech world, even when some companies go public in an IPO (initial public offering), they are still not profitable. While an IPO is viewed as a successful exit by many entrepreneurs and investors, it's just another type of financing: you are selling shares to the public at some price, which is set based on expectations for the company.

Ramaswami compares this to the Endless Wheel of Karma, where each lifetime contains effects that were caused from previous lifetimes, and in each lifetime we create new causes which must be resolved by effects down the road. The only way to get off of this endless wheel of birth, death, and rebirth, is to reach *nirvana*, or an enlightened state.

Your Energetic Pattern is amplified when you have more money; thus both success and failure are closer at hand.

The core factor in how you make decisions as an entrepreneur and how you react to situations that develop in your career and your startup is usually your Energetic Pattern.

A startup is a reflection of the inner lives of the principals. If they are disorganized, the startup is likely to be disorganized. If they like to start the "next big thing" then the startup will find itself doing too many things, as was my own case. If the founders are stubborn and don't like to do too many things, the startup may end up with tunnel vision.

Money in the company actually *amplifies* this problem. An early stage startup may not be able to do too many things because there aren't enough people and there isn't enough money – so they have to prioritize ruthlessly. After raising VC financing (or even after a product is successful, as our first and second products were), the company feels like it has "room to maneuver." This often leads to amplifying an Energetic Pattern, so you have to be more disciplined about looking at clues and at each decision point, figure out if the decision is a good one or if it's just your own Pattern up to its old tricks.

In this chapter, my company started doing too many things once we had money, and this caused us to lose focus on our core products and most importantly, on our bottom line. My Pattern hastened, rather than slowed down, our trip onto the Endless Wheel of Financing.

Note: This doesn't mean that startups shouldn't experiment with ancillary products or markets. By contrast, many first products are not successful, and the company has to move on to other products/markets, so there is no problem with trying "new" things. The main issue was that my Pattern had us doing *too many things, too quickly*. Someone with a very different pattern, say one that was cautious, might not have been doing enough things. You have to find a *Middle Way* between these extremes.

Dreams of Clarity contain messages to us about our life path.

In this chapter, Ramaswami revisits the dream of clarity from the previous chapter. Not only does a dream of clarity contain clues, but he asserts that the dream itself was a clue. When we think of the occult skills of seeing, stalking, or dreaming, each person usually is better at one of these over others, depending on one's own energetic configuration.

He asserted, and subsequent experience showed, that the practice of *dreaming* (i.e. putting ordinary dreams to use) was part of my path. You might say I was a natural. If you're a *dreamer*, than you should pay *more* attention to clues that come from dreams than might others.

The emergence of the dreaming attention is linked to how we live our lives. The more I meditated and focused on my dreaming, the more the dreaming attention emerged. The clues that come from dreaming are tied to our life path, our career, and to our Warrior's Path. These early experiences showed me that dreaming and business together would be an integral part of my Warrior's Path.

19 FINDING MY WARRIOR'S PATH
JANUARY-MARCH, 1996

We finished 1995 with sales of $2.1 million. This was almost 300% of our sales in 1994, which were in the neighborhood of $700,000.

Normally, a 300% increase in sales was a reason for celebration. The only problem was that for us, our expense structure had grown significantly over the last part of the year. And our business plan had called for us to do closer to $3 million that year, most of which we expected to come in the last quarter — October, November, and December. Unfortunately, the fourth quarter sales fell far short from what we expected. Our final number of $2.1 million was off from our expected total by about $900,000, resulting in an unexpected loss of almost a million dollars that year!

This loss was enough to almost completely wipe out the $1 million that we had raised so far, leading to a major crisis for the company.

We also had another $1 million that we could draw upon from our investors, but I was hesitant to do this until I had a solid strategy in mind. The warnings that I had gotten earlier about ramping expenses too high had come home to roost.

It was a cold day at the end of December, just after Christmas, and there was a raging snowstorm outside — what we called a Nor'easter in New England. We had let everyone go home early to miss the storm, and I was the only one left in the

273

office, with a set of preliminary financial statements for 1995 sitting on my desk.

It was a depressing thought that all of that work to grow the company to some 50 people, and to over $2 million in revenues could go out the door if we didn't do something to change the situation and do it soon. I was very stressed out, and decided that I had to make some decisions by New Year's Eve.

What had we done wrong? I wondered and looked out the window. It was about 5 p.m., and the sun had already set. I could see the snow both falling from the sky and flying up from the ground as the wind howled.

We had hired a VP of Sales, we had done an aggressive marketing campaign, and we had gotten a good number of additional customers. We had also released new products and started a consulting group (which seemed to be doing well on its own).

I took a deep breath and realized, as I stared at the snowflakes being buffeted around by the wind, that one of the major issues was that we were doing too many things, with too many products, too quickly. And most importantly, we had been too *aggressive* in our expectations. Sales take time to ramp up. New products take time to get momentum in the marketplace.

In fact, it hit me then that if only we had kept the energetic configuration of a bootstrapped company with limited funds, we would be in much better shape than we were now. We wouldn't have hired so many people so quickly. We would have gone more slowly. We could then have used the cash more effectively over a longer period of time.

As I reflected, I realized that in the end, it had been a combination of my old pattern of moving on to the "next big thing … fast!", along with the high expectations we had raised by getting Venture Capital financing, which had done us in. Normally, a 300% increase in revenues in one year would have been great, by anyone's standards! But we had made the mistake of assuming an almost 400% increase in our business plan.

The last week had been difficult. I wasn't sure if I was the right person to lead the company. After all, I was the one who let it get out of control. I walked to my home in Cambridge through the snow (it was too dangerous to drive), a little depressed and worried that I would lose the company — the Brainstorm that my co-founders and I had built from the ground up. I meditated when I got home and fell asleep early.

That night, I found myself in a surreal setting, on a bridge that seemed to span forever on either side of me. I was under a dark sky with an eerie light.

I looked to one side of the bridge and saw myself, Mitch and Irfan, huddled around a folding table, without any money, but with a lot of promise and energy working on our company in the early days.

I looked to the other side of the bridge and saw the company as it had been for the past few months — lots of money, lots of people, but with diminishing prospects with each dollar that we lost.

I realized that this couldn't really be happening. There was no such bridge. I tried my "consciousness test" and started flying above the bridge. This proved to me that I was in the middle of a dream. I had become lucid.

As I reflected on the meaning of this dream (while still in the dream, a first for me), I realized that this dream was showing me the fact that we didn't make an *appropriate* transition from one side of the bridge to the other. We should have taken more time. It was time to get back to the *fundamentals*, I decided.

Just then, as I looked out to the scene of the big company of the past few months, I saw that beyond our company there were dozens of other companies. And beyond that skyscrapers —a whole financial industry built upon the ways and means that we had built our company — by borrowing money and then rampantly increasing expenses. It was Corporate America built on debt and Silicon Valley built on Venture Capital — both with the same goal, ad infinitum: Growth with a capital G. Growth was the only thing that mattered — for small, VC backed companies it was yearly revenue growth. For public companies, it was quarterly profit growth.

I looked back to the other side of the bridge to see the startup as it had been but there was nothing there but smoke. The smoke slowly cleared and I began to see incredibly tall mountains with snow on them rising off into the distance. *That must be the Himalayas,* I thought to myself.

Just then I saw that Ramaswami was there, meditating on a mountain. There were other monks all around, who I didn't recognize but had the feeling that someday I might, all meditating. An eerie, guttural sound came as they started to chant.

I looked back at the scene of corporate America. Suddenly I saw dark clouds descending over the scene of skyscrapers. A storm was moving in. I heard large noises that made me nervous. Thunder and lightning, and thousands of individuals in suits running from the loud noises toward the bridge. I became very scared and realized that something was wrong. Something was very wrong with Corporate America and it was going to come crashing down.

I turned away and looked at the monks chanting. I became calm. This was a strange scene to me. I started walking toward it. Ramaswami looked up at me and he was reading a book. He held up the book and at first I couldn't see what it was. I tried to fly closer to it but I couldn't fly off the bridge. I was stuck on the bridge. Suddenly my vision enhanced and I saw what it said "Fundamentals of ..." but it was blank after that.

"Fundamentals of what?" I asked out loud.

I looked to the other side of the bridge. There it was — spread out before me — the business world, where I lived during the day, facing a crisis of unimaginable proportions. In fact, our whole way of life was in danger.

I turned to the other side, and there it was – spread out before me — the spiritual worlds. The bridge was a long one, and there was a deep canyon below me. This was a gap that seemed too large to cover — a distance that couldn't easily be bridged.

And there I was, standing in the middle. I couldn't get off the bridge even if I flew. I was stuck in between.

And then I suddenly realized what the book was about. *Fundamentals for Bridging the Gap between the Business World and the Hidden Worlds.* What Ramaswami called The Path of the Career Warrior.

I suddenly understood what the dream was about while I was

still in it.

And then I woke up. I realized that it was a *dream of clarity*, and had meaning on many, many levels.

First, I had lost my way in the business because I had stopped paying attention to the fundamentals of running a business. Not just the fundamentals financially, but the fundamentals of building quality products, having pride in them, and improving them over time. I had focused, like the rest of Corporate America, on only one thing: Growth. And I had gotten us heavily into debt (to the VC's, which wasn't technically debt but it sure started to feel like it as we missed our numbers) to try to make this happen. Suddenly I remembered a conversation I had with Ramaswami about raising Venture Capital.

"It can be a great boon or a great temptation," he had said. "You can stalk the VC-backed company, or you can stalk the startup with no money. Either way, you're likely to learn some valuable lessons — whether you succeed or fail!"

But I wasn't the only one. It was happening all around me. I realized that unless we changed our ways, unless we brought more integrity and spirituality into corporations, the whole world that we have built — like the world of the Romans and other great empires of the past, was going to come crashing down on us. And unless we brought more of our own individual spiritual purpose to our work, that each of us would turn into "zombies" who are cogs in this great machine — this great machine without a soul.

This was a tremendous task — to bring integrity, spiritual purpose, and a knowledge of the hidden worlds into the workplace. No one could do it alone. The Path of the Career Warrior could help in this task. Ramaswami had done his part and was now off tending to his own spiritual needs. Someday, I would have to do my part. That was what he had been trying to tell me about "communication" of these principles.

I wasn't just standing on the bridge. The reason I couldn't leave the bridge was because I was meant to be that bridge. This was part of the contribution I was here to make — part of my own unique Warrior's Path. As I got back to the fundamentals of running a small business, I was to start chronicling the fundamentals of how to bridge this gap that seemed to be so insurmountable to so many of us.

I took a deep breath. I was in my bedroom in the middle of the night. It was dark. The snowstorm was still going outside. I resolved to get back to the fundamentals.

First, I sat down at my desk and started writing an essay: "Meditation and Career Success: Fundamentals of the Path of the Career Warrior."

The next day, I got together our management team, and came up with a plan to trim our costs to try to restore the company to financial health.

I had a strange sense of certainty about me. Somehow, the *dream of clarity* had given me an almost endless supply of energy. It was time to stalk the way we used to be — a company with great prospects but limited means. It was time to go back to the energetic configuration, as Ramaswami called it, of a smaller startup.

The team and I came up with a 60-day plan for cutting costs, reallocating resources, and increasing sales with certain key business partners and customers. We also instituted a profit-sharing plan across all of our employees so that everyone had a stake in what happened. We shut down some extra projects that I had started and rather than worrying about 'the next big thing,' I had to start saying "no" when a new way to spend money was presented to me. It was difficult, but the difficulty didn't phase me at all.

This went on for the next few months. By the end of March, I was able to do two very important things.

The first was something that we hadn't done at Brainstorm for many months: we had a profitable quarter, something that I didn't think was possible only 90 days ago as we stood on the edge of disaster.

The second was that I finished my essay, which recapped some of the lessons I had learned in walking this path from Ramaswami. It was my first attempt to follow my own unique Warrior's Path – to help others bridge the gap between the

278

business world and the spiritual worlds.

A few weeks later, I walked to Harvard Square and left copies of this essay in different places, hoping that students and others would pick it up and find some value in it. I suddenly had a flash of what many of my employees and some of my investors would think if they saw me, walking around town handing out pamphlets on *Meditation and Career Success*. Would they laugh? Would they think I'd lost it? Would they smile dismissively?

But as I walked around, I could feel a golden energy swelling up inside me, and felt a tingling sensation in my forehead, in my third eye area. The energy made me forget all about these worrisome 'what if' scenarios. I sensed gold light all around and a warmth in my belly.

It was a clue, an inner clue, I suddenly realized. A clue that I had *finally* gotten some of the clues. That I had learned *some* of my lessons and was now ready to contribute, in my own way.

I was ready to walk my own unique Warrior's Path.

CHAPTER SUMMARY
FINDING MY WARRIOR'S PATH

A business lives or dies by the expectations that are set on it.

For any business, tripling revenues is great — unless the plan called for quadrupling revenues, and you ramped expenses based on *that* assumption. Then you will have, like I had at the beginning of this chapter, a crisis on your hands.

There's a great scene in the movie, *The Great White Hype*. Samuel L. Jackson's character, a boxing promoter, hypes up a match between an unknown fighter and the heavyweight champion of the world as the "fight of the century." When the match doesn't go as expected and his reputation is ruined, he's asked what he had done wrong. He answers that his biggest mistake was that he "…started to believe his own bullshit!"

Of course, I'm not saying that all business plans that are sold to investors are complete bullshit. However, they are just plans. As Napoleon said, a plan lasts only until the battle starts, then you have to throw it away and start a new one. Any experienced startup guy will tell you that anything in a startup usually takes twice as long as you think it will.

Keeping this in mind, you cannot slavishly stick to a plan, even if that was the plan you sold to investors. You have to be clear-minded enough to see what is happening in the company in reality, and take appropriate actions: sometimes reducing expenses, sometimes aggressively expanding them.

The secret of your Energetic Pattern will run your career and your business.

In this case, it wasn't just that we had stuck to the expense plan and the sales plan took longer to accelerate than we thought it would — the business itself became a reflection of the Energetic Pattern of the founders. As the CEO I had set up the expectation that we could always move on to the next big thing, and we could thus grow big … fast.

As a result, we ended up doing too many things. Having money from VCs made that worse because it gave us the leeway to cover up problems while we did all these "new" things. Other people might have a more cautious or less reckless

Energetic Pattern, and their problem might end up being the exact opposite — they have not expanded aggressively enough.

To succeed in business and in life, you have to be aware of your particular Energetic Pattern. This is part of the reason we meditate — to learn to quiet the mind so that we can perceive this pattern and *see things clearly.*

By following the clues, by clearing our minds, we can find inspiration and energy, from our dreams, from our mentors, to reach beyond our Energetic Pattern and find success.

Your Warrior's Path is the unique combination of lessons you are here to learn and the contribution you are here to make.

To find your Warrior's Path, you must understand both the inner and outer manifestations of your Energetic Pattern. In this chapter, I found inspiration in a dream to not just get my business on track, but to realize some of the potential Ramaswami had been hinting at throughout. Sometimes whether we succeed in business or not is as much the result of the market as it is our efforts – what Ramaswami would call "overlaying our Energetic Pattern along with the patterns of the market." Financial success is not always under our control, since there are so many external factors involved, especially in a fast-moving industry like hi-tech.

Our Warrior's Path is different. It involves not only the challenges we are here to face and learn from (which are a result of our Energetic Pattern), but also the contributions we are here to make (which is also related to our Energetic Pattern!).

By paying attention to the clues, and by understanding what's important to us, we can understand the positive and negative aspects of our own Energetic Pattern. We can tie up many of the loose ends that might be making our Pattern so hard to deal with or erratic.

Most importantly, by focusing on both the positive and negatives aspects of our natural tendencies and life circumstances, the inner and outer manifestations of our Energetic Pattern, we can make our own unique contributions to this world. Only then can we truly find and walk our own unique Warrior's Path!

Appendices

SUMMARY OF THE PRINCIPLES OF THE CAREER WARRIOR

To be a Career Warrior, you don't have to be an entrepreneur or a computer scientist. You simply have to follow the Principles of the Career Warrior in your own life, your own job, and your own career.

Finding your own Warrior's Path isn't about following strict rules. Rather, it is about understanding and practicing these principles in your daily life. It's about looking for more than meets the eye, paying attention to the inner as well as the outer side of events, learning to perceive and regulate energy, and to find and follow the clues in the ultimate treasure hunt: your unique Warrior's Path.

Principle #1) *Everything that is obvious and visible to us has a hidden side.*
- The physical universe all around us simply one dimension of existence.
- When we quiet our minds, we can tune in and hear more than logic; we can hear our intuition.
- For every external activity, there is an internal side, which is impacted by our Energetic Patterns in the hidden worlds.

Principle #2) *Make your career and life a Treasure Hunt. To find the treasure, follow the clues!*
- The future is always calling out to us, if only we can learn to pay attention.
- If something is unusual, and if it repeats, then it's probably important.
- Clues indicate direction, not excuses — you still have to go in that direction to find what they're pointing to.
- Remember, *there are no coincidences.*

Principle #3) *Meditate daily to concentrate, but remember — the most important goal of meditation is expanded awareness.*
- Meditation starts with simply sitting for a few minutes

and focusing on your breath or an object or even an energy center in the body.

- Meditation starts with concentration, but the real goal is awareness of a greater part of you that lives in the hidden worlds.

Principle #4) *To be a Career Warrior, use your work as a form of meditation.*
- In order to enhance your meditation, be mindful at work and work without interruptions.
- Consciously turn your daily tasks into Warrior's Tasks — tasks which have both an obvious and a non-obvious purpose.

Principle #5) *In starting a business or any project, timing is everything.*
- The dual principles of *No Choice* and *Right Timing* are the two most important factors in when to start a business.
- "Start-up" is really a stop-and-go process.
- To be successful, the timing of the market has to match with your internal timing.

Principle #6) *Study Energy in your body and learn how to regulate it.*
- Two central tenets of energy are: Energy is regulated by breath, and Energy follows thought.
- You can use observation to study how your energy is moving and the things that increase or decrease your energy.
- Use Yoga, rhythmic breathing, or visualization to regulate your energy.

Principle #7) *Seek out Places of Power and Times of Power.*
- Tuning into the energy of a place helps to identify Places of Power, or Power Spots.
- You have a built-in Energy Detection Device: your body.

- Take a Warrior's Trip now and then, preferably at a Time of Power, to a Place of Power.
- Notice times of day, times of the month, and times of year where you are flowing with the current and not against it.

Principle #8) *Follow your intuition.*
- To accomplish an occult task, follow your intuition not necessarily your logic.
- No matter how crazy it seems, learn to quiet your mind and tune in (even if it's an ocean talking to you!)
- Trust the feelings in your body, not just logic.

Principle #9) *Use all Four Keys to Manifestation when trying to create something in your life*
- Right Intent, or visualization and putting energy behind your goal.
- Right Patterns, or understanding how your energetic patterns are helping or hindering your success.
- Right Technique, or what to do in the outside world to make your goal a reality.
- Right Timing, or Appropriateness, means whether a particular goal fits with your inner timing and the external timing of the marketplace.

Principle #10) *There are (at least) 7 different types of clues – each of these is a different type of message from the hidden worlds.*
- Write down clues.
- Look for unusual clues and clues that repeat themselves.
- Pay particular attention to synchronicity and dreams.

Principle #11) *To find your Energetic Pattern, recognize External Patterns in your work and your life.*
- If a chain of events repeats in your life or your work, then you have found an External Pattern.
- Examine the decisions that led to a repeat of this External Pattern.

- This will give you a clue about your Energetic Pattern — the sum of all of your hopes, fears, anxieties, and energetic loose ends from this and previous lives.

Principle #12) ***When making decisions, understand if it's your Energetic Pattern at work or not.***
- A clue usually indicates direction.
- But sometimes, a clue is really our Energetic Pattern asserting itself.
- Learn to recognize the difference and learn to "ride the dragon" of your Energetic Pattern, rather than working against it or feeding it.

Principle #13) ***Learn about Seeing, Stalking, and Dreaming.***
- Stalking is kind of like acting but more authentic – you have to become that which you are stalking.
- Dreaming is to put ordinary dreams to use by looking for clues and unlocking the dreaming attention.
- Seeing is perceiving energy and the hidden aspect of any situation.

Principle #14) ***Find and Walk Your Warrior's Path.***
- Your Warrior's Path is the unique combination of lessons you are here to learn and the contribution you are here to make.
- To find it, understand both the inner and outer manifestations of your Energetic Pattern.
- If it's not a little scary, then you are missing part of your Warrior's Path. It may not be exactly what you expect it to be!
- When you find your Warrior's Path, have the courage to pursue it, without worrying about what other people will think!

ABOUT THE AUTHOR

Rizwan Virk ("Riz") is a well-known entrepreneur, author, independent film producer, and angel investor in Silicon Valley. He started his first company on a shoestring budget at the age of 23 and rapidly grew it into a multi-million dollar operation with offices around the country. Since then, he has started grown, and sold several high tech companies in enterprise software, video games, and online advertising. He has also been an advisor and mentor to dozens of other entrepreneurs and filmmakers.

His entrepreneurial exploits have been featured in *Inc. Magazine*, *The Boston Globe*, *The Wall Street Journal*, *Tech Crunch*, *GameSpot*, and were even skewered by the *Daily Show with Jon Stewart*. He writes and speaks regularly about entrepreneurship, video games, film-making, and spiritual growth. Mr. Virk is a graduate of MIT in Computer Science and Stanford's Graduate School of Business.

To learn more, visit his website at www.zenentrepreneur.com.

31354893R00180

Made in the USA
Lexington, KY
08 April 2014